Schenkerian Analysis

Schenkerian Analysis: Perspectives on Phrase Rhythm, Motive and Form, Second Edition, is a textbook directed at all those—whether beginners or more advanced students—interested in gaining understanding of and facility at applying Schenker's ideas on musical structure. It begins with an overview of Schenker's approach to music, and then progresses systematically from the phrase and its various combinations to longer and more complex works. Unlike other texts on this subject, *Schenkerian Analysis* combines the study of multi-level pitch organization with that of phrase rhythm (the interaction of phrase and hypermeter), motivic repetition at different structural levels, and form. It also contains analytic graphs of several extended movements, separate works, and songs. A separate instructor's manual provides additional advice and solutions (graphs) of all recommended assignments.

This second edition has been revised to make the early chapters more accessible and to improve the pedagogical effectiveness of the book as a whole. Changes in musical examples have been carefully made to ensure that each example fully supports student learning. Informed by decades of teaching experience, this book provides a clear and comprehensive guide to Schenker's theories and their applications.

David Beach has taught music theory for over forty years at Yale University, the Eastman School of Music (University of Rochester), and at the Faculty of Music, University of Toronto. He is currently retired, living in northern California.

T0388064

Schenkerian Analysis

Perspectives on Phrase Rhythm, Motive and Form

Second Edition

David Beach

NEW YORK AND LONDON

Second edition published 2019
by Routledge
52 Vanderbilt Avenue, New York, NY 10017

and by Routledge
2 Park Square, Milton Park, Abingdon, Oxon, OX14 4RN

Routledge is an imprint of the Taylor & Francis Group, an informa business

First edition published by Routledge 2012

Library of Congress Cataloging-in-Publication Data
Names: Beach, David, 1938– author. | Beach, David, 1938–. Advanced
     Schenkerian analysis.
Title: Schenkerian analysis : perspectives on phrase rhythm, motive and form /
     David Beach.
Description: Second edition. | New York ; London : Routledge, 2019. |
     Previous edition published under title: Advanced Schenkerian analysis. |
     Includes bibliographical references and index.
Identifiers: LCCN 2018046078 (print) | LCCN 2018048467 (ebook) |
     ISBN 9780429453793 (ebook) | ISBN 9781138319479 (hardback) |
     ISBN 9781138319554 (pbk.)
Subjects: LCSH: Schenkerian analysis.
Classification: LCC MT6.B294 (ebook) | LCC MT6.B294 A38 2019 (print) |
     DDC 781.8—dc23
LC record available at https://lccn.loc.gov/2018046078

ISBN: 978-1-138-31947-9 (hbk)
ISBN: 978-1-138-31955-4 (pbk)
ISBN: 978-0-429-45379-3 (ebk)

Typeset in Bembo
by Apex CoVantage, LLC
Printed and bound by CPI Group (UK) Ltd, Croydon, CR0 4YY

Visit the eResources: www.routledge.com/9781138319554

Music analysis, at its best, is an art, not a science.
Indeed it must be based on a thorough understanding of
counterpoint, harmony and form.
And careful attention must always be paid
to context, to musical detail
as well as to the larger picture.
Most of all—to be truly insightful—
it requires musical sensitivity and imagination.

Contents

Musical Examples

Figures

Preface to the Second Edition

What is Schenkerian analysis? Clearly, if you read the literature, the term means different things to different people. It is possible, of course, to understand Schenker's ideas in terms of a formal theory, complete with axioms and corollaries. The organization of *Free Composition*, which progresses from background to foreground, is revealing in this respect. But what we are talking about here is Schenkerian *theory*, which is to be understood from top down. Schenkerian *analysis*, on the other hand, is a practical tool, a way of approaching and understanding the organization of tonal works and representing that organization graphically in musical notation. It is *musical* analysis, and, as indicated by the statement on the opening page of this book, I view the process as an art more than a science. It requires knowledge, but it also requires musical sensitivity and, yes, musical instinct. It also requires time and practice.

I was fortunate to have been introduced to Schenkerian analysis by Allen Forte in a year-long seminar at Yale University in the early 1960s, and this was followed by individual lessons with Ernst Oster in New York City. In those days you learned through the analysis of individual works. I would spend the time on the train ride back to New Haven taking detailed notes on what Oster had said in my lesson with him, and then put the piece and my notes away before moving on to the next assignment. It was only when I returned to look at my original analysis and my notes sometime later that the true significance of Oster's observations really sank in. This one-on-one interaction plus the luxury of time to absorb the fruits of this interaction was an ideal learning situation, but not possible in a formal course at the college/university level. In this context, one must begin with short musical units and progress rather quickly from there to increasingly larger works to develop the technique and to learn how to present your analytical interpretations logically and clearly. That is a given. But still I believe in teaching analysis through the examination of musical works. Rather than have individual chapters on specific techniques, like voice exchange or reaching over, I like to introduce these techniques through analysis, and, once introduced, to reinforce them through succeeding assignments. That is the way I taught Schenkerian analysis at the Eastman School of Music for many years and that is the foundation of this book.

The changes I have made in this revised edition are of two types. First, I have made several changes in the early chapters to make this part easier to use by beginning students. Second I have substituted new analyses for others in some of the later chapters, ones that I feel are easier to understand and that add new dimensions to the understanding of this fascinating topic.

Organization and Intended Uses

My original conception of this book was that it was directed at those with some background in the subject, potentially upper-level undergraduate and graduate students, and it was at the insistence of the original readers of my manuscript that the title include the word "advanced". I have never been comfortable with this description, in part because of its connotation, but also because it is not entirely accurate, and for these reasons the word "advanced" has been dropped from this revised edition. There are other texts available,[1] but this one differs from the others in two respects: it incorporates the study of phrase rhythm, motive and form into the study of voice leading, and it proceeds as soon as is feasible to complete movements and musical works, since it is there that we can encounter Schenker's conception of musical structure in its entirety. This text is intentionally flexible, adaptable to those at different levels of understanding of Schenker's ideas.

As noted earlier, many of the changes made in this revised edition are directed at making this text more useable for the beginning student. The information provided in the first two sections of Chapter 1—the three basic premises of Schenker's approach to musical structure and the detailed examination of Bach's C Major Prelude—provides crucial information for the beginner, the latter because it provides a glimpse into Schenker's concept of structural levels and the associated terminology, and it introduces the important concept of hypermeter. While I admit to a particular fascination with the third section in this chapter, Schenker's notion of motivic parallelism, I believe the beginning student could skip this section for now and proceed directly to Chapter 2. Systematic instruction with graded exercises begins with Chapters 2–4, which deal with phrases of different types, the interaction of phrase and hypermeter (phrase rhythm), phrase expansion, and combinations of similar and dissimilar phrases to form larger closed units. While it is important that beginning students be exposed to the ideas expressed in Chapter 3 (phrase rhythm), I would not expect the instructor to assign the entire chapter and all the assignments, because some of the examples in the latter part of the chapter are rather difficult. That is, I expect instructors to exercise good judgment in selecting examples and assignments appropriate to the level of the class. Chapter 5 deals with the analysis of representative works in ternary (rounded binary) form, followed by a review of concepts and terminology. This first part of the text (Chapters 1–5) is appropriate for an initial term of Schenkerian analysis. Even if the student goes no further, these chapters provide a solid background in the topic.

More advanced students should review all of Part I (Chapters 1–5) carefully, completing selected assignments to assimilate the information before proceeding to the second part, which is organized into topics. This part consists of chapters on baroque one-part and two-part forms as exhibited in selected works of Bach, on extended rounded binary and ternary forms, on sonata form, and finally a chapter on music and text. There is room for considerable flexibility in the use of this second part, depending on the interests and abilities of a particular class. An important feature of these later chapters, beginning with the last chapter of the first part, is the inclusion of analytical graphs of over fifteen complete works or movements. All these chapters provide suggested assignments and, in some cases, specific questions to answer and/or approaches to take.

Features

As suggested by the subtitle, an important feature of this book is the inclusion of three topics that pertain to Schenker's work, yet are most often treated as ancillary to his concept of multi-level pitch organization in tonal music, if they are discussed at all: phrase rhythm (the interaction of phrase and hypermeter); motivic repetition at different structural levels; and formal design. Though these topics have been addressed in the secondary literature, they have generally been ignored in texts on Schenkerian analysis, the result being an incomplete picture of his approach to music. The process of analysis ought to involve uncovering aspects of formal design, motivic development and metric organization in addition to voice-leading structure. This is the approach that will be followed in this text.

A common misconception among students and in general among those not well acquainted with Schenker's writings is that his theory of tonal hierarchy does not deal with aspects of meter and rhythm, or does so only in passing. But, in fact, there is a wealth of information in the fourth chapter of *Free Composition*, his last work. It is very clear, for example, that Schenker was well aware of what we today call hypermeter, the regular recurrence of metric groups of the same size, most often in multiples of two, and the existence of metric groups at more than one level. See, for example, his analysis of the metric organization of the St. Anthony Chorale (*Free Composition*, Figure 138/3), a short work we will examine in Chapter 5. Schenker's examples and commentary also cover important aspects of the interaction of hypermeter and phrase structure, what William Rothstein has appropriately labeled "phrase rhythm".[2] These include matters such as: (1) metric reinterpretation; (2) successive downbeat measures; (3) phrase overlap, with and without metric reinterpretation; and (4) phrase expansion. These topics will be introduced in this text within the first three chapters, and analyses in subsequent chapters will include aspects of phrase rhythm appropriate to the works being examined.

The second topic is Schenker's concept of motivic parallelism. Traditionally, the term "motive" has been used to describe a recurring musical figure, often identified by its rhythmic articulation. The most frequently cited example is the repeated four-note motive from Beethoven's Fifth Symphony. Schenker, on the other hand, developed quite a different concept of motive, one that is tied, at least in part, to his notion of structural levels. Motive, for Schenker, is a melodic pattern—perhaps a neighbor-note figure or a linear progression—that is repeated in the course of a musical work, sometimes at the same pitch level, sometimes transposed, sometimes occupying the same time-span as the original statement, but also sometimes greatly expanded—that is, occurring at a deeper structural level. In this latter case, the motive is no longer associated with its original rhythmic articulation (unless it is an augmentation). It is defined by the pitch succession, or scale degree succession when it appears in another key. Schenker did not leave us with an essay on his concept of motive. Instead, comments appear here and there in his writings, and motivic parallels (repetitions) are clearly identified in his musical graphs by horizontal brackets. A certain amount of basic information is available in Oswald Jonas's book, *Introduction to the Theory of Heinrich Schenker*, in the brief section titled "Repetition as a Device of Art". But the most thorough treatment of the topic is found in Charles Burkhart's article "Schenker's 'Motivic Parallelisms'".[3] One feature of this article is Burkhart's discussion of Schenker's remarkable analysis of the first movement of Beethoven's Piano Sonata in F Minor, Op. 2, No. 1.[4] In this analysis, Schenker reveals how the pitch configuration of the opening phrase, the ascending third A♭5–B♭5–C6 and the following descending sixth C6–E♮5, becomes the middleground framework for the entire development section leading to the dominant. Not only does this demonstrate Schenker's notion of motivic enlargement, but also indirectly it reveals the potential of Schenker's approach to uncover hidden repetitions of this sort. In this instance, I believe it is also uncovering Beethoven's compositional method.

The third topic is form. In this instance, we have Schenker's views set out in the last chapter of *Free Composition*, which are reflected in texts on the subject. The reason this topic interests me is the clear dichotomy between Schenker's conception of form and that expressed in traditional texts on the subject, like William Caplin's *Classical Forms* (Oxford, 1998), a point of potential confusion for students. Take, for example, the form of a Haydn or Mozart minuet. Traditionally, this form is described as rounded binary, ‖: a :‖ ‖: b a′ :‖. It is binary because it is in two parts, each of which is repeated, and it is "rounded" because of the return to "a" and tonic harmony in the second part. Once you remove the repeats, you are left with a ternary design, a b a′. This is the view taken by Schenker, since voice leading, which is his primary concern, does not account for repeats. In my opinion, both descriptions are correct, not a point of view normally taken by either camp. And I believe it is our obligation to make clear to students the criteria leading to these two descriptions of the same thing. On the one hand we are talking about formal design, and on the other, we are talking about underlying design as related to the voice-leading structure. As we shall see, this becomes further confused when Schenker's ternary design is described as having a two-part structure (interruption form). The point of all this is to say that it is extremely important to be clear what exactly it is that we are talking about when describing form and structure. So in the chapters on ternary (rounded binary) form and sonata form,[5] I will depart from a strict Schenkerian stance to present both sides and to clarify the criteria leading us one way or the other.

The musical graphs are my own. A few are based on previously published material, sometimes only slightly altered but in other instances quite different, or on graphs by Schenker. In each of these cases, the source is acknowledged in a footnote.

Finally, three technical matters. First, the notation of pitch in this book follows the system adapted by the Acoustical Society of America, where middle C is C4. Second, I use a shorthand system I learned years ago from Allen Forte to indicate applied chords in square brackets—for example, [V] V, meaning V of V to V or [ii⁶-V] ii, meaning ii⁶ and V of ii. Third, scores for the assignments are available online through the International Music Score Library Project (Petrucci Music Library) at http://imslp.org.

NOTES

1. Allen Cadwallader and David Gagné, *Analysis of Tonal Music: A Schenkerian Approach* (Oxford University Press, 2010); Allen Forte and Steven Gilbert, *Introduction to Schenkerian Analysis* (Norton, 1982). See also Tom Pankhurst, *Schenker Guide* (Routledge, 2008).

2. William Rothstein, *Phrase Rhythm in Tonal Music*, chaps. 1–4 (Schirmer, 1989, Musicalia Press, 2007). Other works to consult in this area are: Joel Lester, *The Rhythms of Tonal Music*, chaps. 6–7 (Southern Illinois, 1986); Ryan McClelland, "Extended Upbeats in the Classical Minuet: Interactions With Hypermeter and Phrase Structure," *Music Theory Spectrum* 28/1 (2006), 23–56, and "Teaching Phrase Rhythm Through Minuets From Haydn's String Quartets," *Journal of Music Theory Pedagogy* 20 (2006), 5–35; William Rothstein, "Rhythmic Displacement and Rhythmic Normalization," *Trends in Schenkerian Research*, ed. Allen Cadwallader (Schirmer, 1990), 87–113; Frank Samarotto, "Strange Dimensions: Regularity and Irregularity in Deep Levels of Rhythmic Reduction,"

Schenker Studies 2, eds. Carl Schachter and Hedi Siegel (Cambridge University Press, 1999), 222–238; Carl Schachter, "Rhythm and Linear Analysis," published in three parts in *The Music Forum* IV (1976), V (1980), and VI (1987), reprinted in *Unfoldings*, ed. Joseph Straus (Oxford University Press, 1999), 17–117; and Heinrich Schenker, *Free Composition*, trans. and ed. Ernst Oster (Longman, 1979), chap. 4.

3. Charles Burkhart, "Schenker's 'Motivic Parallelisms'," *Journal of Music Theory* 22/2 (1978), 145–175. Other works that shed light on this topic are: Allen Cadwallader and William Pastille, "Schenker's High-Level Motives," *Journal of Music Theory* 36/1 (1992), 117–148; John Rothgeb, "Thematic Content: A Schenkerian View," *Aspects of Schenkerian Theory*, ed. David Beach (Yale University Press, 1983), 39–60; Carl Schachter, "Motive and Text in Four Schubert Songs," *Aspects of Schenkerian Theory*, ed. David Beach (Yale University Press, 1983), 61–76, reprinted in *Unfoldings*, ed. Joseph Straus (Oxford University Press, 1999); Eric Wen, "Illusory Cadences and Apparent Tonics: The Effect of Motivic Enlargement Upon Phrase Structure," *Trends in Schenkerian Research*, ed. Allen Cadwallader (Schirmer, 1990), 133–143.

4. This analysis was published in *Tonwille* 2 (1922).

5. The same issues exist with sonata form, which Schenker describes as a three-part (ternary) form: exposition-development-recapitulation. Yet we all know this design has its origin in a binary form. See, for example, the descriptions of large binary form in Koch's *Versuch einer Anleitung zur Composition* (1782–93) and Reicha's *Traité de haute composition musicale* (1824–26). The form was first described as ternary by A.B. Marx in Volume 3 of his *Die Lehre von der musikalischen Komposition* (1845), but his reasons for doing so were very different from Schenker's.

Acknowledgments

Writing this book provides a wonderful opportunity for me to thank those who have taught me about Schenker's concept of musical structure over the years. First among this esteemed group is Allen Forte, who first introduced me to Schenkerian analysis almost fifty years ago and who suggested some time later that I contact the late Ernst Oster to continue my studies. I was fortunate to have a few lessons with Oster in the late 1960s and early 1970s. Since then I have learned much from my colleagues, especially Charles Burkhart, Roger Kamien, John Rothgeb, William Rothstein, Carl Schachter and especially Edward Laufer, with whom I have had many instructive conversations over the past few years. And I have learned much from my students. All these people share the credit for what is of value in this book. If it is lacking in some way, the responsibility is mine alone.

I would like to take this opportunity to thank all those who have contributed so much to the publication of the second edition of *Schenkerian Analysis*: first, Genevieve Aoki, Editor, Routledge Music; and Peter Sheehy, Senior Editorial Assistant (Music); Abigail Stanley, Production Editor; Marianne Fox, Copy Editor; and Marie Louise Roberts, Project Manager, who was especially helpful in technical matters. And last, but not least, a salute to Massimo Guida for his careful preparation of the new musical examples and graphs for this edition.

David Beach, Santa Rosa, California
June 2018

PART I
Concepts and Terminology

1 Schenker's Conception of Musical Structure

An Overview

Introduction

I have always liked to begin my courses on Schenkerian analysis with an overview of his conception of musical structure. There is a danger, of course, in overloading the newcomer with too much information; despite this, I see definite advantages to this approach. First, it has been my experience that many students, even those with some background in the area, have developed strange notions about Schenker and his work, and this overview can help to dispel some of the misconceptions. Second, it provides a glimpse into where this study will take us. And third, it provides a review of basic concepts and terminology for those with some background.

We will begin by examining what I take to be three basic premises on which Schenker's mature theories are built. First is his observation that melodic motion at deeper levels progresses by step. Second is his understanding that some tones and intervals, such as the dissonant seventh, require resolution. And third is the distinction Schenker draws between chord and harmonic step (*Stufe*), which may incorporate a succession of many chords. We will then examine in detail Bach's well-known Prelude in C Major from the *Well-Tempered Clavier*, Book I. We will begin by examining its harmony and metric organization and then proceed to a consideration of its voice-leading structure. This will give us an opportunity to examine Schenker's concept of structural levels as well as the specific techniques of prolongation involved. Finally, we will consider Schenker's notion of motivic repetition as related to that of structural levels. The chapter will end with a review of concepts and terminology.

Three Basic Premises

Melodic Motion by Step

Schenker's theoretical publications span almost thirty years, from 1906 until 1935, the year of his death. Sometime during this period, most likely early on, he observed that melodic progressions beyond note-to-note connections have a tendency to progress by step. Today this observation seems quite apparent, but historically it has great significance as Schenker's ideas on structural levels began to develop. We will begin by examining four relatively short examples, provided in Example 1.1, from this perspective.

a) The first example is the opening four measures of the Prelude from Bach's Cello Suite in G Major, where each half measure consists of an arpeggiated chord with the top note decorated by its lower neighbor. The reduction below the score shows the underlying progression of two voices over a tonic pedal. The inner voice progresses by step from D3 to G3, while the top voice progresses from B3 to its upper neighbor C4 and back. The controlling harmony is the G major chord, and the progression of the top part *prolongs* the third of the chord by its upper neighbor.

EXAMPLE 1.1a Bach, Cello Suite I, Prelude, 1–4

b) Our second example is the opening of the sarabanda movement from Bach's Violin Partita in D Minor. Here the note-to-note progression of the melody involves motion back and forth between two melodic strands, a top voice and an inner voice, sometimes progressing by leap and at other times filling in the gap by step. This phenomenon is commonly referred to as *compound melody*. (Our first example is also an example of compound melody, consisting of two parts above a stationary bass.) The melodic leaps in the first three measures are between these two strands, but individually each progresses by step. As shown by the representation

EXAMPLE 1.1b Bach, Violin Partita II, Sarabanda, 1–5

of the voice leading below the music, the top voice descends by step from F5 to B♭4. The first two steps in this progression, which fall on successive downbeats, are clear. The entrance of D5 in the third measure is delayed until the last eighth note, and the C5 of measure 4 is displaced by D5 on the downbeat. Nevertheless, it is this C5, which becomes the dissonant seventh in relation to the D⁷ chord, V⁷ of iv, that leads to B♭4 in the next measure. Once you look and listen beyond note-to-note associations, all voices in this example progress by step, including the bass. The E♭4 on the downbeat of measure 4 belongs to an inner line, only temporarily delaying the connection between B♭3 and A3 in the bass within the larger descent of a fifth from D4 to G3.

c) Our third example is taken from Schubert's famous song, "Die Forelle". Here the surface progression involves arpeggiation between inner and outer strands until the step connection between E♭5 (outer voice) and A♭4 (inner voice) at the end of the excerpt. The initial arpeggiation occurs within a single harmony (tonic), as occurred in the opening example, and then the leap from A♭4 to E♭5 and the reverse filling in of that interval occur over the dominant.

This creates a step progression between the top notes of the arpeggiations, F5 to E♭5, harmonized by I to V⁷, as shown in the reduction below the example.

Example 1.1c Schubert, "Die Forelle", 6–10

d) Our final example is taken from the third movement of Beethoven's Piano Sonata in E♭, Op. 7. Here the melody once again opens with an arpeggiation of the tonic triad, which reaches up to G5 in measure 11, at which point the line descends a third with the middle member of the third extended to its lower third. This idea is then repeated a step lower, creating the step progression G5 (measure 11)-F5 (measure 13). This is shown clearly in the interpretation of the voice leading of this passage provided below the music. (Here the notation does not indicate relative duration but the hierarchy of events.) The function of the C minor chord (vi) is shown to be part of a descending arpeggiation in the bass from I to ii⁶, where the bass note A♭ has been omitted and is thus shown in parentheses. It is common practice in Schenkerian graphs to show notes implied by context but not stated explicitly in this manner.

EXAMPLE 1.1d Beethoven, Piano Sonata Op. 7 (III), 9–14

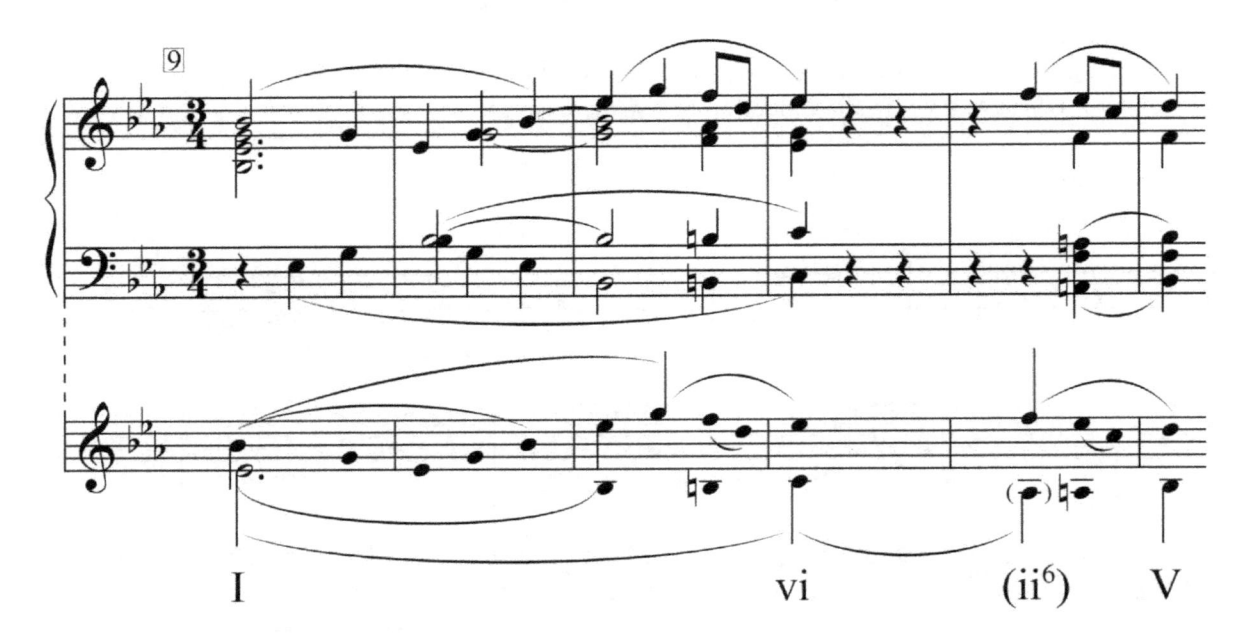

These examples are concerned with connections in relatively close proximity, but as Schenker's notion of structural levels began to take shape, he quite naturally became concerned with connections at more remote levels. Regarding step progressions, he observed that at deeper levels these invariably descend, and at the deepest level they descend to *closure*. The concept of closure, which for Schenker means both melodic and harmonic closure—the simultaneous arrival at scale degree 1 and tonic harmony—is central to his concept of tonality. Closure can occur at many levels—for example, at the end of a theme or musical period, or over the course of an entire piece, in which case we are talking about closure of the fundamental line and fundamental structure. Once again, we are touching on the idea that music operates simultaneously at different structural levels. But we are getting ahead of ourselves; we will get to this shortly.

Resolution of the Dissonant Seventh

The second basic premise that I like to stress early on in introducing Schenker's ideas is his recognition—hardly a new one for his time!—that certain notes of the scale have specific tendencies—for example, $\hat{4}$ and $\hat{7}$ to resolve to $\hat{3}$ and $\hat{8}$. This general notion is reflected in the title of one of his publications, a series of pamphlets with the name *Tonwille*, which literally means "will of the tone(s)". I like to demonstrate with a few examples involving resolution of the dissonant seventh, since it is extremely important not only to be aware of the normal treatment of this dissonance but also especially to be aware when encountering those special circumstances where the seventh is not treated as expected. First, let's observe the resolution of the dissonant seventh under "normal" circumstances.

a) The meaning of the first example, the opening two measures from the second movement of Beethoven's Piano Sonata, Op. 7, is perfectly clear. Here resolution of the F4 on the second beat of measure 1, the dissonant seventh of the dominant, is delayed until the second beat of measure 2. Similar to the initial example in the previous section, the opening of the prelude movement of the first Cello Suite by Bach (Example 1.1a), the third of the tonic harmony is *prolonged* by its upper neighbor.

EXAMPLE **1.2a** Beethoven, Piano Sonata Op. 7 (II), 1–2

b) Our second example is the opening measures from the third movement of Mozart's Piano Sonata, K. 570. Here we have another example of a compound melody, where the lower strand proceeds from D5 on the downbeat of measure 1 and the upper line from the F5 on the fourth beat of the same measure. This third, harmonized by the tonic, is answered by the third C5-E♭5, where the E♭5 is delayed until the fourth beat (like the F5 of measure 1) by its upper appoggiatura. This third is harmonized by the dominant, and E♭5, the dissonant seventh, is transferred in the immediate context to the bass leading to the I⁶ chord on the downbeat of measure 3. However, the longer-range resolution of this dissonant E♭5 is to D5 on the downbeat of measure 4 following a *voice exchange* (see below) with the bass, the result being a descending third F5-E♭5-D5 spanning the four measures, shown in the voice-leading representation by the upward-directed stems and the large slur.

This third progression is harmonized by $B\flat(I) - A (V_5^6) - B\flat(I)$. Each of the melodic thirds is filled in, and in each instance the connecting passing note is providing support. This phenomenon is referred to by Schenker as *consonant passing tone*, a term that at first may seem self-contradictory. By definition a passing tone is dissonant against the harmony of the notes it connects, but it is consonant in the immediate context in which it is harmonized. Again, this is a matter of sorting out levels.

Voice exchange is a common technique of prolongation we will encounter repeatedly in this book. It occurs when notes *belonging to the same two voices* exchange places between statements of the same harmony. Most common is an exchange between outer voices, as in Example 1.2b: B♭4 over D4 exchanging with D5 over B♭3. This phenomenon is highlighted in graphs by crossed lines. Like many techniques of prolongation, voice exchange can occur in the immediate context, as here, or at deeper levels of the voice-leading structure.

EXAMPLE 1.2b Mozart, Piano Sonata K. 570 (III), 1–4

c) Our third example is taken from the first movement of Mozart's Piano Sonata K. 332. It includes the final measures of the first theme area and the beginning of the transition to the second theme and second key area. Here the dissonant seventh of the dominant, the B♭5 of measure 19, is resolved in the immediate context by transfer to an inner part, indicated by the arrow added to the score. However, in the larger context, the resolution is stated in the same octave five measures later, creating a link between the two sections, which otherwise are separated by the strong cadence on F, the following rest, and the dramatic change in dynamics.

EXAMPLE 1.2c **Mozart, Piano Sonata K. 332 (I), 16–24**

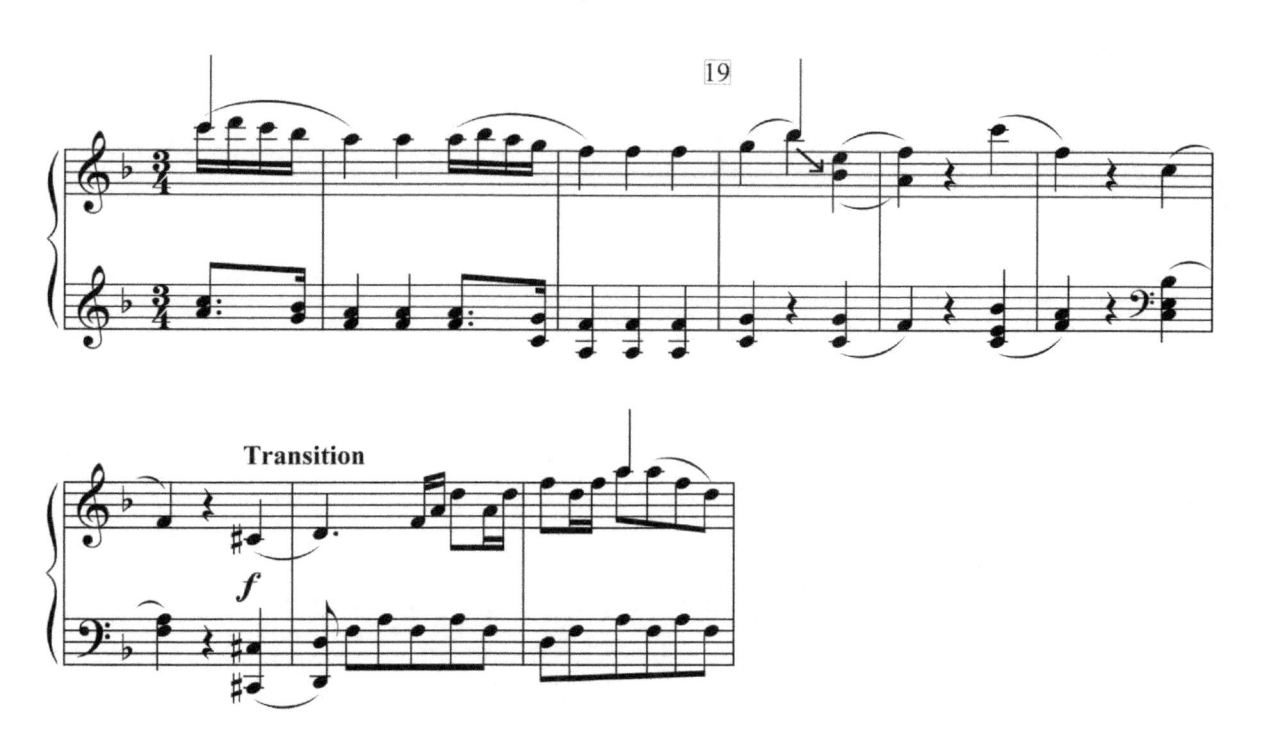

The final example dealing with resolution of the seventh has been given its own number because of its complexity and the manner of presentation. In this instance, we begin with a simple progression involving normal resolution of the seventh (a). At (b) the seventh descends by step to the fifth of the dominant harmony while the seventh is transferred to the bass, where it resolves. At (c) are measures 20–25 of the sarabande movement from the Cello Suite in E♭ by Bach, and below at (d) is an interpretation of the voice leading of these measures. Here we see that the progression from vi to V^7 has been expanded by a connecting applied dominant supporting the rising third C4-E♭4, the latter temporarily displacing the resolution to D4 in the next measure. The second step in the progression shown at (b), the 7–6–5 over the dominant and transfer of the seventh to the bass, is now extended over three measures, internal to which the tonic chord on the second beat of measure 23 offers consonant support for G3 within the third A♭3-G3-F3 (the 7–6–5 of the controlling dominant harmony). One result of the voice leading in these measures is the transfer of the resolution of the leading tone, D4, to the lower octave (E♭3).

EXAMPLE 1.3 Bach, Cello Suite IV, Sarabande, 20–25

(Harmonic) Scale Step

The third idea that is basic to Schenker's thinking is the distinction he makes between chord and harmonic step (*Stufe*), which carries the meaning "controlling harmony". A harmonic scale step may incorporate several chords in succession.

a) Our first example—a virtual showcase of the technique of voice exchange—consists of the opening phrase from Beethoven's Piano Sonata Op. 110. As shown below the score in Example 1.4a, the harmonic progression expressed on the downbeats of the first three measures is the chord succession $I - V^4_3 - I^6$, where each of the first two chords is locally extended by a voice exchange between the outer voices. However, we understand the second of these chords as passing—that is, as connecting I and I^6. The controlling harmony is the tonic, which now progresses through IV, also extended by voice exchange between the outer voices, to V and back to I and C5 on the downbeat of measure 5. The entire phrase, in fact, prolongs the tonic scale step and scale degree 3.

EXAMPLE **1.4a** Beethoven, Piano Sonata Op. 110 (I), 1–5

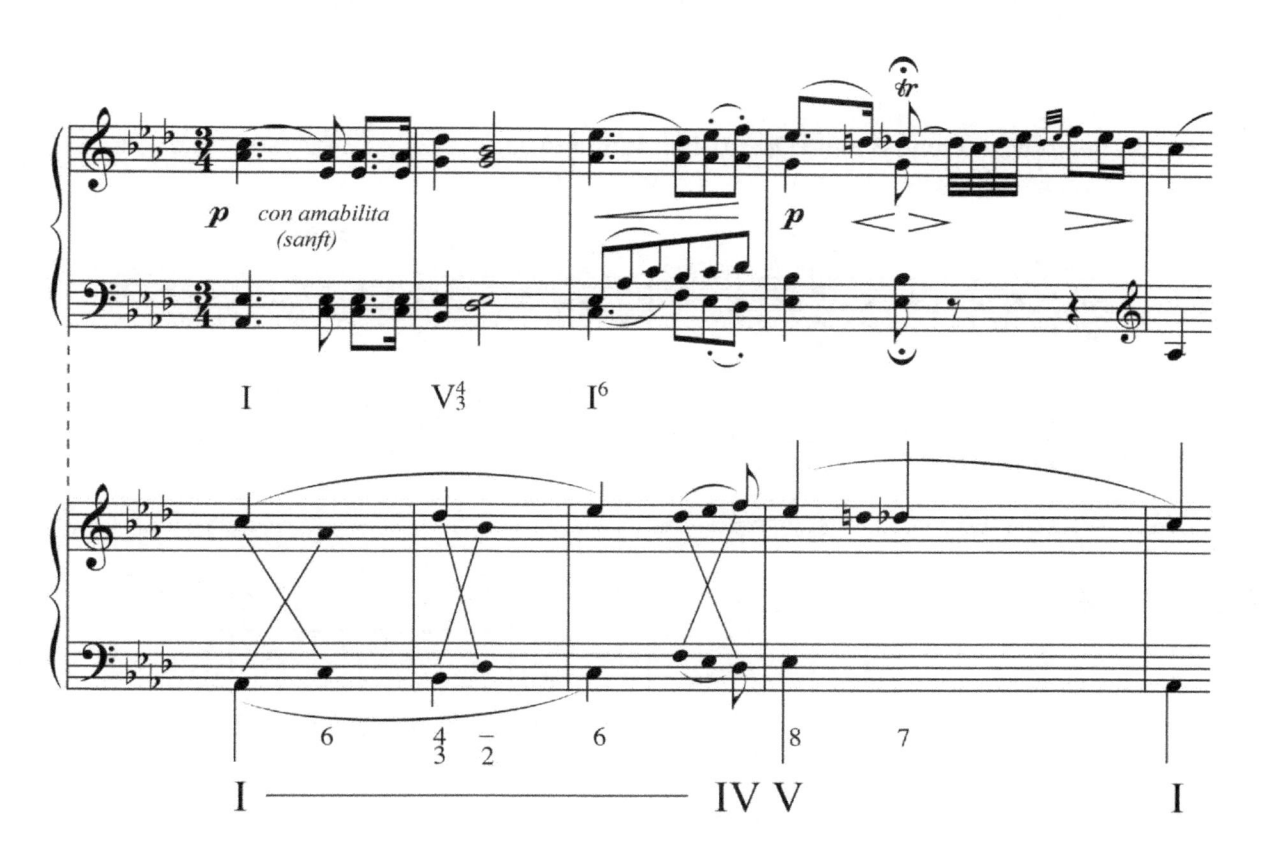

b) Our second example, the opening phrase from the second movement of Beethoven's Piano Sonata Op. 10, No. 1, involves harmonic motion at three levels. In the initial two measures, the tonic harmony and A♭4 are prolonged by the dominant chord supporting the upper neighbor of A♭4.[1] Then in measures 3–4 the dominant harmony and B♭4 are prolonged by a tonic chord that offers consonant support for C5, the upper neighbor of B♭4. This leads to C5 and tonic harmony on the downbeat of measure 5. The first three chords are grouped together, as are the second three. In the first group, the controlling harmony is I, which is prolonged by V, and in the second group it is V that is prolonged by I. At a somewhat deeper level, measures 3–4 are heard as passing between measures 1–2 and 5; the dominant harmony of those intervening measures offers consonant support for the passing tone B♭4 within the ascending third A♭4 - B♭4 - C5. Thus the controlling harmony over the span of measures 1–5 is I, as shown in the representation of the voice leading below the music. This representation shows the continuation of the harmonic progression at this level to continue to the dominant through the subdominant. What about the progression through V_5^6 to I in the seventh measure? Clearly this tonic harmony is not the goal, and thus it must function in a more immediate context than the following dominant, which is the goal of the phrase. Stated somewhat differently, the motion passes through this tonic to the following dominant offering consonant support to C5, the passing tone within the descending third D♭5 (which is displaced by a motion to the covering A♭5, but picked up in the following scale

EXAMPLE 1.4b Beethoven, Piano Sonata Op. 10, No. 1 (II), 1–8

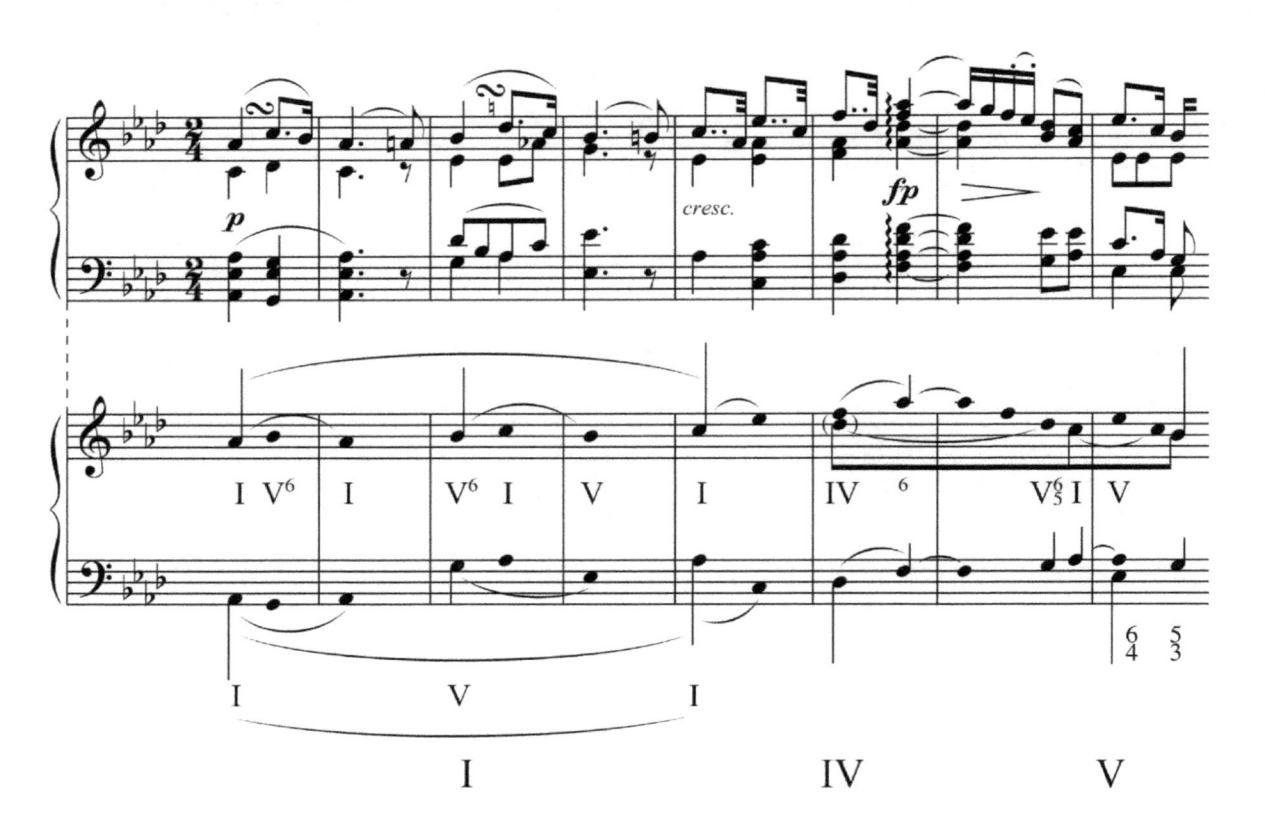

passage leading to D♭5-C5-B♭4. This third is an answer to the ascending third A♭4-B♭4-C5 supported by the tonic scale step. The goals of these thirds articulate a deeper-level step progression C5 to B♭4 shown in the graphic representation by the extended upward-directed stems.

c) The final example in this section is the opening phrase of the development section from the first movement of Mozart's Piano Sonata in B♭, K. 333. This phrase is in the key of the dominant, F major. The chord in the second measure, which is repeated in the third, is vii⁶, a common connector between I and I⁶. In this instance, it does not lead to I⁶, but to a chromatic substitute for it, the diminished seventh chord of ii, thus driving the music forward more forcefully to the following ii⁶. These first four measures fall under the tonic scale step, or stated differently, they prolong the tonic. Looking ahead you will note that I have labeled the chord in the second half of the fifth measure as passing. It is a dominant seventh chord, which logically follows ii⁶. So why have I not labeled it as V⁷? The answer is that it is not the dominant that leads us to the tonic in the final measure of the phrase. That dominant falls in the seventh measure. This chord functions in a different capacity—namely, as a connecting chord between ii⁶ and its chromatic alteration, the diminished seventh chord of V in six-five position, extending the predominant harmony until the cadential six-four in the next measure. The reason I have not labeled the chord in the second half of the fifth

EXAMPLE 1.4c Mozart, Piano Sonata K. 333 (I), 64–71

measure as V^7 is that by doing so it imparts to it a harmonic function it does not have. It has a passing, not a harmonic, role in the progress of the phrase. Labeling all chords can be very misleading if you do not also show their grouping at successive higher levels. Schenker tends to avoid this potential confusion, and when he indicates harmonies on his graphs, he indicates the scale steps (*Stufen*).

Summary

Before proceeding to a consideration of Schenker's concept of structural levels, we should make sure that the ideas and terminology encountered so far are clear. First is *closure*, which for Schenker means the simultaneous arrival at scale degree 1 and tonic harmony. Closure can occur at many levels, in a local context or over the course of an entire composition. Second is the distinction Schenker makes between chord and *harmonic scale step*, or, as I have called it, a controlling harmony that is prolonged by a succession of chords. Most difficult to define is the term *prolongation*, which occurs frequently in the Schenkerian literature. We speak of both melodic and harmonic prolongation. This does *not* mean that the note or harmony being prolonged is present throughout, but rather that this note or harmony is the focal entity to which others are related or from which they derive their meaning *in a given context*. Like closure, prolongation occurs at different structural levels.

The Concept of Structural Levels: A Practical Demonstration

In the previous section, we touched briefly on Schenker's observation that melodic lines at levels beyond note-to-note connections tend to progress by step and that at deeper levels they tend to descend by step to closure. A logical extension of this observation led Schenker eventually to his theory of the *fundamental line*. Since Schenker's focus was on classical tonality, where a key is established and eventually returned to, he inevitably came to the realization that the fundamental line, which occurs over the span of an entire movement or work, must begin on a scale degree belonging to the tonic triad and descend from there to closure. Thus there are only three possibilities: $\hat{3}\ \hat{2}\ \hat{1}$, $\hat{5}\ \hat{4}\ \hat{3}\ \hat{2}\ \hat{1}$, and $\hat{8}\ \hat{7}\ \hat{6}\ \hat{5}\ \hat{4}\ \hat{3}\ \hat{2}\ \hat{1}$. The first note of the fundamental line is called the *primary tone*. (Actually the word used by Schenker was *Kopfton*, which literally means "head tone" or tone at the head/beginning of the fundamental line.) Octave descents at this level occur only in music of the mature baroque, never in classical music, and since we will focus primarily on the classical and early romantic repertoire in this text, we will be dealing almost exclusively with fundamental lines from $\hat{5}$ and $\hat{3}$. Finally, the fundamental line and its support are appropriately called the *fundamental structure*. Various harmonizations for descents from $\hat{3}$ and $\hat{5}$ are listed by Schenker in Figures 15 and 16, respectively, of *Free Composition*.[2] There seems little need to reproduce these possibilities here. Fundamental to all is the bass arpeggiation I-V-I supporting $\hat{3}\ \hat{2}\ \hat{1}$ or $\hat{5} - \hat{2}\ \hat{1}$.

To demonstrate the function of different levels within the context of an encompassing structure, we will examine in detail a short but complete work: Bach's Prelude in C Major from the first volume of the *Well-Tempered Clavier*. This is a work often cited in the literature, including an analysis published in *Five Graphic Music Analyses*,[3] to which we will refer throughout the following discussion. There is much to be learned from this deceptively simple work. The score is provided in Example 1.5.

EXAMPLE 1.5 Bach, Prelude in C Major (WTC I)

EXAMPLE 1.5 *continued*

The first step in the analysis is to make a reduction—actually a simplification of the score, one harmony per measure. Next we will examine the harmony in detail, labeling all chords in the first nineteen measures and beyond that point as appropriate. It is important for us to understand harmonic syntax at this as well as at deeper levels of organization, and this piece offers an excellent opportunity for a review of this component of musical organization. Finally, in this initial stage of analysis, we should examine the metric groups to determine if there is an underlying *hypermeter*. For those of you unfamiliar with this term and the concept it represents, hypermeter refers to the regular grouping of measures where individual measures function much like beats within a measure. By implication, there are accented and unaccented measures in hypermetric groups just as there are accented and unaccented beats in a measure.

A complete reduction of the score with harmonic analysis and indication of metric groupings, shown by the Arabic numerals between the staves, is provided in Example 1.6. One note about the reduction: to simplify, it has been notated in four parts throughout, one result being the transfer of the original "tenor" voice (left-hand) to the upper register through measure 23. Looking at the harmony, we see that the opening four measures establish the key by means of a standard progression and that E5 ($\hat{3}$) is prolonged by its upper neighbor. The six-three chord in measure 5 may be understood as arising from a 5–6 linear motion, but in retrospect it may also be heard as a supertonic harmony in the key of the dominant, which is reached through the following progression leading to the cadence in measure 11. The chord in measure 8 is built over a bass suspension delaying the ii⁷ harmony in the key of the dominant. The next two measures following the cadence on V are a diminished seventh chord of ii progressing to ii⁶, and this is followed by an answer to that progression a step lower. This is followed by a four-measure replica of the progression leading to V a fifth lower, now leading to I in measure 19. Thus the first nineteen measures are to be understood as a prolongation of I. The following four measures are a transition to the dominant. The first harmony, V of IV, leads to IV⁷ and the expectation is that the dissonant 7 will resolve to 6, thus transforming the subdominant into a supertonic. Eventually this takes place following a chromatic passing chord (a diminished seventh chord), but by the time the 7 arrives at 6, the bass has moved up to A♭. The following eight measures prolong the dominant, internal to which the fifth of the chord (D4) progresses up to the seventh (F4). The final four measures are tonic, but typical of Bach, he adds ♭7 to the tonic, propelling the music forward to a final IV-V-I progression over a tonic pedal. At the last minute Bach picks up scale degree 2 in the upper register to come to closure on C5.

The clue to the metric organization is evident in our examination of the succession of harmonies. We have already noted that the four-measure progression leading to the cadence on V (mm. 8–11) is reproduced a fifth lower in mm. 16–19, strongly suggesting an underlying quadruple hypermeter. Note that the strong dissonance, the bass suspension in measure 8 and again in measure 16, falls on a hypermetric downbeat. If we now examine the metric groupings beginning in measures 8–11, we see and hear that the remainder of the prelude follows this pattern. This means that the irregular group falls at the beginning. One might explain the organization of the opening seven measures as overlapping fours, where the fourth measure is reinterpreted as the first of the next four-measure group: 1234/1234. Schenker's solution in *Five Graphic Music Analyses*, reproduced here, is more consistent with his concept of prolongation. The designation 1---agrees with the initial prolongation of the

EXAMPLE 1.6 Reduction of Bach Prelude in C Major

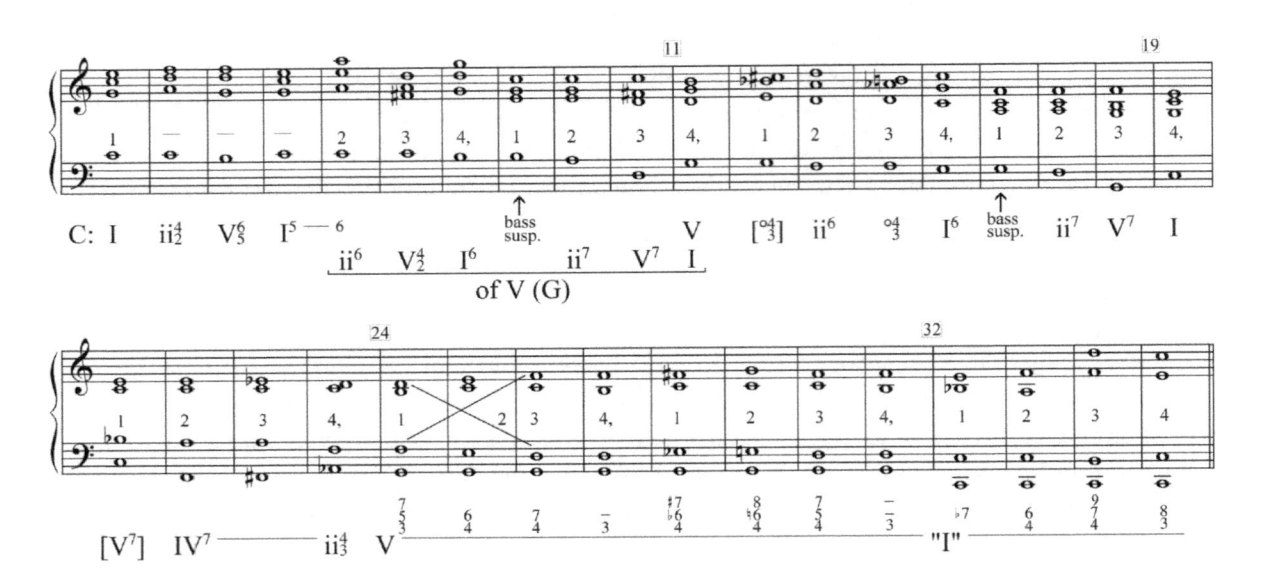

tonic harmony and $\hat{3}$, and it is only following the required establishment of the key (mm. 1–4) that the music begins to move away from the point of reference.

A two-level "sketch" or analytic graph of this prelude—based on the one in *Five Graphic Music Analyses*—is presented in Example 1.7. Notes of the deepest level of structure—the fundamental line ($\hat{3}$ $\hat{2}$ $\hat{1}$) and the supporting bass (I–V–I)—are indicated by half notes. Events of the next level are indicated by quarter notes. We have already noted that the music returns to the tonic harmony and the primary tone, now an octave lower, in measure 19. The means by which this prolongation is accomplished is the *linear progression* (the harmonized progression by step) of the octave E5–E4 running in parallel tenths with the bass, which is broken only in the approach to the cadences in measures 11 and 19. The progression in tenths is indicated by curved lines when top voice and bass are in alignment and diagonal lines when they are not. The descent of the octave is divided into a fourth and a fifth, which is indicated by the slurs within the larger slur encompassing the octave progression. The numbers 1 and 2 above mm. 4–7 and again above mm. 12–15 indicate that the descent of an octave in the top voice is twice elaborated by *covering motions* (temporary projections of an inner voice above the main melodic voice) in pairs, first the motions to A5 and G5 extending E5 and D5, respectively, and then later the chromatic motions C♯5–D5 and B4–C5 covering the chromatic descent from B4 through B♭4 to A4 and through A♭4 to G4. Note that the slurs originate from the notes being prolonged by the covering motion—for example, E5 to A5, and D5 to G5 in mm. 4–7, not the opposite (A5 to D5 and G5 to C5). This seemingly minor point underscores the care one must take in graphic notation. There are circumstances like this, also in the bass in mm. 9–10 and 17–18, where the second note in the pair is understood to extend the first. But there are also circumstances where, for example, the incomplete neighbor progressing to the note it embellishes or the special circumstance where scale degree 4 in the bass leads to scale degree 5 at a cadence, in which case the note is not slurred to the point of origin but to where it leads. As circumstances

EXAMPLE 1.7 Analytic graph of Bach Prelude in C Major

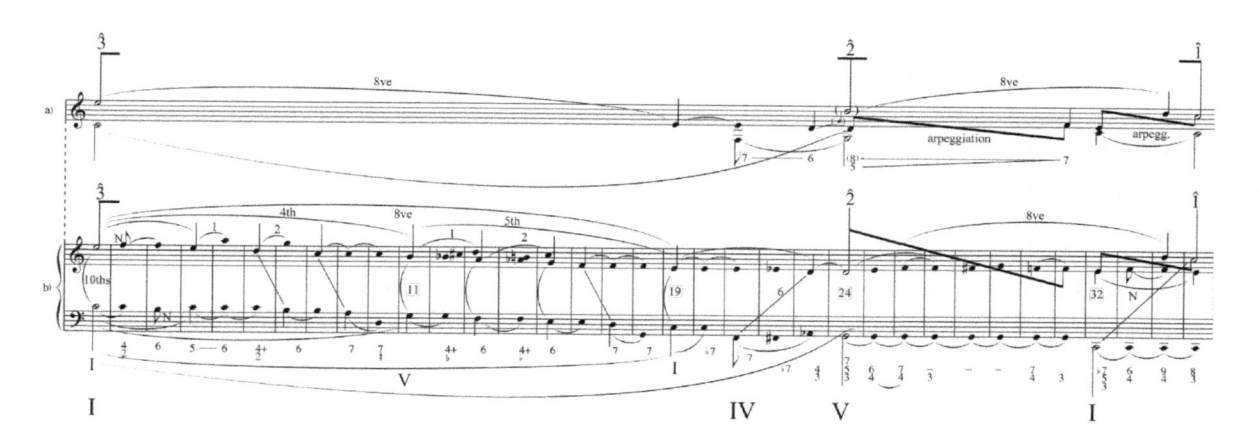

change, so must one's interpretation and notation of it. We shall return to this point several times as we progress through this text. The final observation to be made regarding the first nineteen measures is the prolongation of E5 by its upper neighbor and the bass C4 by its lower neighbor in mm. 1–4. The eighth note is used to designate the lower structural status of the neighbor in relation to the note it prolongs. By now it should be clear that the use of note values in analytic graphs does not denote relative duration but status in the prolongational hierarchy.

As noted earlier, the transition to the dominant, measures 20–23, is a bit more difficult to interpret because of the chromaticism and displacement. The diagonal line between bass and top voice indicates that the melodic D4, which anticipates $\hat{2}$ in the lower register, is to be understood as associated with the bass note F—that is, as the 6 in a 7–6 motion over F. This is more clearly indicated in level (a) of Example 1.7. The main feature of the following eight measures is the motion from D4 to F4, from the fifth to the seventh of the dominant, which is answered in the final four measures by the sixth E4-C5 rather than the third E4-C4, thus ending the prelude in the original register. The notation used here indicates the double *unfolding* of one interval answered by another (see definition at the end of this chapter). The notation used here is often over-employed, thus making a sketch too "busy"; it is better reserved for circumstances where the analyst wants to highlight visually a particular phenomenon, which normally occurs in pairs. The slur from D4 (m. 24) to D5 (m. 34) indicates the coupling of the lower to the upper register in answer to the earlier coupling from upper to lower in measures 1–19. Finally, note the inner voice motion E4-F4-E4 in the final four measures, which imitates the initial melodic gesture of the piece. If one can speak of a motive in this prelude, this is it.

Level (a) of Example 1.7 is the equivalent of level 1 in Schenker's analysis, one step removed from a representation of the fundamental structure, which Schenker shows separately as the top one of three levels. Here the fundamental structure is represented by the half notes. The figured-bass designation below the structural dominant shows that the seventh is to be understood as coming not only from the fifth but also conceptually from the octave.

Fundamental to Schenkerian theory is an understanding that music consists of multiple levels of structure operating simultaneously, very much like visual art. We speak of the musical surface (all the notes in the score), the *foreground* (somewhat below the musical surface), the *middleground*, the *background* and finally the ultimate level, the *fundamental structure*. Continuing the analogy to visual art, let's say to a painting, we can speak of the surface, the individual brush strokes, the organization of these brush strokes into shapes, and then these into larger patterns or colors, which finally are seen as part of the entire picture. Everything—every brush stroke, every shape, every grouping—has its place in the hierarchy. Such is the case with music, at least the type of music we are considering here. But what constitutes these various levels? The extremes, the surface and the fundamental structure, are not an issue here. But what belongs to this or that level in between is not so easy to define, and thus is best discussed in relation to a specific work. Considering the C Major Prelude, perhaps it would be fair to designate the reduction given in Example 1.6 as the foreground. Then the black notes with stems in Example 1.7b designate the linear progressions of the middleground, and Example 1.7a represents the background. But it must be understood that the meaning of these terms—foreground, middleground and background—is relative depending on the composition being examined.

Motive and Structural Levels

In our discussion of the C Major Prelude, the phenomenon of hypermeter—of a regular recurring number of measures—was raised. This is indicated in Schenker's graph of this piece in *Five Graphic Music Analyses*, and there are indications elsewhere in Schenker's writings that he was aware of this idea and of its importance. Yet this aspect of musical organization was never developed by Schenker, and it has fallen to contemporary theorists such as William Rothstein to develop the concept more fully.[4] Likewise with the topic we will now consider: the repetition of motives at different as well as at the same structural level. Again, we know that Schenker was aware of this phenomenon because he points out such occurrences in some of his analyses. But he never developed the idea, and we have Charles Burkhart to thank for highlighting this aspect of Schenker's thinking for us.[5] When we speak of a motive occurring at a different level, it could appear either contracted or enlarged; however, most frequently it is the latter. Once a motive appears at a more remote level of structure—say at the middleground—it no longer is identified with the original rhythmic articulation. In essence, it is defined solely by its pitch succession, or, in the case of a transposed statement, by its scale degree succession in relation to the local key. A simple but elegant example of this phenomenon—one often cited in the literature[6]—occurs in the opening measures of Mozart's Piano Sonata in C major, K. 545. See Example 1.8. As shown by my additions to the score, the A5-G5-F5-E5 of measures 3–4 are immediately repeated and expanded in the following four measures, which is followed by its continuation to D5, first supported by ii⁶, then V at the half cadence.

A more complex example of motivic repetition and enlargement occurs in the opening phrase of Mozart's Piano Sonata in B♭, K. 333, which is reproduced in Example 1.9a, below which is my interpretation of its voice leading as well as its motivic repetitions. The motive to which I am referring is the descending arpeggiation of the tonic triad F5-D5-B♭4, and its several statements are highlighted in my graph by the beamed notes. The initial statement of this idea opens with an appoggiatura, G5, and though the first four notes are played equally (as four sixteenth notes), Mozart's notation reveals his understanding of this note

EXAMPLE 1.8 Mozart, Piano Sonata K. 545 (I), 1–12

Example 1.9 Mozart, Piano Sonata K. 333 (I), 1–10

as a decoration of F5. This is an important detail that is exploited by Mozart not only later in this movement but also in the finale. This initial idea is answered by a statement a step lower, E♭5-C5-A4. The resolution of the dissonant seventh of the dominant, E♭5, is to D5 supported by tonic harmony in measure 4. As indicated in my graph by the extended beams and scale degrees with carets, the underlying voice leading of these opening measures is F5-E♭5-D5 harmonized by the progression I-ii-V-I.

Beginning in measure 5 we have a two-measure idea, actually a reiteration of the fifth motive that is subsequently repeated in varied form. How are we to interpret this? Does the statement of the motive of a fifth from F5, once again decorated by the upper neighbor G5, suggest the retention of F5 and that the preceding descent of a third is to be understood as embedded within a more inclusive descent? That is a possibility. But when we look to the goal of this gesture, we note that there is a specific relationship between its end points—namely, a voice exchange between the outer parts. In other words, the function of the fifth descent here in measures 5–6 is not to reinstate F5 ($\hat{5}$) but rather it serves as a motivic reference—a diminution motive—within the prolongation of $\hat{3}$ and the tonic harmony. The varied repetition of this idea has been placed in parentheses to show that it or the statement before it could be omitted, and the Arabic numerals between the staves indicate that it is this repetition that expands an eight-measure phrase to ten. Following this repetition, there is one more statement of the descending fifth motive and completion of the structural descent transferred to the upper register. Note the substitution of the leading tone for scale degree 2 over the dominant and the employment of the diagonal line to show the association of C6 with the bass supporting the dominant harmony. In summary, then, this phrase contains five statements of this motivic idea, all at the same level, but serving different purposes in the voice-leading structure. But it is also true that the motive is represented at the middleground level, as shown in Example 1.9b. That is, the entire phrase articulates a descending fifth divided into thirds: F5-E♭5-D5 (mm. 1–4), which is extended twice by a voice exchange and elaborated by the fifth motive, and then D6-C6-B♭5 in measures 9–10, again elaborated by a statement of the motive. This division of the fifth into two thirds and the elaboration of scale degree 5 (F) by its upper appoggiatura (incomplete neighbor) are exploited by Mozart in the development section of this movement.

The score of the development section is provided in Example 1.10. On the score, the notation 8/1 is written between the staves in measure 71 to indicate that the last measure of the initial phrase is simultaneously the first measure of the following material. This is a very common procedure in tonal music—a *phrase overlap* with *metric reinterpretation*—to keep the music moving forward without constantly stopping at a cadence and then beginning again. Also written on the score are points of stability: V (prolonged through the initial phrase)— III♯ (the D major chord prolonged in measures 81–86)—and finally I (measure 94) at the beginning of the recapitulation. Some of you might wonder why the D major chord is labeled III♯ rather than V of vi. The answer is simple enough. Though introduced from a G minor chord (downbeat of measure 80), it never functions as a dominant—that is, it never realizes its potential as a dominant. Rather, it functions to divide the space between V (F) and I (B♭). In short, the development section as it connects to the recapitulation appears to be organized around the large-scale representation of the descending fifth motive that permeates more immediate levels of structure throughout the first as well as the third movements of this sonata: F–D–B♭. The fact that this passage is organized around the progression V–III♯–I is hardly proof that Mozart was thinking in terms of *motivic enlargement* when he wrote this passage, since this very progression is a common means of connecting V to I. But the notion of motivic derivation gains credibility when we observe that the means by which Mozart prolongs the F is by progressing twice to its upper neighbor G, as he has done in the opening gesture of the movement.[7]

A bass-line sketch of this passage is provided in Example 1.11. The extended stems and large slurs show the descending arpeggiation to B♭ (I). Before progressing to D, the bass line is directed up to G, the first time in measure 73 to an unstable harmony (G7), which is returned to F, now F7, via the chromatic passing tone G♭, and then a second time via the chromatic passing tone F♯ as the point from which to lead logically to the D major chord. Following the extension of the D major chord by its chromatic upper neighbor supporting the augmented sixth chord E♭–G–C♯, the bass moves to the passing dominant in four-three position in the upper register to prepare the return to the opening. This registral shift is not shown in Example 1.11 in order to show more clearly the descending bass arpeggiation. Rather than progress immediately to the tonic, Mozart introduces the dominant seventh harmony in root position, which is now decorated by its chromatic upper neighbor G♭. It is remarkable to see that a work that may have originally been improvised, as apparently some of the sonatas were, is so rich in motivic associations.

EXAMPLE **1.10** Mozart, Piano Sonata K. 333 (I), 64–94

EXAMPLE 1.10 *continued*

EXAMPLE 1.11 Bass-line Representation of Mozart's Piano Sonata K. 333 (I), 64–94

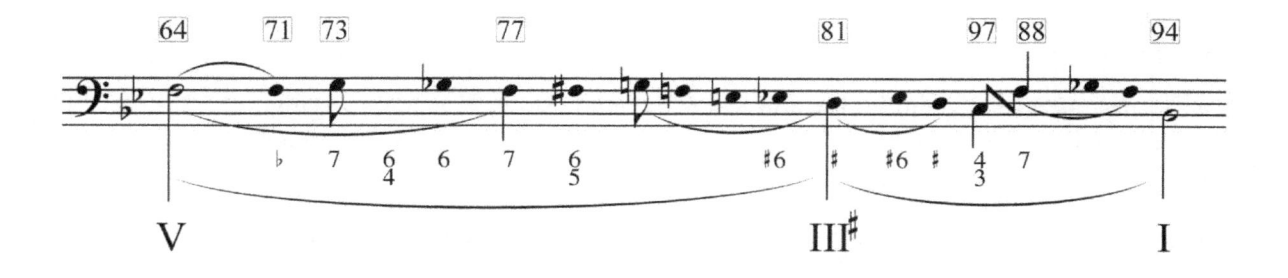

REVIEW: TERMINOLOGY AND DEFINITIONS

Ahead are definitions of important terms encountered in this introductory chapter.

1. *Structural levels* are identified by Schenker as three levels in addition to the most basic level, the fundamental structure: *foreground, middleground* and *background*. In longer works, more than one level of the middleground is frequently identified.

2. The *fundamental structure* consists of the *fundamental line* ($\hat{3}\hat{2}\hat{1}$, $\hat{5}\hat{4}\hat{3}\hat{2}\hat{1}$ or rarely $\hat{8}\hat{7}\hat{6}\hat{5}\hat{4}\hat{3}\hat{2}\hat{1}$) and its harmonic support. The first note of the fundamental line is called the *primary tone*.

3. *Closure* refers to the simultaneous arrival at $\hat{1}$ and tonic harmony at the conclusion of the fundamental structure or at more immediate levels, in which case it is often referred to as *local closure*.

4. *Prolongation* refers to the process by which a note or a chord retains its control over surrounding events.

5. *Linear progressions* are stepwise harmonized progressions of the middleground. According to Schenker, linear progressions span consonant intervals only: thirds, fourths, fifths, sixths and octaves. We have observed all of these in their descending form in this chapter.

6. *Voice exchange* is an extremely common technique of prolongation involving the exchange of two notes belonging to the same harmony between the same two voices. Exchange between outer voices is most common.

7. *Substitution* at the cadence refers to the common substitution of the leading tone for scale degree 2 in relation to V at either a half or a perfect authentic cadence.

8. *Unfolding* involves motion between two parts, often between the top and an inner voice. This motion may occur between different notes belonging to the same harmony (most common) or belonging to different harmonies. This phenomenon is notated graphically by adding an upward-directed stem on the lower of the two notes, a downward-directed stem on the upper of the two, and a slanted beam connecting the two stems. Stems are often added to both notes in the opposite direction as well to identify them as part of a linear progression in a particular voice.

9. *Hypermeter* refers to the regular grouping of measures, most often in multiples of two, in a composition. Where this occurs, the measures are accented (strong) or unaccented (weak) in much the same ways as beats have relative accentuation in a measure.

10. *Phrase overlap* refers to a common situation where the last measure of one phrase simultaneously becomes the first measure of the next phrase, in this way allowing the music to proceed without unnecessary stops.

11. *Metric reinterpretation* refers to the reassigning of function of a hypermeasure—for example, 4 becoming 1 (4/1 or 4 = 1). Metric reinterpretation occurs frequently in conjunction with phrase overlap, but it also occurs independently.

12. *Motivic parallel* refers to repetition of a motive, which can occur at the same or at different structural levels.

NOTES

1. The upper neighbor Bb is displaced by C5, resulting in a clearly articulated descending third C5–Bb4–Ab4, an important detail that is related to thirds articulated at deeper levels. A thorough analysis of the phrase should take into account this clearly articulated idea and its repetition. However, from a structural perspective, this C5 is an appoggiatura, and the underlying melodic progression of measures 1–2 is Ab4–Bb4–Ab4.

2. Heinrich Schenker, *Free Composition*, trans. and ed. Ernst Oster (Longman, 1979).

3. Heinrich Schenker, *Five Graphic Music Analyses* (Dover, 1969).

4. William Rothstein, *Phrase Rhythm in Tonal Music* (Schirmer, 1989).

5. Charles Burkhart, "Schenker's 'Motivic Parallelisms'," *Journal of Music Theory* 22 (1978), 145–175.

6. See, for example, Oswald Jonas, *Introduction to the Theory of Heinrich Schenker*, trans. and ed. John Rothgeb (Longman, 1982), 3–4.

7. Whether this motivic parallel was intentional must remain unanswered. But one thing is certain: we would not even be entertaining this possible connection if we had not considered musical connections at deeper levels.

2 The Phrase and Parallel Phrases

In the following three chapters we will examine the phrase and the period in some detail and, in some cases, from diverse though compatible points of view. The purpose of these chapters is not to present an exhaustive catalogue of phrase types or of phrases in combination, but to explore some principles that are fundamental to Schenker's thinking. We will begin in this chapter with the individual phrase and the combination of two phrases in the antecedent-consequent relationship. Chapter 3 will deal with aspects of phrase rhythm and phrase expansion, and Chapter 4 will round out this study with a consideration of the combination of contrasting phrases to form larger closed units. This extended exercise will prepare us well to deal with short compositions in ternary (rounded binary) form in Chapter 5, which rounds out Part I.

Before embarking on this exercise, a word about notation. The analytic graphs in this and subsequent chapters show the underlying voice leading and thus purposely omit almost all surface embellishments (e.g., passing and neighboring tones), unless they play a significant role in the composition. The reasons for their omission are simple. Their inclusion would make the graph too crowded and difficult to read, and would make it harder to show important underlying connections. But this does not imply that these decorative notes are not important, only that they have no significant role in the underlying structure. Still, it is important that you identify these elements and understand why they have been omitted. A worthwhile exercise is to examine carefully each musical excerpt presented with the corresponding graph with this in mind. Each one of these examples should be studied carefully.

The Phrase

First we must define the term "phrase". At the most basic level we are talking about a musical unit that expresses tonal motion leading to a point of rest (a cadence). Under most circumstances a phrase has a clearly defined beginning, middle and end. There is no requirement regarding length, though the norm in the second half of the eighteenth and in the nineteenth centuries is four or eight measures, depending on many factors, including tempo. The only requirement is that it expresses a well-formed musical idea. We will begin by examining four phrases from three different periods. The first (see Example 2.1a) is the opening phrase of the courante movement from Bach's Cello Suite No. 1.

A good place to begin is an examination of the motivic repetitions in the opening measures. In addition to the opening gesture, the descending arpeggiation, the most

EXAMPLE 2.1 Bach, Cello Suite I, Courante, 1–8

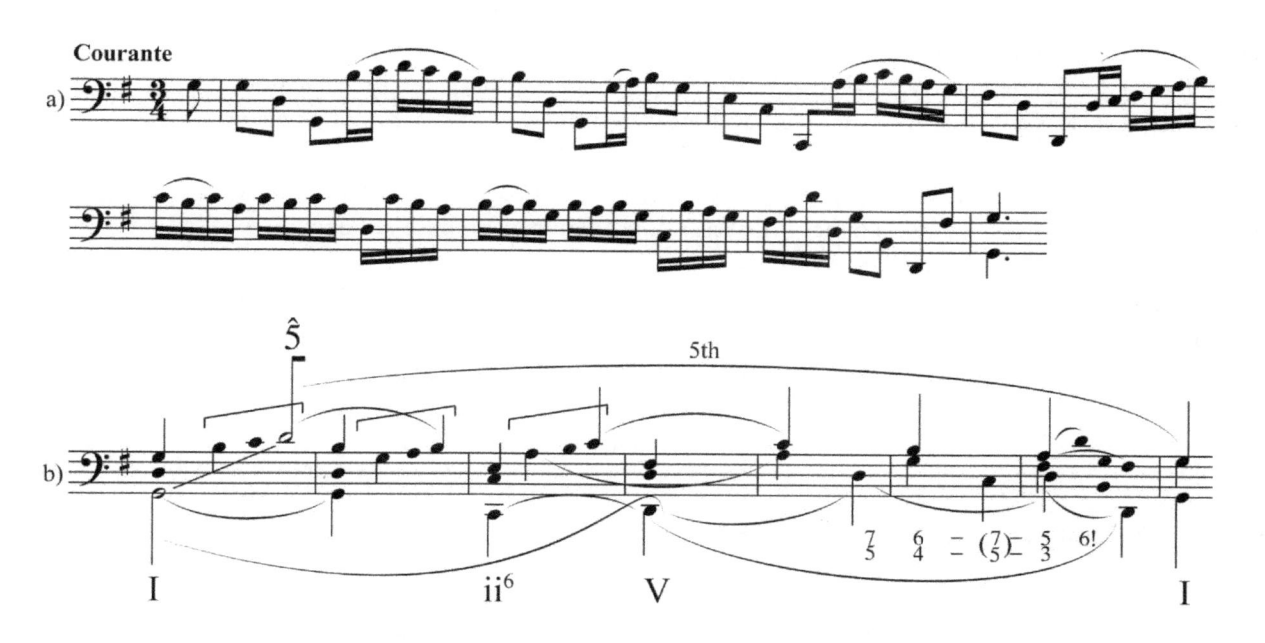

important motivic component is the rising third B3-C4-D4 and its continuation. Though this idea is answered a third lower in measure 2, the rhythmic continuation is different. Bach could have written four sixteenth notes at the end of the second measure, but he chose to reserve this gesture—the real answer to measure 1—until the third measure. One result is the establishment of a duple grouping of measures (duple hypermeter) with alternating strong (accented) and weak (unaccented) measures. It also informs our hearing of these measures and thus our interpretation of them. That is, we hear the third A3-B3-C4 in measure 3 as an answer, a step lower, to the third B3-C4-D4 in measure 1. Looking ahead, we see that the third A3-C4 is picked up in measure 5 (another strong measure), from which point the thirds continue to descend to local closure in measure 8. The point of departure for this descent is the opening third B3-C4-D4 in measure 1.

A graphic representation of the voice leading of this phrase is provided in Example 2.1 at (b). The repetitions of the rising third motive are indicated by brackets, which is a common method of indicating motivic repetition employed by Schenker in his graphs. The primary tone ($\hat{5}$) and the remaining tones of the descending fifth are encompassed by a large slur, and the steps along the way are clearly indicated by upward-directed stems. The descent in thirds from measure 5 on requires some comment. One might expect the third G3-B3 in measure 6 to receive consonant support, but instead we hear the descent of the thirds A3-C4, G3-B3, and F♯3-A3 in measures 5–7 all in relation to the bass note D—that is, as a motion from the seventh to the fifth of the dominant in the top part, as indicated by the figured-bass symbols below. The bass note C3 on the last beat of measure 6 also requires some comment. Had Bach continued the sequential pattern established in measures 5 and 6, we might expect this C to progress down by step in the next measure. Instead, it seems to function as a lower neighbor of D3, to which it returns briefly on the fourth sixteenth in measure 7. But what of the bass note B2 that actually does follow in measure 7? What is its function? It appears to provide consonant support for the passing tone G3 within the third A3-G3-F♯3 extending the second scale degree on its way to *closure*. (As noted in Chapter 1, the concept of closure is fundamental to Schenker's conception of musical structure. The term refers to the simultaneous arrival at scale degree 1 [melodic closure] and tonic harmony [harmonic closure]. Closure can occur at all levels of structure—e.g., at the end of a period or phrase, like here [referred to as local closure] or of the fundamental structure.) Considered in relation to the controlling harmony (V), this passing G3 is a dissonance. But at the level that it receives support, it is a consonance—that is, a consonant passing note connecting A3 and F♯3.

Example 2.2a presents the opening phrase of Beethoven's Piano Sonata Op. 2, No. 1, a phrase cited by many, including Arnold Schoenberg and Heinrich Schenker. For Schoenberg, this phrase represented a prime example of what he called a musical *sentence*,

EXAMPLE 2.2 Beethoven, Piano Sonata Op. 2, No. 1 (I), 1–8

the main components of which are a basic idea (tonic version, mm. 1–2) and its repetition (dominant version, mm. 3–4), which together form the presentation. This is followed by the continuation, which consists of fragmentation (repetitions of the descending third motive) and a cadential idea. A characteristic of this phrase is the process of acceleration, the shortening of statements of the basic idea/motive—from two measures plus upbeat to two measures to one measure in length—in the drive to the cadence.[1] Schoenberg's primary focus here is describing the building blocks of the form (the basic idea and its motivic components), their treatment and their assembly into a coherent unit. Schenker too was concerned very much with motivic development, but within the context of voice leading. While their approaches are different, they are not mutually exclusive. Both approaches provide valuable insights into the music.

A graph of the voice leading of this phrase is provided as Example 2.2b. Repetitions of the descending third motive (measures 2, 4, 5 and 6) are marked by brackets. Measures 2–5 are shown to prolong Ab5 and the tonic harmony by means of a neighboring chord, after which the melodic line ascends to C6 in parallel tenths with the bass, shown by the curved lines. The ascent of a third is clearly delineated in both voices by a slur. The diagonal line from the opening bass note (measure 2) to C6 (measure 7) indicates their association. While the primary tone is frequently established right from the very beginning, Schenker points out that there are circumstances under which the introduction of the primary tone is delayed, in which case it is approached either by arpeggiation or by an ascending progression by step, as here.[2] There is not enough information here for you to decide on a primary tone. This decision is based on an examination of the remainder of the movement. A remarkable feature of Schenker's analysis[3] is his revelation that the primary features of this opening phrase, the ascending third Ab5-Bb5-C6 and the descending sixth C6-E♮5, become the framework for the entire development section of this movement. This is a prime example of what is referred to as *motivic enlargement*, a type of motivic parallelism.[4] A special feature of this descending sixth is its articulation—namely, the step progression C6 to Bb5 and then the unfolding of the interval Bb5-E♮5, which promises an answering Ab5-F5 that occurs only much later in the movement, transposed to the lower octave, after the restatement of this opening phrase at the beginning of the recapitulation. This particular articulation is reflected in the enlarged statement in the development section—that is, the C and Bb receive a different articulation than the continuation to the inner voice tone E♮. This analysis by Schenker reveals his remarkable insight into Beethoven's compositional method.

Our third example is the opening phrase of Beethoven's Piano Sonata Op. 13, another example of a musical sentence, in this case one that modulates from the tonic (C minor) to the relative major (III). As shown by the brackets on the score (Example 2.3a), the basic idea or motive of measure 1 (tonic form) is repeated in measure 2 (dominant/diminished seventh form) leading to i⁶. The continuation involves two condensed statements of this idea leading to V⁶, and this is followed by the secondary dominant in four-two position leading to iv⁶ on the third beat of measure 4. This is the pivot in the modulation to Eb (iv⁶ = ii⁶ in the new key). Arrival at III in measure 5 supports a "new" idea, which is really a reworking of the previous repeated motive.

The main features of the dramatic initial idea are the opening tonic chord, the ensuing voice exchange between the outer parts in which the top voice reaches up to Eb4, and the following diminished seventh chord leading to V supporting D4 over B♮3. This gesture is answered by a diminished seventh chord in the main key involving another voice exchange between the outer voices, which then resolves to a tonic chord in first inversion. As shown in the graph in Example 2.3b, the underlying melodic progression across these two statements of the basic idea is a rising third E♭4-F4-G4 accompanied by a bass motion from C3 (i) to E♭3 (i⁶). The continuation, which follows in the upper octave, begins with a variant of the opening idea that is immediately repeated. Here the voice exchange, which reaches up to E♭5 in the top part, occurs within the diminished seventh chord of V, which leads to D5 supported by V⁶. Rather than resolve back to E♭5, the second statement of this idea leads to E♮5 as part of a secondary four-two chord leading to F5 over A♭3 (iv⁶), the pivot in the modulation to III. From this point the top voice reaches up to A♭5 to introduce G5 from above. Resolution to the E♭ chord first occurs in the lower octave, and G5 is subsequently introduced on the third beat of measure 5 following an ascending third, a gesture that recalls the melodic progression uniting measures 1 and 2 in the lower octave.

A middleground graph of these measures is provided in Example 2.3c. The large slur here as well as in the graph above it shows the overall motion from the opening E♭ leading to G5. Like the preceding example, the primary tone has been reached by a harmonized ascending step progression (*Anstieg*), only here the point of arrival comes after a local change of key.

The final phrase to be examined here, the opening nine measures of the Brahms Intermezzo Op. 117, No. 2, is reproduced in Example 2.4a. Though its style characteristics are very different from the Beethoven phrase (it was written just short of 100 years later), its underlying voice leading is decidedly classical. First let's examine the phrase's harmonic organization and its motivic repetitions. The harmonic progression is indicated between the staves. The chord on the downbeats of measures 1 and 2 is a tonic chord in six-three position, but the function of the chord introducing them is not clear, though eventually we may surmise it to be an incomplete diminished seventh chord (missing the leading tone A♮). On the third beat of measure 2, the root and seventh are added to the tonic harmony, and this becomes the initiating point for a descending fifth sequence of diatonic seventh chords directed first at ii⁷ (m. 5) and then V⁷ (m. 6). The remainder of the phrase is an extension of the dominant harmony through measure 9, creating an overlap with the consequent phrase. The primary motivic component is the opening gesture, clearly defined by its rhythmic character and the repetition of its middle note (C5) in the descending third D♭5-C5-B♭4. This motive and its repetitions are notated on the score. The first time this motive is extended is in the statement beginning on the upbeat to measure 5, where the descending third E♭5-D♭5-C5 is first introduced and supported by ii⁷, and then repeated in the next measure supported by the dominant. The remainder of the phrase extends this idea further, eventually to include the opening gesture at the phrase overlap.

A musical graph of the opening phrase of the Brahms Intermezzo is provided in Example 2.4b. Note that the B♭, the root of the tonic harmony, has been added in parentheses. (The first tonic chord in root position without a seventh is the last chord in the piece!) The first repetition of the identified rhythmic motive introduces the primary tone (F5) on the downbeat of measure 2, and, as noted earlier, the addition of the root (bass) and the seventh (top voice) of the tonic harmony initiates the following sequence. The graph shows the texture of the phrase as consisting of three voices, and the numbers between the staves indicate the intervallic pattern of the top two parts in relation to the bass. The addition

EXAMPLE 2.3 Beethoven, Piano Sonata Op. 13 (I), 1–5

EXAMPLE 2.4a Brahms, Intermezzo, Op. 117, No. 2, 1–9

EXAMPLE 2.4b Graph of Brahms Op. 117, No. 2, 1–9

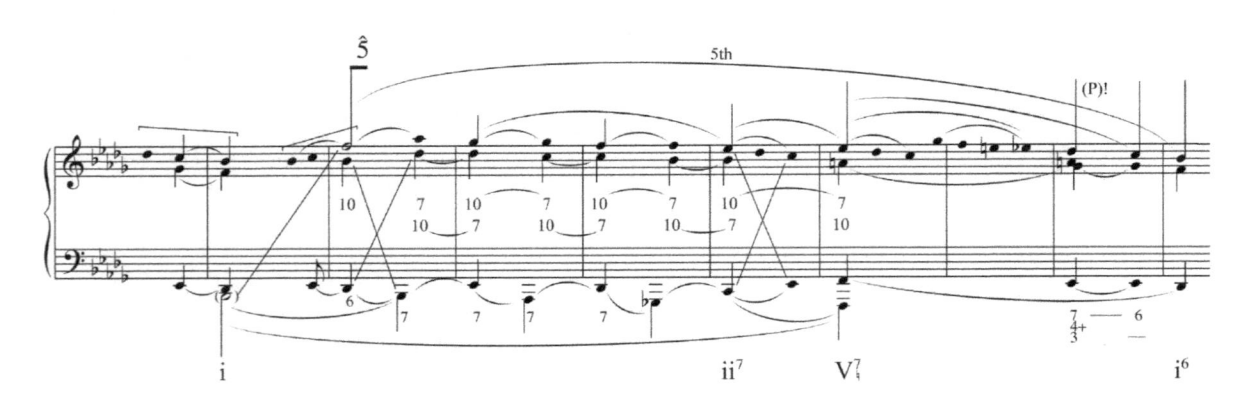

of the seventh (A♭5) to the tonic harmony in measure 2 introduces the upper neighbor of F5—namely, G♭5. However, rather than return to a stable F5, the sequence continues beyond this point to the E♭5 on the downbeat of measure 5. Thus this G♭5 is not marked as a neighbor note, but rather as the initiating point of a descending third leading to the E♭5, which is notated by a slur. The arrival at this point coincides with the initial statement of the descending third E♭5-D♭5-C5, articulated by a voice exchange within the ii⁷ harmony, which is subsequently repeated, now supported by the dominant. Our expectation, of course, is that this E♭5, the dissonant seventh of the dominant, will resolve to a stable D♭. Instead, what follows is an enlargement of the descending third supported by an extended dominant that is transformed into a diminished seventh chord in four-three position leading to a repetition of the opening gesture. It is this manner of return to the opening gesture that leads to the idea of the opening chord being an incomplete diminished seventh chord.

One might be tempted to interpret the harmony in measure 8 as a minor chord built on G♭, thus supplying consonant support for the D♭, but the continuation makes it clear that Brahms means the A♮ he has written, not B♭♭. The D♭ is not stable; it is an extended passing tone within the restated third E♭5-D♭5-C5. And it is the extension of this passing tone that results in the expansion of an eight-measure phrase to nine. This is a remarkable passage. Scale degree 3 never receives consonant support within the descending fifth. Though very different from the Bach phrase examined earlier, the two share this common characteristic.

Antecedent-Consequent Phrases

In this section we will examine seven examples of periods formed by parallel phrases (antecedent-consequent pairs). The term "parallel" here means that the phrases begin with the same material. Of the various types—interrupted, sectional, continuous and progressive (modulating)—we will focus on the first of these, since this construction has particular significance in Schenkerian analysis. In this chapter, we will treat these periods as if they are complete short pieces—that is, we will notate their structures as fundamental, using open note heads (half notes) for the deepest level of structure. However, you must understand that our notation of them will change once they are placed in their larger contexts. Our interpretation would not change—only our notation.

Our first example is the opening eight measures of the theme used by Schubert as the basis for a set of variations in his Impromptu, Op. 142, No. 3. The score is provided in Example 2.5 at (a) and our interpretation of its structure at (b). The primary tone ($\hat{3}$) is clearly articulated from the very beginning. It is prolonged initially in measure 1 by a voice exchange with the bass and from measure 1 to its restatement on the downbeat of measure 3 by a motion to its upper neighbor E♭5 in measure 2 supported by the dominant. The third D5-B♭4 (m. 1) is answered by the diminished fifth A4-E♭5 (m. 2), which resolves back to D5-B♭4 (the latter supplied in parentheses in our interpretation) in measure 3. The leap in measure 3 from D5 to G4 is from an outer to an inner voice; the D5 over the bass note E♭ is to be understood as a displacement of C5, as occurs an octave lower in the left-hand part. This gesture is then answered in the next measure by a leap from C5 to F4 supported by the progression $\left[V_5^6\right]$ V. Overall the melodic progression is from D5 to C5 ($\hat{3}$ to $\hat{2}$) supported by the motion I to V. This example introduces another concept fundamental to Schenker's theory—namely, that of *interruption*, which refers to the cessation of melodic motion short of *closure*—that is, at $\hat{2}$ supported by V. Interruption, like closure, can occur at multiple levels of structure, and in Schenkerian graphs its presence is signaled by two short parallel lines. Within the context of a parallel period, the interruption comes at the end of the antecedent phrase, and local closure then follows at the end of the consequent phrase, following the restatement of the primary tone, as occurs in this and several of the following examples.

Before proceeding to further examples, let's take a look at the notation employed in Example 2.5b. The notes of the fundamental structure, the fundamental line and its harmonic support, are indicated by open notes with stems (half notes). Furthermore, the notes of the fundamental line are marked by scale degrees with carets above, in this case $\hat{3}$ $\hat{2}$ // $\hat{3}$ $\hat{2}$ $\hat{1}$. I have also used slurs to indicate melodic connections at this and at other levels of structure. The notation of the bass line at this level follows a common convention in Schenkerian graphs—namely, a large curved slur from tonic up over the dominant; furthermore, the note preparing the dominant, commonly scale degree 4, is notated as an eighth note slurred to the dominant, as here at the end of the antecedent phrase.

The melodic line in this excerpt consists of two strands (compound melody), and I have notated the upper strand with stems up, the lower one with stems down; I have also indicated the leaps between the two with slurs. This same procedure is followed in the bass line in measures 1–3 and 5–7. Melodically the primary tone D5 is prolonged by its upper neighbor tone E♭5, which is notated as an eighth note to indicate its place in the pitch hierarchy. As a general rule, Schenkerian notation indicates relative levels in the structural hierarchy, the deepest level shown as half notes, then quarter notes, eighth notes and unstemmed note-heads. Structural connections, like the prolongation of D5 here in measures 1–3, are marked by slurs.

Our second example is the opening period from the third movement of Mozart's Piano Sonata K. 333. The score is reproduced at a in Example 2.6, below which I have provided two levels of interpretation at b and c. The top melodic line is shown at level b by the notes with the upward-directed stems. The first two notes of this line, F5 and E♭5, each initiate a statement of the descending fifth motive so prominent in the first movement,[5] but in the second of these the middle note, C5 (in parentheses) is displaced by G5. The resolution of the dissonant E♭5 is delayed until the third quarter of the next measure following a voice exchange with the bass. Note that the pitches of the underlying ascending line in this third measure are each introduced by their upper appoggiaturas (incomplete neighbors). This ascending line proceeds to E♭5 supported by ii⁶, after which it descends by step to C5 over the dominant, the point of interruption. Though we have identified the progress of the top line to this point, it remains partially uninterpreted here. That is, the notation suggests that the notes of the melodic progression are all equal structurally. They are not.

Below level b I have provided an analysis of the harmony at two levels. Schenker would not mark all the detail I have shown at level 1, but only the underlying progression at 2. But I think it is useful, particularly for the beginning student, to understand harmonic syntax at the chord-to-chord level as long as this is done in conjunction with an examination of harmony in the broader context, as I have indicated at level 2. Note the designation I⁵⁻⁶ in the first measure; the inner-voice note G4 arises from a melodic motion (F)-G, not from harmonic considerations. Chords arising from linear motion are never marked as harmonic entities in Schenkerian graphs. The second level of harmonic analysis indicates that the first

EXAMPLE 2.5 Schubert, Impromptu Op. 142, No. 3, 1–8

part of the phrase through the third quartet of measure 3 is controlled by the tonic harmony; said differently, this passage constitutes a tonic prolongation. Thus, by definition, the initial descent F5-E♭5-D5 occurs within this extended tonic area, prolonging the initiating tone, F5. This leads us to the interpretation at level c, which shows this initial descent embedded within the descending fourth leading to the interruption. What is crucial to understand is that the melodic E♭5 on the fourth quartet of measure 3 is not functioning in the underlying structure as the upper neighbor of D5, but as part of the descending line from F5 to C5. This brings up an interesting issue regarding performance. The notation of the right-hand part in measure 3 suggests that each of the four quarters is equal, but is each to be played equally, or should there be slightly greater emphasis given to the fourth quarter? To a certain extent Mozart has provided the solution for us by adding the bass note E♭ at this point, thickening the texture.[6] But what of the consequent phrase, the first two measures of which replicate those of the antecedent phrase? Why have I interpreted the initial descent differently than before? The answer is that the continuation, the context, is different. The line continues its descent to local closure. Note the extension of C5 ($\hat{2}$) by a descending third to the leading tone at the cadence. We will encounter this phenomenon—substitution at the cadence—frequently throughout this book.

EXAMPLE 2.6 Mozart, Piano Sonata K.333 (III), 1–8

Our next example, which has a similar structure to the one just examined, is the second subject from the first movement of Mozart's Piano Sonata in D Major, K. 311. The score is provided in Example 2.7a and my interpretation of its voice leading at b. The melody begins with a pickup, a decorated ascending third to the primary tone (5̂), which is prolonged in the first measure by a leap up to A5 and the return by step to E5 supported by tonic harmony. In the next measure, D5 is introduced by its lower appoggiatura, and then prolonged, first by its upper neighbor and then by a motion down a third to B4. The D5 is first supported as a consonance by ii, then as the dissonant seventh of the dominant. Instead of resolving directly to C♯5 on the downbeat of measure 3, the lower note of the third D5-B4 resolves first to A4, introduced by its lower appoggiatura G♯4, and C♯5 is reached via the passing tones B4 and B♯4. This motion A4 to C♯5, from inner to outer voice, is supported by a voice exchange with the bass. Here again care has to be taken to distinguish inner from outer parts by direction of stems in our analytic graph. So, what do we have so far? An elaborated descending third E5-D5-C♯5 supported by the progression I–ii–V⁷–I. Like the preceding

Example 2.7 Mozart, Piano Sonata K. 311 (I), 17–24

example, it may appear to the novice that there are two possible interpretations of this descending third. Either it is the primary descent to $\hat{3}$, which is subsequently decorated by its upper neighbor note before progressing on to $\hat{2}$ in the next measure, or it is a preliminary descent prolonging $\hat{5}$ and thus embedded within the encompassing descent to the interruption, as shown in Example 2.7 at b. In fact, you do not have a choice, at least from a Schenkerian perspective. The reason is that the descending third takes place within a tonic prolongation, and thus by definition it prolongs the initiating tone.

The consequent phrase begins parallel to the antecedent phrase, but it changes on the downbeat of the third measure, where the preceding D5 resolves directly to C♯5 supported by A. Furthermore, the line continues from there to closure with the common substitution of the leading tone for $\hat{2}$ over the dominant. This time the descent E5-D5-C♯5 is not embedded within a larger progression but continues to closure. This is *not* an inconsistency, but rather points to an important axiom of Schenkerian analysis—namely, that interpretation is dependent on context, and here the context—the continuation beyond this descending third—has changed. Regarding notation, the diagonal lines indicate the association of notes not occurring simultaneously, and the designation 4/1 in the last measure indicates a metric reinterpretation and phrase overlap resulting from the final measure of the theme becoming the first measure of the following phrase.

Example 2.8, level a, the opening eight measures from the second movement of Mozart's Piano Trio K. 542 (piano solo), presents an interesting comparison to the preceding example. Considering the antecedent phrase alone, a logical interpretation might appear to be an interruption from $\hat{5}$ (E5), stated on the downbeat of measure 1 and prolonged until the entrance of D5 on the second beat of measure 3. There are two problems with this idea, the first being the status of C♯5 and its tonic support on the last eighth note of measure 3. It is clearly passing within the descending third D5-C♯5-B4, not a structural pitch but a local connecting note. Furthermore, as we look ahead to the consequent phrase, we see (and, of course, hear) that the C♯5 on the downbeat of measure 7 leads directly to C♯5 supported by the dominant and on to local closure. There is no D5 connecting E5 to the C♯5, unless we were to supply one in parentheses on the last eighth note of measure 6. Despite the weak placement of C♯5 at the beginning of both phrases, this is our primary tone, and E5 is an example of what is called a *covering tone*, a prominent pitch that covers the primary tone.

You should take some time to examine the notation employed in the graph (Example 2.8a), including the use of slurs to show connections at various levels. Following the initial voice exchange between the outer and inner voices, the primary tone, now in the inner voice covered by E5, is prolonged by its upper neighbor, notated as an eighth note and marked "N". I hear the decorated B4 in the second half of measure 1 as passing to A4 in measure 2, which is led back immediately to C♯5 on the downbeat of measure 3 via the harmonized passing note B4. The following descending third, which leads to $\hat{2}$, is shown as a local event (no stems).

Our next example, the second subject from the first movement of Mozart's Piano Sonata in B♭, K. 333, is longer and presents several challenges to the analyst. The score is provided in Example 2.9 and a graph of its voice-leading structure in Example 2.10. Each of the eight-measure phrases is clearly divided into four-measure units, articulated by a weak cadence on I in the fourth measure. Thus the first four measures of both the antecedent and consequent phrases are to be interpreted as prolonging the tonic, and the descent to A4 in the fourth measure of each as prolonging the primary tone C5 ($\hat{5}$). If we now examine the contents in some detail, we see that the opening gesture (measure 1) fills in the descending arpeggiation

EXAMPLE 2.8 Mozart, Piano Trio No. 3, K. 542 (II), 1–8

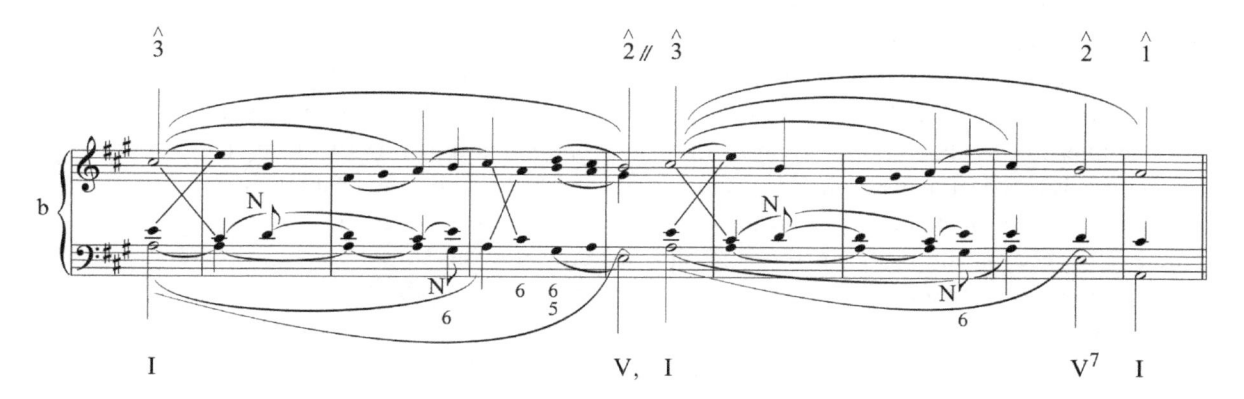

of the tonic triad with the primary tone decorated by its upper neighbor, D5. This neighbor note is provided consonant support (IV) in the second measure before returning to C5 supported by tonic harmony in six-three position, above which the top voice reaches up to F5 to cover the primary tone. This motion to F5 takes on greater significance in the final four measures of the consequent. Here, in measures 1–2, there is a suggestion of a rising fourth C5-D5-E5-F5, but E5 does not receive support. This covering motion is marked in Example 2.10 by a bracket. Moving on to the third measure, the repeated motion G4-A4 (the repetition is not shown in Example 2.8) is shown as an extension of the inner voice tone F4. Then, in measure 4, Mozart picks up the C5, now as seventh above the bass note D, and the line progresses through B♭4 to A4. As with earlier examples examined, this descending third, here C5-B♭4-A4, is embedded within the more encompassing descent to interruption.

The second half of the antecedent phrase opens with D5, the upper neighbor of the primary tone supported by ii⁶. The top voice then begins to move down by step in parallel tenths with the bass. Here is a potential trouble spot for the novice. A common student error is to mark this D5 as a neighbor note returning to the primary tone in the sixth measure. But this is not correct. The motion continues beyond this point to the seventh measure, where there is a change in surface design. Thus this D5 does not return to a point of stability, but rather passes through the C5 in measure 6 to B♭4, as shown in Example 2.10. The line continues to descend to an implied G4 ($\hat{2}$) at the cadence where the leading tone is substituting for it. The harmonization of the structural descent here is weak, progressing in parallel tenths rather than strong root movement.

The second half of the consequent phrase presents some interesting challenges. It opens with D5, as in the fifth measure of the antecedent phrase, but from there the top voice progresses up to B♭5, supported by ii⁶, from which point the line descends to B♭4 in the next measure, now as seventh of the dominant, where it resolves to A4 supported by I. This is followed immediately by a voice exchange with the bass, A4 over F3 to F5 over A2. What are we to make of this? Note that the motion to F5 at the end of the sixth measure of the phrase resolves the leading tone E♮5 that here is supported by dominant harmony. In other words, the D5 in the fifth measure, which is associated aurally with the C5 in the first measure, does not move down as before, but progresses through E♮5 to F5, thus realizing the potential inherent in the opening two measures of the antecedent phrase. The bracket above this ascending fourth indicates that it is a motivic parallel, actually an enlargement, of its earlier statement in the first two measures. Here the first six measures of the phrase, not just the first four, compose a tonic prolongation, and the resolution of B♭4 to A4 in the inner voice is thus interpreted as prolonging the A4 from the fourth measure. The structural descent to closure, then, occurs at the very end of the phrase beyond the limits of the tonic prolongation.

Our final example in the interruption category is the opening theme from the second movement of Beethoven's Piano Sonata Op. 31, No. 2. This is more difficult to interpret than previous examples in this chapter, so I recommend to beginners that they skip to Example 2.13. But more advanced students should definitely grapple with the issues and challenges it presents. The music is provided in Example 2.11 and a graph of its voice-leading structure in Example 2.12. For the first time in this text, but certainly not the last, you are faced with making an informed choice between $\hat{3}$ and $\hat{5}$ as primary tone. Both D5 and F5 are important pitches, but only one of them can be interpreted as primary. Let's begin with $\hat{5}$. The F5 in measure 2 is clearly connected to the same pitch on the third beat of measure 6, after which it moves down by step to C5 ($\hat{2}$) supported by V in measure 8. But there is a problem interpreting this as a structural descent to interruption. The only support for D5 is a passing six-four. If we look ahead to the consequent phrase, we see that the only potential support for D5 in a structural descent from $\hat{5}$ is the submediant harmony on the downbeat of measure 15. So we must abandon this idea and take a look at $\hat{3}$ (D5) as the primary tone. In this case, there is strong support from the very beginning.

The second challenge is dealing with all the registral changes, and it is for this reason that Example 2.12 consists of two levels. The lower one preserves octave placements as Beethoven has written them, but the top level presents a registral simplification to show connections more clearly. Taking the D5 in measure 2 as the primary tone, we can interpret its initial prolongation by means of its upper neighbor stated an octave lower in measure 4, which resolves to D4 in measure 5. But what about the third A5-C6 in measure 4, which is stated as a clear answer to D5-F5 in measure 2? As suggested in Example 2.12a, we might interpret the registrally diverse melodic gestures as prolonging the primary tone by lower, then upper, neighbors. In measure 6, the opening melodic third is restated as the tonic harmony is altered to become a diminished seventh chord of ii, which progresses to ii⁶ on the downbeat of measure 7. This harmony supports the descending third E♭5-D5-C5 while the E♭ of the bass is altered to E♮, now in an inner voice, to direct the motion more strongly to the dominant supporting $\hat{2}$ in measure 8. This progression is simplified in Example 2.12a.

In the subsequent phrase, the statements of the third C6-E♭6 in measures 12 and 14 are heard as answers to the opening melodic statement of the third D5-F5 a step lower, but transposed to the upper register. Thus we hear the return to D5, supported by vi on the downbeat of measure 15, both as the goal of a descending motion of a third and, as suggested in Example 2.12a, as the prolongation of $\hat{3}$ by its upper neighbor. The long-range bass arpeggiation B♭-G continues to E♮ supporting a diminished seventh chord of the dominant. Rather than resolve the chromatic passing tone directly to C5 ($\hat{2}$), Beethoven writes an intervening six-four

EXAMPLE 2.9 Mozart, Piano Sonata K. 333 (I), 23–38

"correcting" the Db to D♮. Scale degree 2 does not follow, but rather we find once again the leading tone substituting for $\hat{2}$ in the descent to closure. This modal inflection, Db–D♮, is a response to the earlier Gb–F, which is "corrected" to G♮5–F5 in measures 15–16, where we clearly hear this gesture as covering the primary line. Regarding the hypermeter, it is clearly duple/quadruple throughout. In previous examples the final harmony has normally fallen in the final measure of a hypermetric group, sometimes, as in Example 2.7, reinterpreted as the first measure in the subsequent phrase. Here, as with the opening phrase of Beethoven's Op. 13 (Example 2.3), the end of the phrase falls on a hypermetric downbeat.

As a final example in this chapter, we will examine an antecedent-consequent pair in which the tonal motion is continuous, not interrupted. This example is the first sixteen measures of the Menuetto movement from Beethoven's Piano Sonata Op. 10, No. 3. The

EXAMPLE 2.10 Graph of Mozart K. 333 (I), 23–38

EXAMPLE 2.11 Beethoven, Piano Sonata Op. 31, No. 2 (II), 1–19

EXAMPLE 2.12 Graph of Beethoven Op. 31, No. 2 (II), 1–19

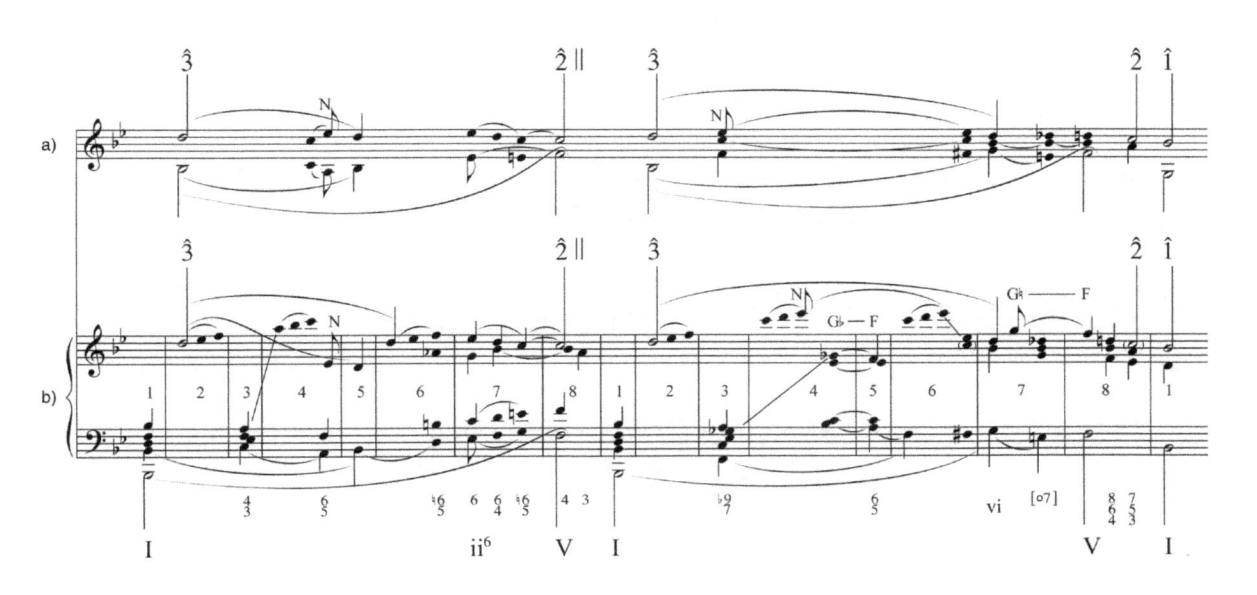

score is provided in Example 2.13 and a graph of its voice leading in Example 2.14. There is an important difference between this example and the previous ones examined in this chapter. Though the consequent phrase begins with the same motivic material as the opening, it does so at a different tonal level, a step higher. The context has changed, and this will lead us to reconsider the role of the cadence in measures 7–8. A brief look at the opening phrase reveals that we are dealing once again with a motion to $\hat{2}$ supported by V at the cadence, but when we look ahead we see that the primary tone $(\hat{3})$ is never reinstated, and thus there can be no interruption. This means that the prolongation of the tonic continues beyond the cadence on the dominant. What, then, is the function of this dominant if not to support an interruption? It is a *divider*—that is, a dominant that articulates the phrase division, and as such is understood as part of the tonic prolongation.

Before settling on an overall interpretation, let us take a look at the antecedent phrase. Melodically it opens with a leap from the inner voice tone A4 to F♯5 $(\hat{3})$, from which point the line begins to descend. As shown in Example 2.14, the immediate goal of this motion is the D5 in measure 3 supported by tonic harmony in six-three position. In short, there is a voice exchange between the outer parts in these three measures. Internal to this progression, F♯5 progresses down a third to D5, which falls on a change of harmony in measure 2. That is, this D5 is rhythmically displaced. This third is then answered by the third a step lower, C♯5-E5, thus filling in the connection between F♯5 (m. 1) and D5 (m. 3). From this D5, the line skips down to A4, picking up the inner voice, and the melodic line then descends by step to F♯4 supported by tonic harmony on the second beat of measure 6. The first two steps in this inner voice descent, A4 and G4, are both decorated by escape tones on the third beats of measures 4 and 5. Not shown in the sketch are the accented passing tones on the downbeats of measures 5 and 6, which, despite the phrasing, maintain the illusion of descending thirds. This is followed by yet another descending third, G4-F♯4-E4, in measures 6–8 supported by the cadence. So all the ingredients are here to read an interruption, but, as noted earlier, this potential is denied by the continuation.

The opening three measures of the consequent phrase are parallel to the opening three measures of the antecedent phrase a step higher. Once again there is a voice exchange

EXAMPLE 2.13 Beethoven, Piano Sonata Op. 10, No. 3 (III), 1–16

EXAMPLE 2.14 Graph of Beethoven Op. 10, No. 3 (III), 1–16

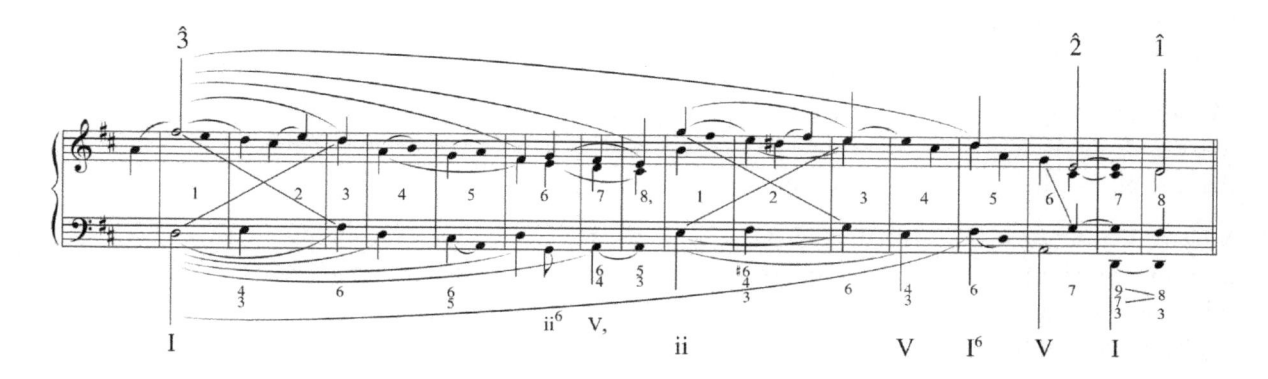

between the outer parts, and this is followed by a connecting dominant seventh chord in four-three position leading to D5 supported by tonic harmony in six-three position on the downbeat of measure 13. This is followed immediately by the cadence leading to closure in the lower octave. The limit of the tonic prolongation, then, falls in measure 13 just before the leap to the lower register and the ensuing cadence, and once we look at the end points of the prolongation, we see that the underlying relationship is a large-scale voice exchange. In this one example, we see the voice-leading technique of voice exchange operating on two levels: first in measures 1–3 and again in measures 9–11, and then at a much deeper level encompassing measures 1–13. With this last one there is a clear disjunction between formal design and underlying structure. If we were now to try to show this large-scale voice exchange in our detailed graph, the result would be too many crossing lines, so in this instance I have decided to describe rather than show this level of organization.

If there are basic principles to take away from this chapter, principles to guide you in your own analyses, they are: (1) not to lose sight of details in your search for underlying structure, since the two are often related; and (2) to be aware that interpretation is dependent on context. Many of the examples examined in this chapter exhibit a similar design and underlying structure (parallel period with interruption), yet they are different, requiring unique interpretations.

SUGGESTED ASSIGNMENTS

Phrases

1. Beethoven, Piano Sonata Op. 31, No. 2 (III), 1–16. What is this phrase type called? Provide a sketch. Note: scale degree 2 in the local descent to closure is replaced by the leading tone; it should be provided in parentheses in your sketch.

2. Beethoven, Piano Sonata Op. 10, No. 3 (II), 1–9. There are several unusual features of this phrase, one being that the primary tone is not stated until measure 7 in relation to a diminished seventh chord of V, though it is anticipated in measure 1. Your sketch should show a connection between measures 1 and 6, a relationship articulated musically by the restatement of the opening motive a step higher. As with the preceding example, the leading tone substitutes for scale degree 2 at the cadence.

Parallel Phrases

1. Beethoven, Piano Sonata Op. 2, No. 1 (II), 1–8. The motion from C5 to F5 in measures 5–6 covers the fundamental line.

2. Mozart, Piano Sonata K. 494 (rondo theme). No problems here, though a decision has to be made regarding the status of the tonic chord in measure 4 (and measure 10). Note that the phrases here are six measures in length.

3. Mozart, Piano Sonata K. 310 (II), 1–8. Here you are faced with a potentially difficult decision regarding primary tone: $\hat{3}$ or $\hat{5}$? The opening gesture strongly suggests $\hat{3}$, but subsequent linear motion to interruption and later to closure is generated from $\hat{5}$. You might try two sketches. If $\hat{3}$, where is its continuation? If $\hat{5}$, how do you explain A5?

4. Mozart, Piano Sonata K. 332 (I), 41–56 (second subject). Note that both the antecedent and consequent phrases are divided into two subphrases. What is the function of the F5 on the downbeat of the fifth measure?

5. Mozart, Piano Sonata K. 576 (I), 1–8. In this example, the consequent phrase begins on a scale step other than the tonic. How does this affect the structure? What is the function of the dominant at the end of the antecedent phrase?

6. Beethoven, Piano Sonata Op. 14, No. 1 (II), 1–16. When is the primary tone first stated?

NOTES

1. All this is clearly set out in William Caplin's *Classical Form* (Oxford University Press, 1998), pp. 9–11 and Example 1.1. Sentence structure is very common in classical music. Consider, for example, the opening phrase from the second movement of Beethoven's Piano Sonata Op. 10, No. 1, which we examined in Chapter I (see Example 1.4b). The sequence of formal units—the presentation of a basic idea (tonic version) followed by its repetition (dominant version) and a four-measure continuation to the cadence—is the same as the opening phrase from the first movement of Op. 2, No. 1.

2. Schenker uses the term *Anstieg* (which literally means "ascent") to describe this phenomenon, by which he means the initial ascent by step to the primary tone.

3. Heinrich Schenker, *Der Tonwille* 2 (1922).

4. Schenker's analysis of this movement is outlined in Charles Burkhart's article "Schenker's 'Motivic Parallelisms'," *Journal of Music Theory* 22/2 (1978), 145–175.

5. This example was originally placed within the section "Motive and Structural Levels" in Chapter 1. Like the first movement of this sonata, this excerpt from the third movement articulates statements of the motive F-D-Bb and contains references to G as a displacement of F. Though the first and third movements are different in many respects, they are related motivically.

6. Schenker's early career was as a performer, a pianist, and though his ideas on musical structure became increasingly theoretical as they developed, there was always a practical link between the theory and performance.

3 Phrase Rhythm and Phrase Expansion

Phrase Rhythm

The term "phrase rhythm" refers to the interaction of phrase, a unit of tonal motion with a clearly defined beginning that leads to a point of rest (cadence), and hypermeter, the existence of recurring patterns of accented and unaccented measures. The components of a hypermetric group or unit, called hypermeasures, function much the same as beats within a measure. By definition, then, hypermetric units are beginning accented with the first measure of the unit receiving the greatest stress. In *Free Composition*, Schenker has pointed out that hypermeter most naturally occurs in multiples of two. The most common hypermeter is quadruple, but duple is fairly common as well. Hypermetric groups containing an odd number of measures are relatively rare, and when we do encounter them, they often occur in pairs. A famous passage with extended triple hypermeter often cited occurs in the Scherzo movement of the Ninth Symphony, where Beethoven writes "ritmo di tre battute". In this instance, he is telling the conductor to conduct in three, and what is being conducted are measures, not beats, in a fast tempo; in other words, the hypermeter.

While a very large portion of the music of the classical and romantic periods exhibits hypermetric organization in whole or in part, we cannot assume its existence. This brings up an interesting question. How do we identify the existence of hypermeter? In general, hypermeter is a phenomenon that is readily perceivable: it is based on repetition of tonal and or rhythmic patterns. In some types of works—for example, those based on dance types, such as the minuet, the scherzo or the mazurka—the regular recurrence of four-measure units is most clear. In longer movements—for example, sonata form—we can expect the rhythmic organization at this level to be more flexible. This is where phrase rhythm becomes interesting, where phrase and hypermeter are not always congruent and where various events conspire to stretch but not destroy the underlying pattern.

Before turning to the fascinating topic of phrase expansion, I would like to explore briefly two important phenomena we will encounter. The first of these is the occurrence of successive downbeat measures, an interesting example of which is found in the opening phrase from the second movement of Beethoven's Piano Sonata Op. 10, No. 3, which is provided in Example 3.1. This phrase is nine measures long, and a cursory examination might suggest that the last measure falls on a hypermetric downbeat following two hypergroups

EXAMPLE **3.1** Beethoven, Piano Sonata Op. 10, No. 3 (II), 1–9

of four. But closer examination suggests that both the fifth and sixth measures are accented. Thus a more accurate description of the metric organization of these nine measures is: 1 2 3 4, 1, 1 2 3 4. Note that this interpretation agrees with the repetition in measure 6 of the opening motive.

Next is the common phenomenon of phrase overlap or elision, which we have encountered several times in the previous chapters. When the first of the two phrases ends in the final measure of a hypermetric unit, which is most common, then the phrase overlap will occur in conjunction with a metric reinterpretation. We have already observed this with the second theme from the first movements of Mozart's Piano Sonata K. 311 (see Example 2.7). Refer also to Example 1.4c, the opening phrase of the development section from the first movement of Mozart's Piano Sonata K. 333; though not indicated on the example, the eighth measure is also the first measure of the following phrase. A further illustration is provided in Example 3.2, measures 49–56 from the first movement of Mozart's Piano Sonata

EXAMPLE 3.2 Mozart, Piano Sonata K. 332 (I), 49–56

K. 332. This music is the consequent phrase of the second theme, the last measure of which is the first of the following transition. Here 4 becomes 1.

However, when the first phrase of the pair ends on a hypermetric downbeat, then the phrase elision occurs without a hypermetric reinterpretation, quite a different effect from the situation described earlier. We observed this phenomenon once in the opening phrase from the first movement of Beethoven's Piano Sonata Op. 13 (Example 2.3). Another illustration is provided in Example 3.3, taken from the development section of the first movement of Beethoven's Piano Trio Op. 1, No. 3. The hypermeter of this phrase (quadruple) is clearly articulated, and the phrase ends on a hypermetric downbeat, where the next phrase begins.

EXAMPLE 3.3 Beethoven, Piano Trio Op. 1, No. 3 (I), 168–176

Phrase Expansion

There are two general types of phrase expansion: those that expand the phrase externally and those that are internal to the phrase.[1] By far the easier of the two to identify is external, though the more fascinating category includes the interesting ways composers have found to stretch a phrase from within, thus creating additional tension. External expansions occur before or after the phrase and are thus not part of its hypermetric organization, though the expansion may have its own organization if it is of sufficient length. In this category we might find, for example, a two-measure extended upbeat or, at the end of a phrase, a cadential extension. If you think about it for a moment, you will realize that external expansions exist in music at many levels. We are focused here on the phrase, but for a moment let's think big. What is a slow introduction or a coda in, say, a first movement of a classical symphony? Both expand the movement externally, just as an extended upbeat or extended cadence expands the phrase. They are easy to identify. However, it is not so easy always to identify internal expansions. We are helped greatly in this regard when we have before us the model on which the expansion is based. Think, for instance, of an antecedent-consequent phrase pair in which the antecedent is eight measures in length, but the consequent eleven. With the model before us, we can often determine quite readily what has been expanded and how. But many times we are faced with what appears to be an expanded phrase without the model to compare it to. How do we know it is expanded? In some instances, the expansion is obvious—for example, a repetition of a segment of the phrase or a parenthetical insertion that is differentiated clearly from what surrounds it. We have already encountered an instance of the first of these, the opening phrase from the first movement of Mozart's Piano Sonata in B♭, K. 333 (see Example 1.9). In this instance, a two-measure segment (measures 4–5) is repeated in slightly embellished form, thus expanding the phrase from eight to ten measures. But what if the cause is not so clear? In circumstances such as this, we must rely on our understanding of the norm for, say, the classical style if we are studying a classical work. That is, we have in our minds and ears the prototype, and it is this "norm" that helps us to understand whether, in fact, the phrase has been expanded, and if the answer is affirmative, then most likely we can identify what has been expanded and how this has been accomplished.

Internal expansion can result from any of the following processes: (1) by repetition of a portion of the phrase; (2) by avoidance of the cadence, typically by a deceptive progression; (3) by parenthetical insertion; and (4) by a composed-out deceleration, typically at the end of a phrase. We have already seen an example of the first type, and we will have an opportunity to witness the other three in the following section. The second and third types are related, and we normally notate them in a similar fashion by placing parentheses around the expansion. The difference is in their content. Avoidance of closure normally involves repetition of the cadential pattern (same material), but a parenthetical insertion involves new material, often radically different in some way. Frequently this too serves to delay the cadence.

EXAMPLE 3.4 Beethoven, Piano Trio Op. 1, No. 3 (I), 110–124

EXAMPLE **3.4** *continued*

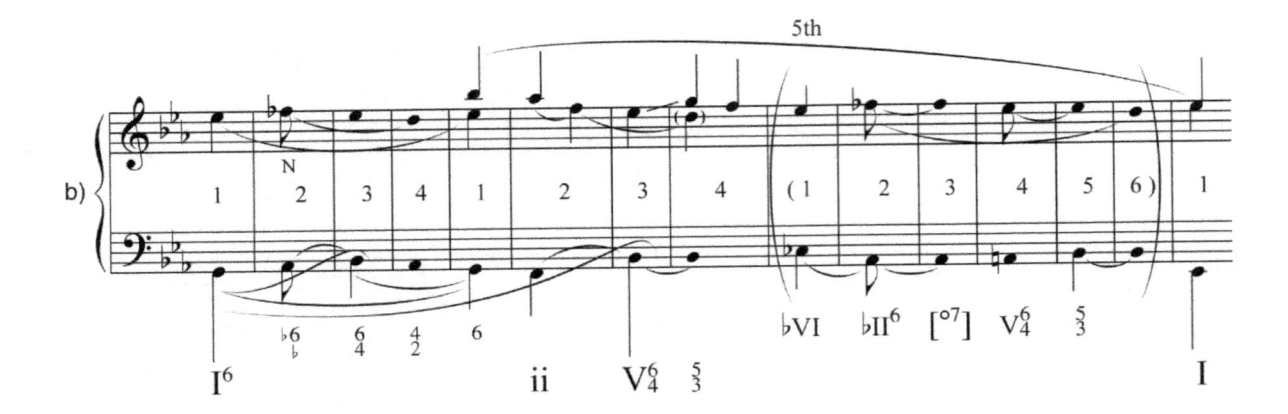

Expanded Phrases

Our first example is the final phrase leading to the codetta at the end of the exposition from the first movement of Beethoven's Piano Trio Op. 1, No. 3, which is reproduced as Example 3.4a. The repeated pattern of the harmony, beginning with the I^6 chord in the local key, confirms the already established quadruple hypermeter. Our expectation is that closure will come in the ninth measure, a hypermetric downbeat. But this is delayed by a six-measure insertion beginning with the submediant harmony from the parallel minor mode; this insertion is an expanded version of the initial four-measure unit. When closure is achieved, it overlaps with the first measure of the codetta. A graph of this expanded phrase is provided in Example 3.4b. It shows the main feature of the opening four measures as the prolongation of E♭5 by its chromatic upper neighbor, F♭5. In the fifth measure, B♭5 is brought in above the E♭5, and from that point there is a descent of a fifth to closure. Note that the 6 of the cadential six-four is delayed until the following measure, a common modification of the standard cadence pattern. Initial arrival at E♭5 is then harmonized by the ♭VI chord, which generates the parenthetical passage delaying closure until six measures later.

Our next two examples of phrase expansion are found in the first two phrases from the second movement of Mozart's Clarinet Quintet, K. 581. A simplification of the score—transposed clarinet part plus supporting bass line and figured bass—is provided in Example 3.5. The two phrases are indicated by circled Roman numerals. The first expansion occurs at the end of the first phrase in the eighth and ninth measures. Our expectation, based on our familiarity with the style, is that we will reach the half cadence in measure 8, so it comes as a surprise when Mozart draws out the content of the seventh measure to occupy two measures, thus creating a nine-measure phrase. This is an odd place for a written-out deceleration, which more typically would come later in a movement. Mozart has caught us off guard, so to speak, and he will keep our attention throughout the movement by inserting other surprises. In this instance, our surprise is created by hearing what Mozart has written in relation to our expectation. This norm is written above the score, and the expansion of the seventh measure to two is signaled by a dash in the indication of hypermetric groups between the staves.

EXAMPLE 3.5 Mozart, Clarinet Quintet K. 581 (II), 1–20

The second instance of phrase expansion occurs near the end of the second phrase, where Mozart avoids closure by harmonizing scale degree 1 by a diminished seventh chord rather than the expected tonic. This parenthetical insertion to the phrase is not subtle, like the first expansion. It is accompanied by a leap to the lowest register of the clarinet and then a leap back to the original register, this time to close as expected. This insertion, indicated by parentheses, is not counted as part of the hypermetric organization, as shown between the staves. In fact, these three measures could be omitted entirely without affecting the underlying structure, but by doing so, the wonderful effect of this insertion would be lost.

A graph of the musical structure of these two phrases, which form a musical period, is provided in Example 3.6.[2] The first phrase progresses from the primary tone $\hat{3}$ to $\hat{2}$ supported by a motion from I to V, and the second phrase then prolongs $\hat{2}$ / V, leading to closure in measure 20. In the first phrase, the primary tone, F♯5, is prolonged by its upper neighbor G5, first in measures 1–4 and again immediately following. The final motion up to G5 initiates a descending third leading to $\hat{2}$ supported by V. Meanwhile the prominent inner voice tone A4 is extended first by an ascending fourth to D5 in measures 1–4 and then by its upper neighbor in the following measures. The one tricky area to deal with in this phrase is the expanded seventh measure. The harmonic progression as written is V-I-V-I-ii⁶. The issue is whether we hear the second of these as passing, thus harmonizing the passing note D5 in the third C♯5-E5 supported by V, or the third of these as passing, thus supporting the passing tone E5 in the third D5-F♯5 supported by I. The graph in Example 3.6 indicates the latter option, which is influenced by the norm, but the other possibility is equally feasible. Perhaps it is this ambiguity within a style that is so transparent that adds to the tension created by this stretching of the phrase, this deceleration (rather than the opposite) as we approach the goal.

EXAMPLE 3.6 Graph of Mozart K. 581 (II), 1–20

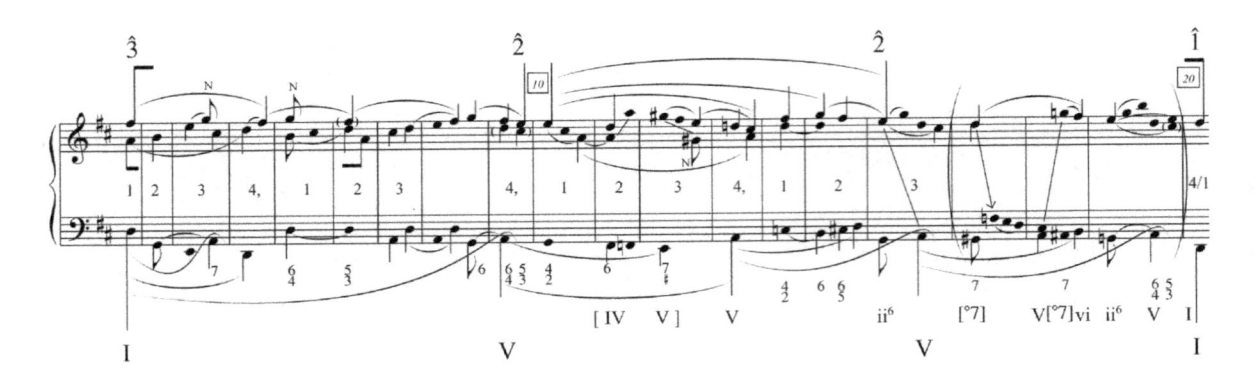

As noted earlier, the second phrase prolongs the dominant and $\hat{2}$ until the very end of the phrase. In measures 10–13, E5 is prolonged by a descending third E5-D5-C♯5, internal to which the final note is approached by a diminution of this same third. This is a tricky spot to notate clearly, especially with the temporary transfer of the inner voice above. Care has to be taken to differentiate the thirds and their place in the hierarchy by some means. Here this has been accomplished by the length of the stems. In the larger context, the descending third of measures 10–13 is embedded within an ascending motion to G5, E5 (m. 10)-F♯5 (m. 14)-G5 (m. 15), and this G5 then descends immediately to E5 ($\hat{2}$) supported by V on its way to closure. Here again in measure 16 the leading tone is substituting for $\hat{2}$ over the dominant. The following three-measure insertion is placed in parentheses. While this passage could be omitted in theory, we must show in our interpretation how it fits into the overall voice leading of the phrase.

Our next example in this section is the second theme from the first movement of Mozart's Piano Sonata in A minor, K. 310. The score is provided in Example 3.7. An examination of this passage reveals that the theme begins with a four-measure idea supported by the harmonic progression I⁶-ii-V⁷-I. The phrase then begins anew with an elaboration of this idea, but now extended to five measures, and this expanded idea then becomes the first part of a phrase directed at closure in the local key (III), which is avoided at the last minute. Here, then, is a situation where we have the model as a point of reference, which in this instance is not a complete phrase but a four-measure idea that is used as the basis for the ensuing phrase.

An interpretation of this passage is provided in Example 3.8. The G major chord, V in the new key, is provided in parentheses at the beginning of the sketch to show that G5 is established in the preceding passage as the primary melodic note in the local context. Thus we can understand the initial motion to C6 as temporarily covering G5, which is picked up at the end of the first measure. The G5 then moves down a step to F5 supported by ii, and over the next two measures it is transferred to the lower octave, now as the seventh of the dominant, which resolves to E4 supported by tonic harmony in measure 4. The underlying voice leading of the melodic voice, the sweeping gesture from C6 down to E4, is a registrally expanded descending third. Simultaneously the

EXAMPLE 3.7 Mozart, Piano Sonata K. 310 (I), 23–35

harmonic progression I⁶-ii-V⁷-I supports an ascending line G4-A4 (left-hand part)-B4-C5 (right-hand), the last delayed until the third beat of measure 4. If you have any difficulty following this interpretation of the underlying voice leading, you should play the passage slowly as written several times, and then the graph. Your ear should confirm the analysis. Once you have become comfortable with the underlying structure of measures 1–4, the analysis of the following phrase becomes much easier. Right from the beginning, the primacy of G5 is clearer than before, as is the role of C6 as a covering pitch. In the next measure the notes A5-F5 -D5 are elaborated by turn figures, so this time G5 has moved to its upper neighbor A5 rather than to progress down by step. This is the beginning of the expansion. What follows in the third measure is a copy of measure 2 a step lower. Here is a potential trouble spot for the inexperienced analyst, who might be tempted to mark this A5 as a neighbor note returning to G5 in the next measure and to do the same in the bass. But if we look at what Mozart has written, including the change in the left-hand accompaniment pattern in the second measure, we see (and hear) that the motion continues through the third measure. From a harmonic perspective, what has become expanded is the supertonic harmony from one measure in the model to two-and-a-half measures here, while the following dominant is shortened from one to a half of a measure. This expanded supertonic harmony supports a descending third A5-G5-F5 running in parallel tenths with the bass, from which point the F5 is transferred to the lower register, supported by the dominant, which resolves as before to E4, the goal of the descending third, supported by tonic harmony. In the latter half of this measure, the addition of the B♭4 to the tonic harmony directs the motion to the subdominant, and the continuation clarifies the role of the preceding descent as prolonging G5. That is, the elaborated descent of a third occurs within a tonic prolongation and is thus embedded within the descent of a fifth spanning the entire phrase. The goal of this motion, C5, has been supplied in parentheses. The entire phrase, excluding the initial four-measure model, is nine measures in length rather than eight due to the expansion of the initial four-measure unit to five. Schenker would note that there is an organic connection between the number of notes involved in the expansion (the descending third A5-G5-F5) and the number of measures,[3] though the length of the following dominant is shortened from the original statement, and thus it is not clear how he would count the measures of this phrase. Clearly an expansion has taken place, regardless of whether there is an organic connection between the number of elements and the number of measures involved, so Example 3.8 shows these measures as an expanded eight, where the last measure overlaps with the following phrase with metric reinterpretation.

Our final example in this section is the opening theme from the first movement of Schubert's String Quartet in A Minor D. 804. The score is provided in Example 3.9 and an interpretation of its three phrases—appropriately labeled a¹, a², and a³, since each opens with the motivic fifth E5-C[♯]5-A4—in Example 3.10.[4] The first phrase is preceded by a two-measure pickup, and the phrase proper is eight measures in length, clearly divided into four plus four, establishing a quadruple hypermeter. The primary tone, E5 ($\hat{5}$), is prolonged by a descent in parallel thirds leading to B4 over G♯4 supported by the dominant. The final four measures of the phrase prolong the dominant, above which the melodic line reaches back to E5. The first four measures of the second phrase introduce a new element, the prolongation of E5 by its upper neighbor F5, which in the next measure is altered to F♯5-E5, and then repeated. This is followed by the ♭II chord, which is transformed into the subdominant/ augmented sixth chord leading to the dominant. Beginning in the fifth measure of the phrase the quadruple hypermeter persists, as indicated by the lower set of numbers between the staves. Above this I have shown how these eight measures can be understood as an expansion of four, first by repetition of a two-measure segment (the F♯5-E5 idea) and then by the extension of the predominant ♭II-iv⁶. Above the system I have provided a simplification of these measures normalizing registral placement. The third phrase is written in the parallel major mode, anticipated in the preceding phrase by the repeated F♯5-E5. In the first four measures, E5 leads up to A5 via G♯5 above a descent through D5 to C♯5. The notation employed here to connect the D5 to G♯5 signifies an *unfolding*;[5] it could be replaced by a slur. The remainder of the phrase leading to closure is six measures in length, which I have shown

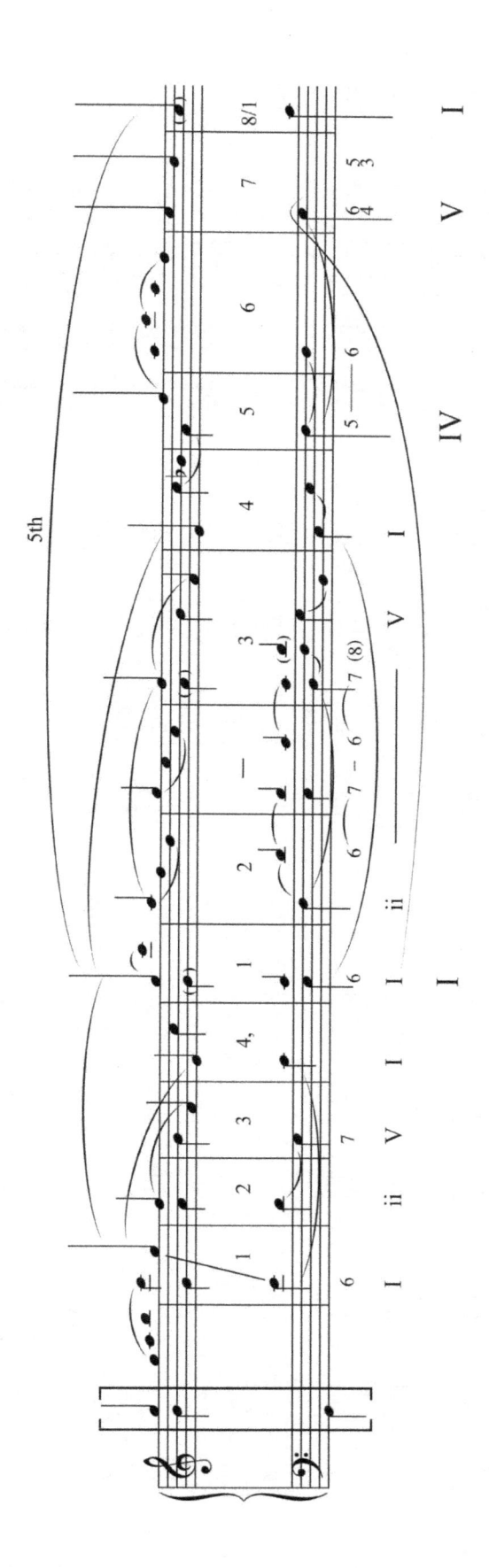

EXAMPLE 3.8 Graph of Mozart K. 310 (I), 23–35

EXAMPLE 3.9 Schubert, String Quartet D. 804 (I), 1–32

EXAMPLE **3.9** *continued*

to be an expansion of an underlying four created by the extension of the subdominant harmony by means of a voice exchange. I would not expect a beginning student to hear or spot this prolongation, internal to which the harmony progresses II–V–I. However, the terminals of this voice exchange are clearly marked by Schubert, as indicated above the system. That is, both the F♯5 and later the D5 are displaced by their upper appoggiaturas (incomplete neighbors), the first marked *f* and the second *fp*. Finally, note that the final measure of the phrase is simultaneously the first of the following phrase, a phrase overlap with metric reinterpretation.

Antecedent-Expanded Consequent

An excellent example to illustrate various aspects of phrase expansion is Chopin's Prelude in G Major, Op. 28, No. 3. This short work consists of two phrases, an antecedent that is expanded externally and a consequent that is expanded both internally and externally. The score is provided in Example 3.11 and two separate graphs of the voice-leading, one showing considerable detail and the other only the underlying structure, are provided in Examples 3.12 and 3.13, respectively.

EXAMPLE 3.10 Graph of Schubert, String Quartet D. 804 (I), 1–32

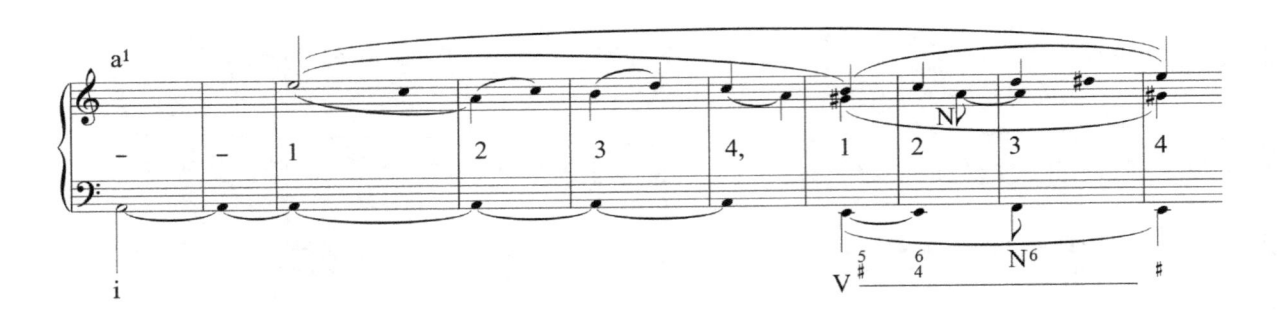

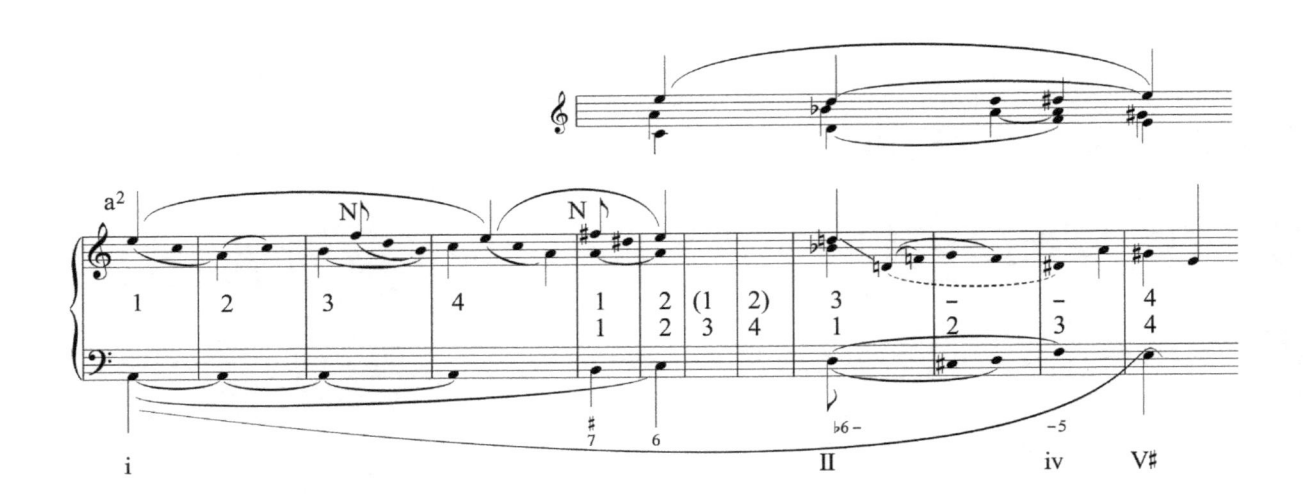

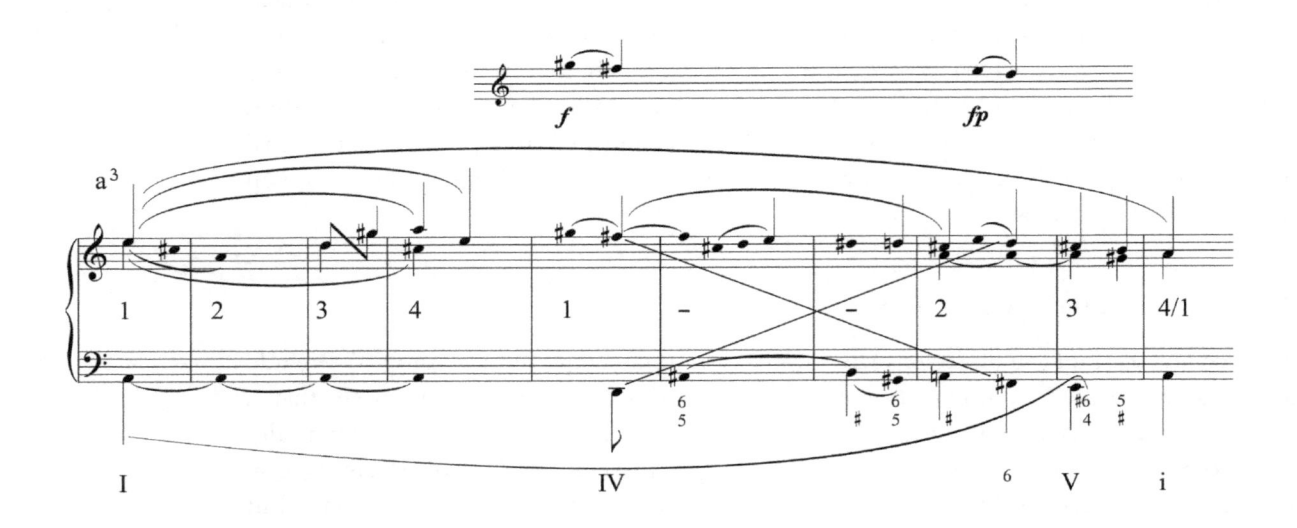

EXAMPLE 3.11 Chopin, Prelude in G Major, Op. 28, No. 3

EXAMPLE **3.11** *continued*

EXAMPLE 3.12 Graph of Chopin Prelude in G

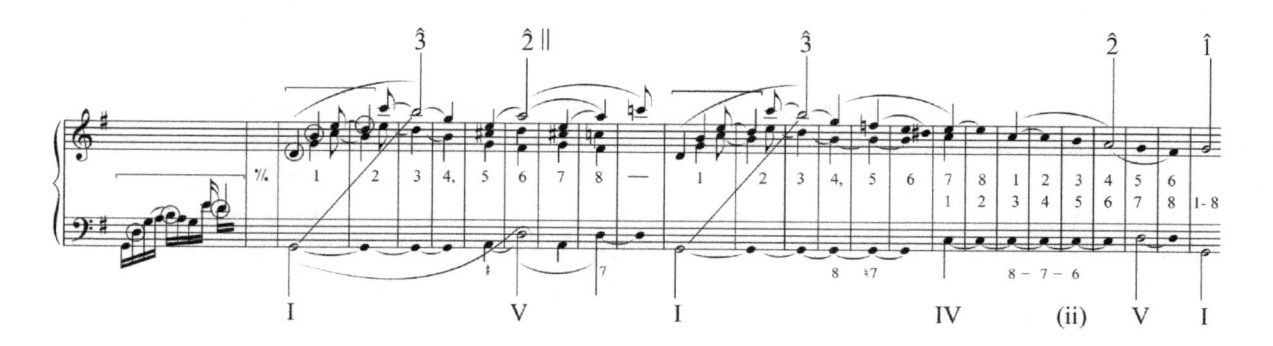

EXAMPLE 3.13 Background structure of Chopin Prelude in G

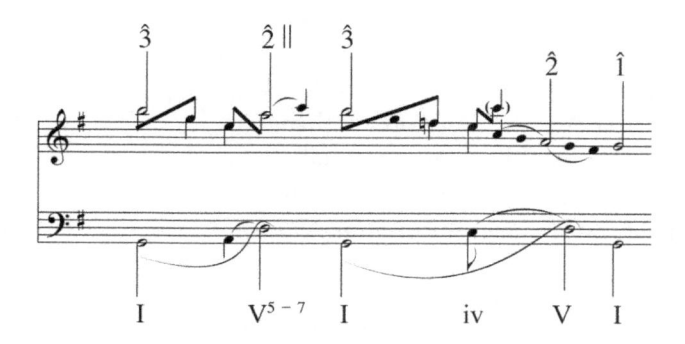

The prelude opens with a two-measure extended upbeat introducing the antecedent phrase. As shown both on the score and on Example 3.10, the repeated left-hand figure emphasizes the pitches D3–B3–D4, the last introduced by its incomplete upper neighbor E4, which forms the basis for the arpeggiation to B5 ($\hat{3}$) in the third measure of the antecedent phrase. Arrival at the primary tone initiates a descending third B5–G5, which is answered in the next two measures by E5–A5, harmonized by II♯ (V of V) to V. This latter gesture is then repeated, the only difference being the addition of the seventh to the dominant. This completes the eight-measure antecedent phrase, but Chopin does not begin the consequent phrase immediately. Instead he extends the dominant for another measure, adding the seventh in the upper register in anticipation of the return to B5($\hat{3}$) in the next phrase. So what we have is an antecedent phrase that is introduced by a two-measure upbeat and extended by an additional measure at the end. Its tonal structure articulates the interruption $\hat{3} - \hat{2} ||$ supported by I–V.

The consequent phrase begins as expected with a repetition of the initial four measures of the antecedent phrase. However, in the fifth measure, F♮5, the lowered seventh of the tonic, is introduced, and this is subsequently resolved to E5 supported by IV two measures later. This completes eight measures, which are clearly divided into four plus four, and the ninth measure of the phrase is heard as the hypermetric downbeat. At the same time, the seventh measure, where the subdominant harmony is first introduced, might be viewed as the beginning of an eight-measure group, at least from a harmonic perspective. It is this thought that leads to the speculative overlapping groups of eight indicated between the staves in Example 3.12.[6] Returning now to a consideration of the tonal content of this expanded phrase, the subdominant harmony is rearticulated in the ninth measure, now with C5 as the top-sounding pitch, which initiates a descending third C5-B4-A4 over a sustained harmony, which then leads to a cadence and closure (m. 26), which is subsequently extended for eight measures. So, the consequent phrase is expanded internally as a result of the motion to the subdominant, which is extended for several measures, and externally by extension of the final tonic. Example 3.13 shows only the middleground-background structure of the prelude. Regarding the consequent phrase, the unfolding B5-F♮5 is answered not by E5-C6, as expected, but by E5-C5, and it is this registral change that leads to closure in the lower octave.

Our next example, the second subject from Schubert's *Quartettsatz* (D. 703), involves an expanded consequent created by the last-minute avoidance of closure. The score is provided in Example 3.14, and on the score I have indicated an interpretation of the metric groups (between the violin 1 and 2 parts) and harmonic analysis (below the systems). An interpretation of the voice-leading structure is provided in Example 3.15. This graph has been organized with the consequent phrase below the antecedent to show as clearly as possible the relationship between the two. There is one important change in notation from the earlier graphs: the notes of the fundamental line (fundamental in the local context) are connected by a beam rather than a slur. This alternative notation is used to facilitate showing as clearly as possible the completion of a line across a ten-measure parenthetical insertion.

The antecedent phrase is twelve measures in length, created by an initial four-measure group leading to the subdominant and then an eight-measure group beginning from the subdominant harmony, which supports a transposed statement of the head motive, the ascending arpeggiation of the tonic triad, identified by a bracket in Example 3.15. From an analytic perspective, the only potential problem spot in these opening measures is the identification of the descending third from the primary tone E♭5($\hat{5}$)−D♭5−C5, where the middle member of this third is extended by its own third D♭5-C5-B♭4. Arrival at C5 in measure 4 coincides with the introduction of the lowered seventh, G♭3 in the bass leading to IV[6] supporting the restatement of the head motive, now a fourth higher. This is followed by a return to E♭5 and tonic harmony, from which point the line begins to descend to $\hat{2}$ supported by V, the point of interruption. Here again one must take great care to distinguish structural from decorative pitches in the descent. The pitch F5 in the second half of measure 34 is a consonant escape tone displacing E♭5. That is, from a structural perspective, E♭5 (m. 34) leads to D♭5 (m. 35). This pattern, further expanded, persists. The E♭5 on the last eighth of measure 35, itself introduced by the appoggiatura F5, displaces D♭5 on its way to C5 (m. 36). Likewise, the E♭5 in measure 36 is an appoggiatura to the D♭5. As we have seen in several previous examples, this note does not function as a neighbor to a stable third scale degree, but instead it initiates a descending third passing through C5 to $\hat{2}$. These measures are worth your very careful attention to separate supported notes from those that elaborate the underlying structure. In the case of this last third, D♭5-C5-B♭4, the end pitches are eighth notes, and the passing tone is a dotted half note, so clearly duration cannot be used as a reliable criterion for structural significance. Note also Schubert's bowings, which do

EXAMPLE 3.14 Schubert, *Quartettsatz* (D. 703), 27–61

EXAMPLE 3.14 *continued*

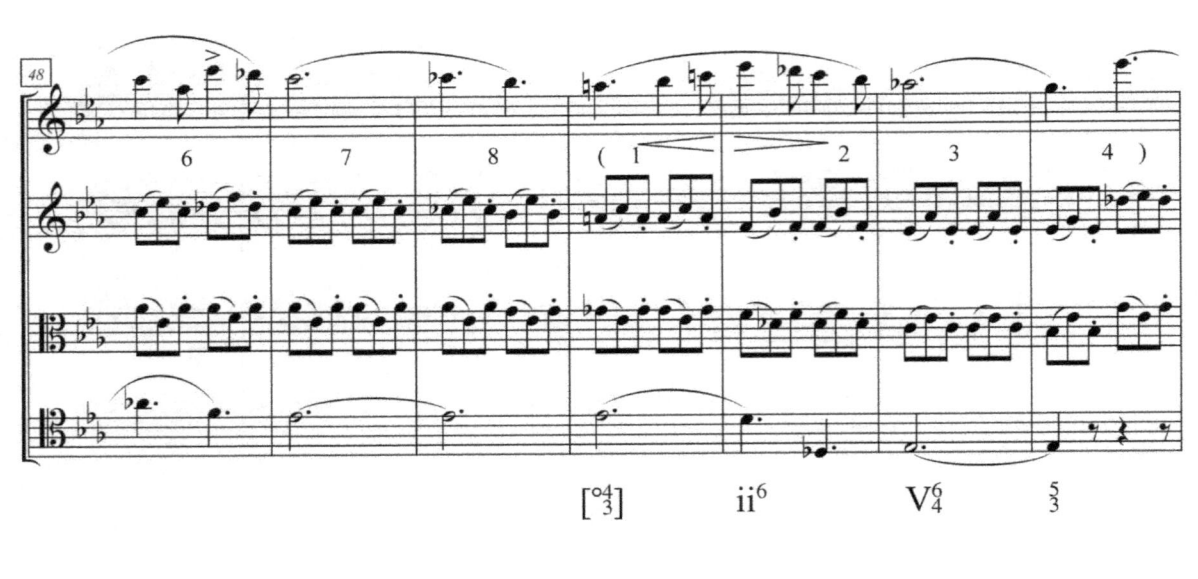

not align with the underlying structure. What determine the structure are the harmony and underlying counterpoint.

The consequent phrase begins an octave higher than the antecedent phrase, as one frequently finds in Schubert's music, but this has been notated in the lower octave in Example 3.15 for ease in reading. The first significant change occurs in measure 50 with the addition of the chromatic passing tone C♭5, marked by an arrow in the graph. Though Schubert could have completed the motion to closure in the next measure, this would not have been convincing. The insertion of this C♭ signals a change, and that change comes in the form of the harmonization of scale degree 1, not by the tonic but by a diminished seventh chord in four-three position, directing the motion to ii⁶, which is followed by the cadential six-four to five-three. Once again Schubert could have completed the motion to closure and,

EXAMPLE 3.15 Graph of Schubert, *Quartettsatz*, 27–61

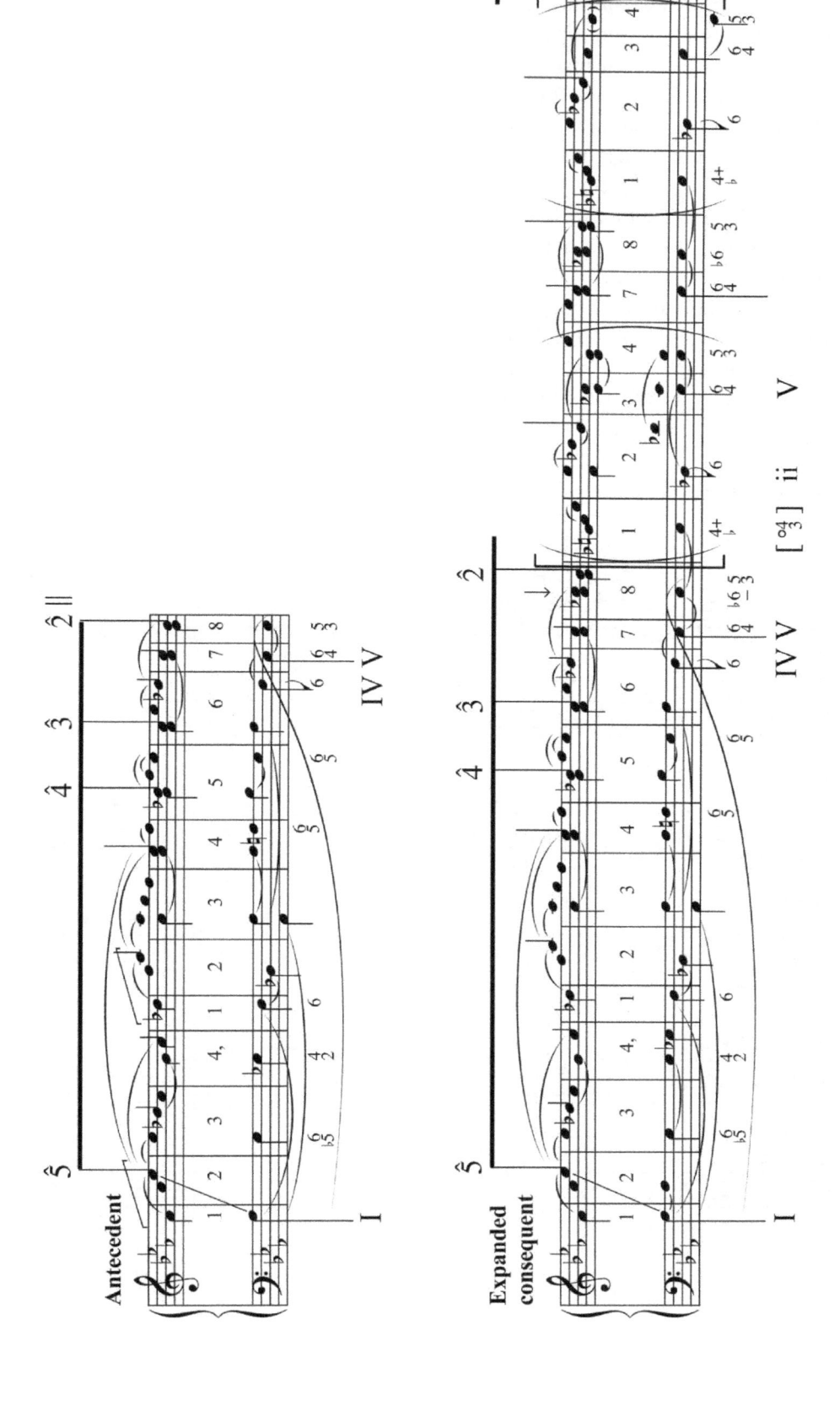

if he had, we would have placed parentheses around the previous four-measure insertion. But instead he repeats the last two measures of the phrase proper, and then inserts a slightly varied version of the earlier four-measure insertion, this time finally leading to closure in the lower octave. The notation used in Example 3.15 attempts to capture the layers of expansion involved. The square brackets mark the entire ten-measure delay of closure, while the parentheses mark the two four-measure insertions within.

The penultimate example in this chapter, the opening section from the third movement of Beethoven's Piano Sonata, Op.7, presents us with a somewhat more complicated situation.[7] The score is provided in Example 3.16 and a graph of the voice-leading structure in Example 3.17. Here we are presented with an antecedent phrase of eight measures and a modulating consequent that is expanded internally, not just before the close, as in our previous example, but mid-phrase. Furthermore, because the consequent phrase leads to a close in the dominant, it follows a different path from the antecedent phrase after repetition of the opening four-measure segment. So the antecedent phrase does not serve well as a model; we must rely instead on our understanding of the norm in this situation.

EXAMPLE 3.16 Beethoven, Piano Sonata Op. 7 (III), 1–24

EXAMPLE 3.17 Graph of Beethoven Op. 7 (III), 1–24

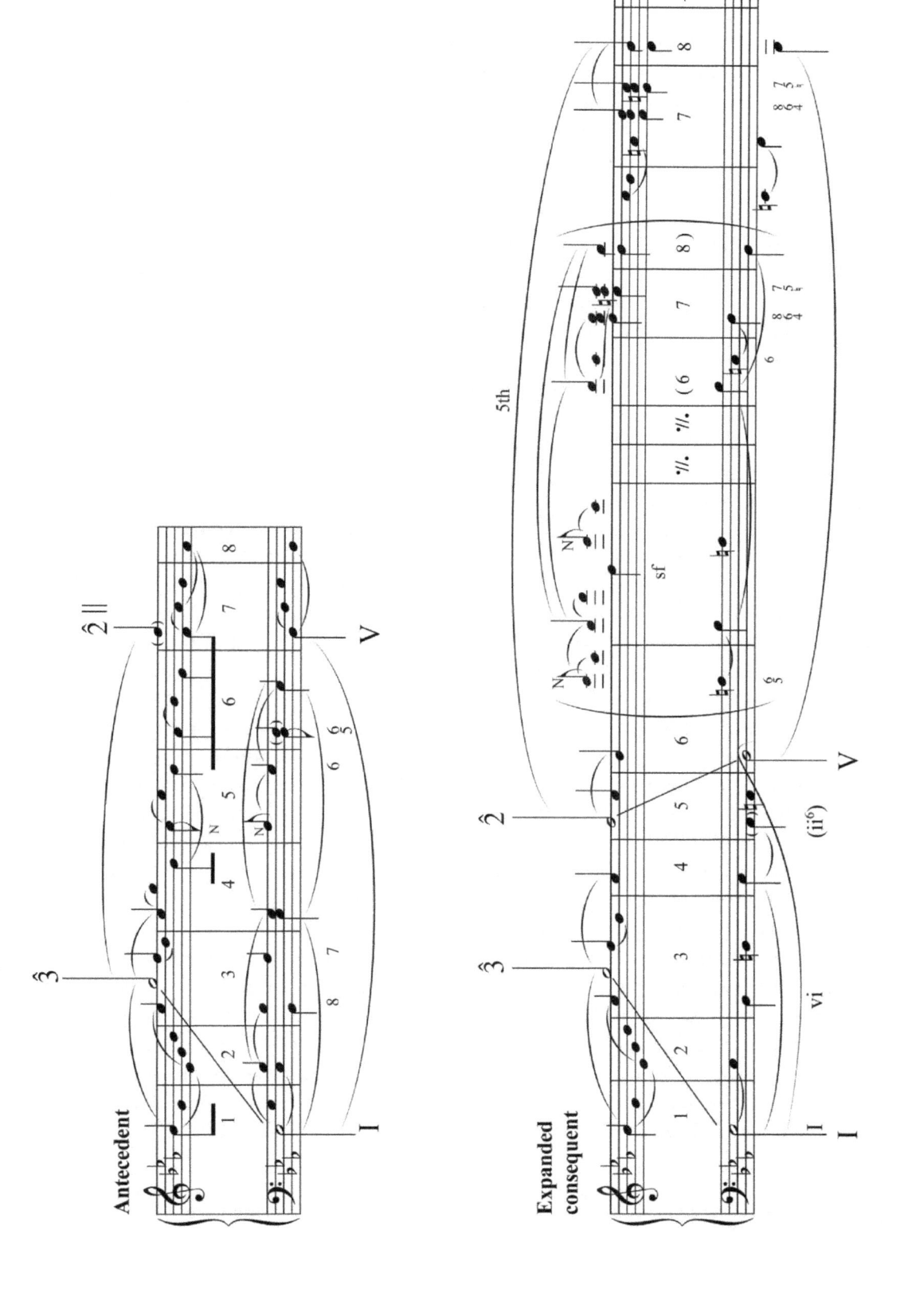

The first issue facing inexperienced analysts is determining the primary tone, which may not be immediately apparent. The movement opens with an arpeggiation leading to G5, but the second half of the phrase clearly descends by step from B♭4 to F4—in other words, to interruption. One's attention is certainly drawn to this linear descent. Clarification of this matter comes in the consequent phrase, where attention is shifted to G5 and its continuation. Here B♭4 is not initiating a descent, but rather is the goal of the motion. So G5 is the primary tone, and the descent from B♭4 in the antecedent phrase is a descent from a prominent inner voice tone. This decision helps very much in notating a graph of the structure. We must find a way to show G5 as primary and, at the same time, to show the prominent inner voice. See Example 3.17, top system, which employs a combination of slurs and beams as well as different note values to represent the structural interpretation as clearly as possible. The one notation requiring explanation is the addition of F5 in parentheses in measures 7–8 and $\hat{2}$ || above it. Motion to local interruption occurs only in the inner voice, but by implication G5 must also be understood to move to $\hat{2}$ over the dominant. The top part cannot remain on $\hat{3}$ once the phrase has reached this goal.

Example 3.17 is organized like Example 3.15 with the consequent phrase below. Here the descent G5–F5–E♭5 is answered immediately a step lower, F5–E♭5–D5, initiating the descent of a fifth to closure in the key of the dominant. Earlier mention was made of understanding the norm in this situation. Much more will be said about this later when we get to ternary (rounded binary) form in Chapter 5. For now, the following brief explanation should suffice. In the initial section of a major key work in this form, one scenario we can anticipate is a descent of a fifth from $\hat{2}$ to closure in the key of the dominant. That is precisely what happens here. However, the descent does not take place in a continuous fashion, but is interrupted by an insertion marked by a change of register and dynamics following the descent of the third F5–E♭5–D5 in measures 13–14. Within this insertion, the third scale degree in the key of the dominant is rearticulated as the focal point no less than four times by its upper neighbor in the upper register before descending to B♭5 on the downbeat of measure 21. Completion of the line in the upper register signals the end of the parenthetical insertion. This is followed immediately by a connection to the lower register and a repeat of the third an octave lower (D5–C5–B♭4), completing the descent of a fifth initiated in measures 13–14. Example 3.17 shows these intervening measures as a parenthetical insertion expanding the underlying phrase of eight measures. Note also the addition of an extra measure at the end, represented by a dash. This measure is extra only in relation to the underlying voice leading. It is quite necessary to create balance (m. 24) and to dissipate some of the forward momentum generated in the previous measures.

Our final example, the opening section from the first movement of Beethoven's "Appassionata" Sonata Op. 57, is difficult, not only longer but also more complex than others we have examined so far. I recommend beginners skip it, but there are rewards for those who do tackle it. In this excerpt we encounter not only phrase expansion but also motivic repetition and enlargement, and we will also discover metric reinterpretation and successive downbeat measures in the hypermetric organization. In many ways this example is a summary of ideas presented so far. The score is provided in Example 3.18 and a graph of its structure in Example 3.19.

The antecedent phrase is sixteen measures in length, the second eight a prolongation of the dominant. The primary tone ($\hat{5}$) is established right from the beginning with the opening gesture, the descending arpeggiation of the tonic triad from C4, which is immediately confirmed by the statement of C5 in measure 3 (supported by V⁶) and its subsequent prolongation by its upper neighbor D♮.5. This gesture, C5 - D♮.5 - C5, is marked with a bracket in measure 3.19 because it and its minor-mode counterpoint, with D♭ rather than D♮., become important motivic components that are developed in the course of the movement. These opening four measures are answered by their repetition a step higher, establishing a quadruple hypermeter, as indicated between the staves in the graph. The result is an expanded statement of the neighbor-note motive: C5(mm. 3–4)-D♭5(mm. 7–8)-C5(mm. 9–10), where the terminal pitches of this gesture are prolonged locally by the neighbor note D♮. The prolongation of the dominant in measures 9–16 involves arpeggiation from C5 to B♭5, 8–7 of the dominant, above insistent reiterations of D♭-C in the bass. Resolution of the B♭5 is transferred to an inner voice at the cadential vi⁶-V⁶ supporting one more statement of D♭-C in the top part. Within the prolongation of the dominant we can trace the descent of a fourth with wide registral distribution, C5-B♭5-A♭3-G3.

The first few measures of the modulating consequent are an intensified reworking of the opening material. The sudden outbursts of *ff* are counter to the established hypermetric pattern established in the beginning measures, resulting in an unsettled feeling. A change is clearly coming, and it does come in measure 23, where the C5-D♮.5-C5 of the previous two measures is answered by C5-D♭5, the latter harmonized as the seventh of the dominant in the key of A♭ major (III). This leads to an extended digression, which serves various purposes, including providing us, the listeners, with time to adjust our expectations. Also, the parenthetical insertion delays the resolution of the dissonant seventh *in the same octave* until the second measure of theme 2 (measure 36), a further enlargement on the C5-D♭5-C5 version of the motive, now harmonized by the progression I-[V⁷]-III. Internal to the digression, E♭6, the octave of the prolonged modulating dominant, is introduced by its upper neighbor F♭6 in measure 27, and then transferred to E♭5 in measure 31 to reintroduce the dissonant seventh two measures later. The seventh is subsequently transferred down to D♭4 to resolve to C4 at the beginning of the second theme. This downward octave transfer is answered by the upper transfer to C5 in measure 36.

The metric organization of this material is interesting in several respects. First, the arrival at the A♭ harmony in measure 35 is heard as a hypermetric downbeat, but the following measure is also heard as accented. Here we are encountering a phenomenon that is not uncommon in the tonal repertoire, *successive downbeat measures*. Measure 36, the return to C5 and completion of the enlarged neighbor-note motive, can be considered at some level as the delayed eighth measure of the extended phrase begun with the upbeat to measure 17, though I have not marked it as such, since the intervening material has established a new pattern. Locally the eighth measure of the phrase is shown simultaneously as the first measure of the digression. This is the first of two hypermetric reinterpretations that occur within this passage.

EXAMPLE 3.18 Beethoven, Piano Sonata Op. 57 (I), 1–36

EXAMPLE 3.18 *continued*

EXAMPLE 3.19 Graph of Beethoven Op. 57 (I), 1–36

SUGGESTED ASSIGNMENTS

1. Mozart, Piano Quartet K. 478 (II), 1–19. This theme consists of an eight-measure antecedent leading to interruption and an eleven-measure consequent. How is the consequent expanded? Prepare a detailed graph of the voice-leading structure.

2. Mozart, Piano Sonata K. 332 (I), 71–86. The initial phrase of this closing theme is six measures in length ending with an imperfect authentic cadence. The following phrase is ten measures in length leading to a perfect authentic cadence. In your graph, show how this second phrase is expanded.

3. Schubert, Symphony No. 9 (II), 1–29. This antecedent-consequent pair is expanded externally at both ends, and the antecedent phrase has one extra measure. What is expanded to create this extra measure? Prepare a graph of the voice-leading structure, including the external expansions.

4. Consider the opening section of the first movement of Mozart's String Quartet in F Major, K. 590. This movement opens with a six-measure phrase divided into two three-measure segments. This is followed by a nine-measure phrase leading to the dominant. How might these nine be considered an expansion of six? What motivic ideas are repeated and developed in this passage?

5. Schubert, Piano Trio in E♭ (D. 929), I: 1–35. On the score, indicate your interpretation of the harmony and hypermetric organization, noting any phrase overlap, metric reinterpretation and phrase expansion. Only then tackle the task of preparing a graph interpreting the voice leading.

NOTES

1. A clear discussion of the topic of phrase expansion is contained in the third chapter of William Rothstein's *Phrase Rhythm in Tonal Music* (Schirmer, 1989).

2. This graph is a slightly condensed version of Figure 1 in the author's "Motivic Enlargement and Phrase Expansion: Illustrations From Two Works by Mozart," *Journal of Schenkerian Studies* 3 (2008), 1–17.

3. Schenker makes the following statement at the beginning of the section on expansion: "The concept of expansion does not include those 6-, 10- and 12-measure groups which serve a diminution organically", by which he means that the expansion is the direct result of the number of elements involved (e.g., three measures to accommodate a descending third). Thus I suspect he might not count this as a legitimate instance of phrase expansion. See the English translation by Ernst Oster, p. 124.

4. Schubert repeats only phrases 1 and 3 in the recapitulation.

5. See the discussion of unfolding at the end of Chapter 1.

6. It is interesting to look at Chopin's slurs in these measures, which do not always align with the hypermeter.

7. This work was discussed by the author in "Phrase Expansion: Three Analytical Studies," *Music Analysis* 14/1 (1995), 27–47.

4 Contrasting Phrases

Formal Type: a b

In previous chapters, we have dealt almost exclusively with musical periods comprising parallel phrases. In this chapter, we will broaden our investigation to include periods or musical themes that incorporate contrasting material. We will begin by examining a theme by Mozart that consists of two contrasting phrases that together form a complete musical idea. The theme is the second subject from the first movement of his Piano Sonata in F Major, K. 280. Its statement in the exposition is reproduced in Example 4.1, and a graph of its voice-leading structure is provided in Example 4.2. It is possible to describe this theme as an extended musical sentence, where measures 1–4 constitute the initial presentation (I-V), the next four its answer (V-I), and the remainder as the continuation. However, as noted earlier, my inclination is to describe this particular theme as consisting of two contrasting though complementary phrases, the first divided into two subphrases, each of four measures.

The formal organization of the theme based on the description just given is a(4) a′ (4) b(9). Note that the contrasting b phrase consists of nine measures, ending on a hypermetric downbeat and overlapping with the following phrase. Within the local context, the primary tone is G5, 5 in the key of C major, and over the course of the theme the top part will descend a fifth to local closure. The first phrase (measures 27–34) descends a third: G5-F5-E5. As we shall see, this is a preliminary descent prolonging G5 and tonic harmony, which connects to G5 supported by I⁶ at the beginning of the contrasting phrase. As shown in Example 4.2, the initial descent within the tonic scale step occurs as follows: G5 (m. 28) -F5 (m. 32)-E5 (m. 34). At the same time, the goal of this motion, E5, is approached by an ascending third broken into two steps: C5-D5 . . . D5-E5. This is shown in the graph by the broken beam.

The second phrase begins from G5 supported by tonic harmony in first inversion. The addition of B♭4 (inner voice) propels the music forward and initiates a sequence involving the technique of *reaching over*. What that term is describing is the procedure of reaching above one note to approach the next step in an ascending line from above. Here the ascending third F5-G5-A5 is accomplished first by reaching up to A5 above F5 to approach G5 from above, then B♭5 above G5 to reach A5 from above. Statement of this A5 is delayed until the second beat of measure 41, from which point the line descends a third to F5 supported by ii⁶. As shown in Example 4.2, this F5 supported by ii⁶ initiates the descent to local closure,

EXAMPLE 4.1 Mozart, Piano Sonata K. 280 (I), 27–43

but with scale degrees 3 and 2 not stated in this voice. These notes are clearly implied by our understanding of the norm for this cadential progression, including the substitution of the leading tone for scale degree 2. We can expect the following phrases to make explicit what is here implied by context, and, as always, Mozart follows through.

The sequence established at the beginning of this second phrase warrants careful examination. The intervallic pattern of the outer voices beginning in measure 36 is 8–10 8–10 (8), where the 10s result from reaching over, thus avoiding parallel octaves. Meanwhile the inner voice of this sequence is progressing in a series of (5)-6 motions above the bass, which avoids parallel fifths. Finally, a word about the notation of the process of reaching over. The A5 (and later the B♮5) is an extension of F5 and is thus connected to it by a slur, not slurred to the note it introduces (G5). Stated differently, A5 prolongs F5 until it moves up to G5.

Though we will study this entire movement in a later chapter, it is instructive in this context to see how Mozart treats this theme in the recapitulation, where it appears in the tonic key (F major). Here the two parts of the theme are separated by a six-measure insertion, the main purpose of which is to move the second part an octave lower to prepare closure in the original register. The score of measures 109–131 is reproduced in Example 4.3, and a graph of the voice leading up to the beginning of the second phrase is provided in Example 4.4.

Little comment is required of the first eight measures, which support an initial descent of a third from scale degree 5 (C6) within a tonic prolongation. As before, the third— here A5—is also approached from below. This is followed by the inserted imitative passage beginning in measure 117, which starts once again from C6 supported by tonic harmony. The harmonic basis of this passage is a circle of fifths progression leading back to tonic harmony in first inversion, now with C5 rather than C6 as the top note, from which point the descent to closure follows in this lower octave. Example 4.4 does not continue beyond measure 123, since this would duplicate the equivalent phrase in Example 4.2 a fifth lower.

The inserted connective passage presents some interesting choices, not only analytic decisions but also related notational issues. Overall the passage articulates a descending fifth with a transfer to the lower octave in the sixth measure. A legitimate question might arise in your mind regarding my choice of G4 as the main note in the sixth measure. If the sequence had continued the established pattern, the next melodic note would have been G5, and if Mozart had followed this through to completion, it would have taken eight measures rather than six to complete the descending fifth. Furthermore, the passage would have ended on F5, not F4, which would not accomplish the mission of getting to the lower octave. So Mozart makes the adjustment in the sixth measure, one result being the statement of G4 on the second beat of the measure while the inner voice tone B♭4 is transferred to the bass to lead to the third of the tonic chord in measure 123. Up to this point this passage had progressed one harmony per measure; in this measure there is an acceleration of this pace with two chords in order to reach the goal on the downbeat of the next measure: $ii - V_2^4$.

The melodic content of this passage is based on the arpeggiation motive employed in contrary motion, so a conscious decision was made to retain this feature in the graph rather than present these chords as verticalities. Second, two registral changes were made (left-hand part, measures 118 and 120) to show the continuity of the voice leading more

EXAMPLE 4.2 Graph of Mozart K. 280 (I), 27–43

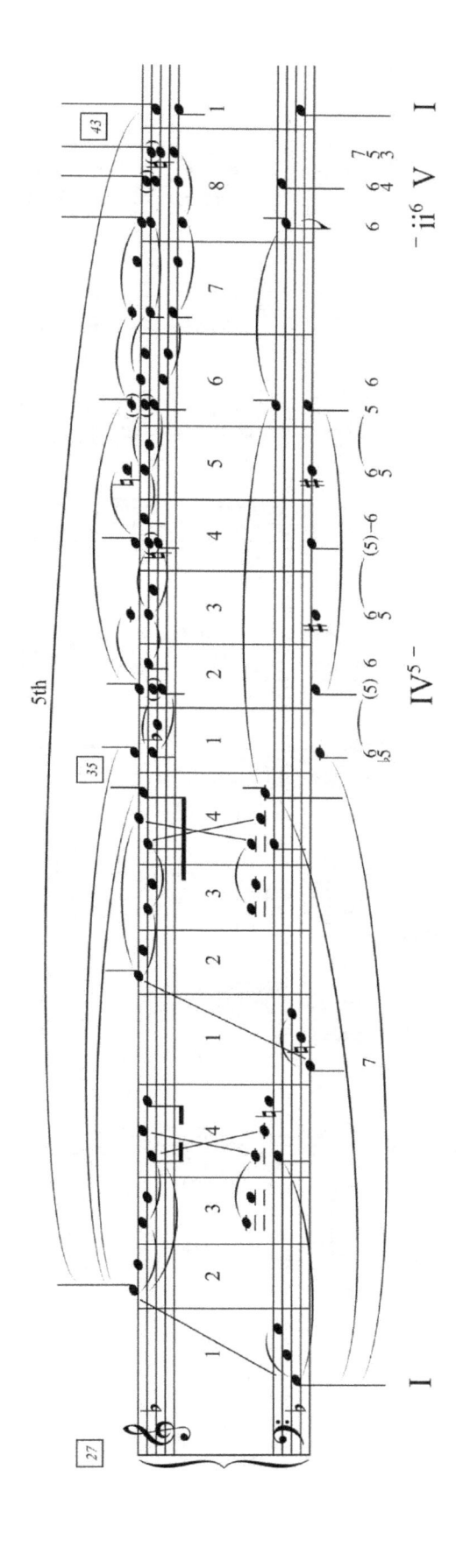

EXAMPLE 4.3 Mozart, Piano Sonata K. 280 (I), 109–131

EXAMPLE 4.4 Graph of Mozart K. 280 (I), 109–131

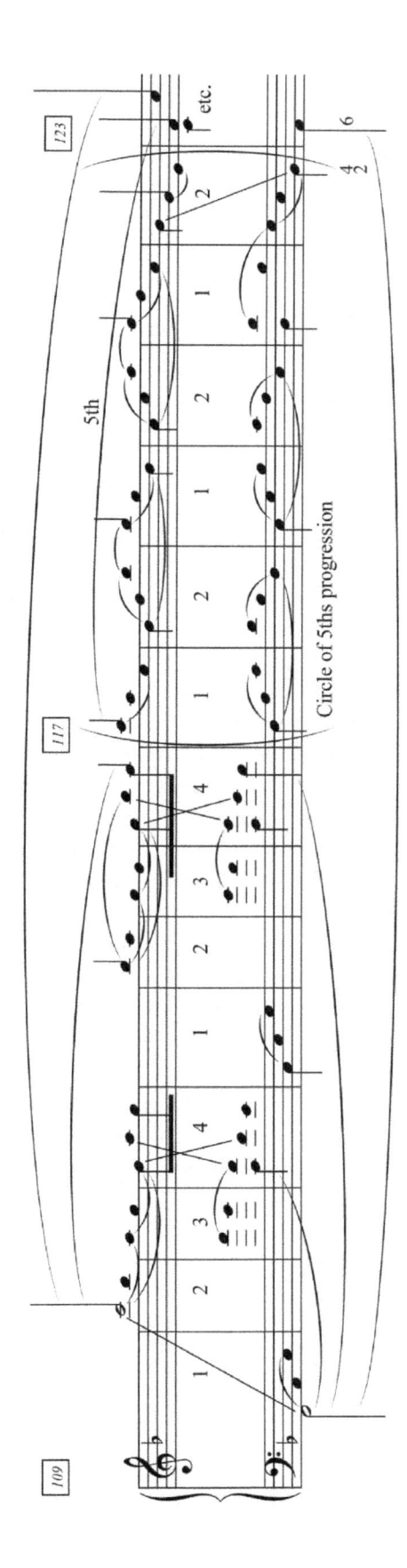

clearly. And finally, a decision was made that it is the seventh of the chord rather than the octave that is the more important note in the voice-leading pattern. To explain briefly, that last note in the right-hand part in measure 119 could be written as E5, but it is the following note, D5, the seventh of the chord, that leads us to C5 in the next measure. Furthermore, this D5, now dissonant, was prepared by the consonant D5 on the downbeat of the previous measure. A further reduction would show the following sequence of chords: $I^7 - IV_2^4 - vii^7 - iii_2^4$, etc.

Our next example, the opening theme from Beethoven's Piano Trio Op. 1, No. 3, presents a different situation. An annotated score is provided in Example 4.5 and a graph of the voice-leading structure in Example 4.6. Here we have two contrasting ideas, labeled a and b, respectively, juxtaposed to form a larger unit. Taken by itself, the first of these might be labeled as an introductory phrase; it certainly has that character. The following material, beginning with the upbeat to measure 11, sounds like theme 1. This material is a musical sentence, consisting of a presentation of eight measures divided into four (i–V^7) plus four (V^7–i), followed by the continuation, which extends the dominant for twelve measures. However, if you listen to the rest of the movement, this introductory phrase returns at important points—at the beginnings of the following transition, the development and the recapitulation—and is thus an integral part of the movement. Perhaps the best description is to label a as the introductory phrase and the remainder, b, as the theme. However we label the components of this section, the voice leading remains the same.

The opening phrase is ten measures in length, which we might understand as an expansion of eight due to the insertion of two measures between the two hypermeasures of four. In this context, these two measures prepare the following augmented sixth chord. If you look ahead, you will note that Beethoven makes use of this A♭ chord to begin the following transition rather than to start again from the tonic. The main features of the opening six measures are the prolongation of C by its lower neighbor in the lower of the two voices and above this the arpeggiation C4-E♭4-G4, which then moves up to A♭4 as a result of the 5–6 motion above C. The following augmented sixth chord is extended by a voice exchange above which the violin states F♯5, which is subsequently decorated by a turn figure before resolving to G5 supported by the dominant in measure 10. At this point we cannot determine the primary tone, but with the ensuing phrase it is immediately clear that the primary tone is E♭5 ($\hat{3}$), which in the course of the next eight measures is prolonged by its upper neighbor. At the end of the phrase, the return to E♭5 is covered by a motion to G5, which prepares the following continuation, where G5 covers an implied D5 ($\hat{2}$), the resolution of E♭5. This portion of the opening section has not been included in Example 4.6, since it prolongs a single harmony (V). However, on the score I have circled the pitches of the ascending third from the leading tone B♮4 to D5, which is stated twice (mm. 19–21 and 23–25). Furthermore, once arriving at D5 in measure 25, it is prolonged by its upper neighbor, finally bringing these two pitches together. The parentheses around that D5 in Example 4.6 could be removed with justification; it is there simply to show that it is not stated initially.

EXAMPLE 4.5 Beethoven, Piano Trio Op. 1, No. 3 (I), 1–30

EXAMPLE 4.6 Graph of Beethoven Op. 1, No. 3 (I), 1–30

Formal Type: a a′ b a″

The next three selections each consist of four phrases with the formal scheme a a′ b a″, where the first two phrases have parallel construction. This is a common pattern for the initial sections of movements with a larger formal design. The first of these is the opening section, measures 1–16, from the second movement of Beethoven's Piano Sonata Op. 2, No. 1. The score is reproduced as Example 4.7, and a graph of its voice-leading structure is provided in Example 4.8.

In some respects this is a simpler excerpt than those we have just examined in this chapter, but it is deceptively simple. There are some interesting issues regarding voice leading and graphic notation. The four phrases are each four measures in length, and a brief examination reveals that the melodic note articulated at the beginning of each of the phrases over a root position tonic chord is $\hat{3}$. This is the primary tone. In addition, note that the first phrase leads to an interruption and the second phrase completes the motion to local closure, as does the last phrase, only an octave higher. With these basic analytic decisions settled, our task of preparing a clear graph showing some, but not all, of the detail is made much easier.

In the first phrase, the main melodic motion of the first measure is A4–F4, which is embellished by a stepwise descent from the covering tone C5. Beethoven's notation indicates this C5 is an appoggiatura to the following B♭4, the upper neighbor of $\hat{3}$. But we must be careful not to discount this detail in our analysis, since it not only has aural significance here as the initiating point of the following descent, but this pitch becomes increasingly important later in this and later phrases. The goal of this motion—which is paralleled by an inner part a sixth lower—is F4, and this F4 then leads to E4 over the dominant in the second measure. This E4 then returns to F4 as the inner voice is led down to A3 (I⁶) on the downbeat of measure 3, immediately after which C5, the covering tone, is reinstated before descending to A4 over root position tonic harmony at the end of the measure. There is a connection between the A4 and tonic harmony on the downbeat of measure 1 and their restatement just before the motion to the interruption. The largest slur shows the overall motion of $\hat{3}$ to $\hat{2}$ harmonized by I to V. The slur below that and the corresponding one in the bass show the prolongation of A4 and tonic harmony, and the next level shows the connection of the covering C5 in measures 1 and 3 before the descent back to A4.

The first change in the consequent phrase comes in the second measure, where the covering C5 is led up to F5 as the bass progresses once again to A3 (I⁶). This is followed by a standard cadential pattern initiated by the subdominant. In the right-hand part I have included only the most essential notes in the motion to closure: B♭4, harmonized by IV leads to A4 (cadential six-four) and then to G4, momentarily obscured by decorative pitches before being articulated strongly on the next downbeat as an appoggiatura leading to F4. Again a note about slurs: the motion from C5 to F5 in measures 5–6 is indicated by a slur. Then the A4 on the second beat of measure 7 is shown as a passing note within the third B♭4-A4-G4. This is an important point. This return to A4 is *not* the end point of a tonic prolongation as it was in the initial phrase, and thus a slur connecting this point to the A4 at the beginning of the phrase would be incorrect. Rather, the motion passes through this point on its way to G4.

The b phrase consists of four measures of dominant harmony, above which the top line arpeggiates twice to C6, the second time to introduce the passing seventh leading back to $\hat{3}$,

EXAMPLE **4.7** Beethoven, Piano Sonata Op. 2, No. 1 (II), 1–16

EXAMPLE 4.8 Graph of Beethoven Op. 2, No. 1 (II), 1–16

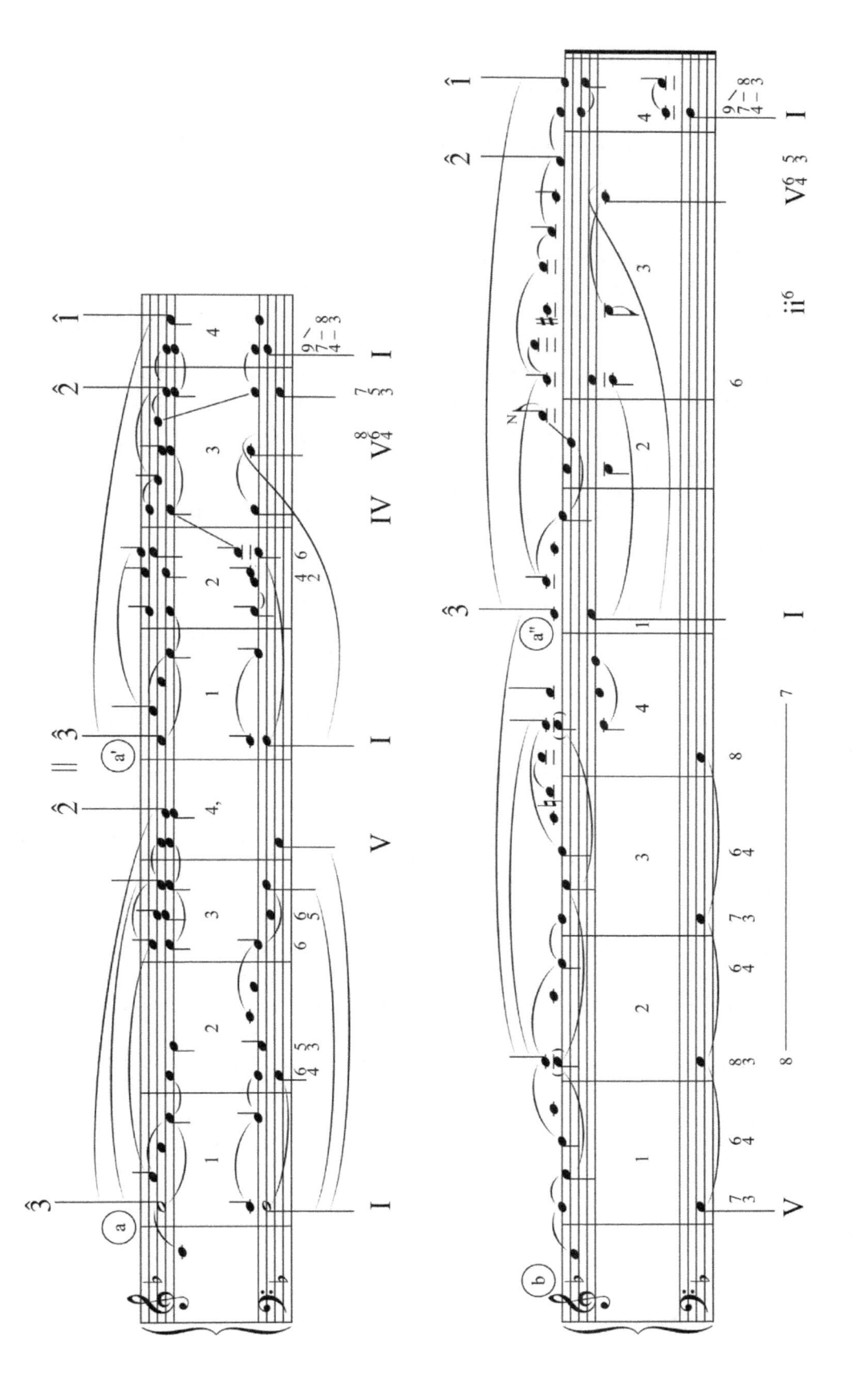

this time in the upper octave. In this last phrase, even greater emphasis is placed on the covering line. C6 is reintroduced on the downbeat of the third measure by its harmonized upper neighbor, and then led back to D6, supported by ii⁶, via the chromatic passing tone C♯6. This motion covers the progression to B♭5, which, as before, passes through A5 to G5 on the way to closure.

A second example of this formal scheme, also in F major, is provided in Example 4.9. It is the opening theme from the second movement of Schubert's "Trout" Quintet, D. 667. The interaction between the two instruments sharing the melodic material, piano and violin, adds another layer of complexity. The imitation between the two is highlighted on the score by open-ended brackets and connecting lines. A graph of the voice leading is provided in Example 4.10.

As already noted, the first two phrases are parallel in construction, the first leading to interruption and the second completing the motion to closure. In the antecedent phrase, the melody is in the piano part. Identification of the primary tone is not immediately apparent in the first measure, but by the third measure it becomes clear that it is A5 ($\hat{3}$). So C6 on the second quarter of the first measure, which is given an accent by Schubert, is to be interpreted as a covering tone extending $\hat{3}$. As shown in Example 4.10, the D5 on the third quarter of the measure, which is approached by a leap of a seventh from C6, may be conceptually understood to have its origin in C5, an octave lower. This line leads immediately to F5, and from there the harmonized progression of an ascending third leads back to A5. In the third measure, the primary tone is prolonged by its upper neighbor, and in the fourth measure A5 gives way to G5 ($\hat{2}$) supported by the dominant. Note, however, that no attempt has been made to represent the inner voice (viola). That certainly could have been done, but as we continue it would be increasingly difficult to show all the parts without making the graph almost impossible to read.

In the answering phrase, the melody is switched to the violin. The one "new" event here is the imitation of the opening melodic gesture, the leap of a third A5–C6, between violin (measure 5) and piano (measure 6), which has been represented in Example 4.10 by the open-ended brackets. This is an important detail that is subsequently exploited by Schubert, and, as we shall see, one that results in the establishment of competing hypermetric groups.

The piano once again takes the lead in the third phrase, which is contrasting in some respects, but also clearly derived from previous material. The imitation between piano and violin intensifies. First we have the imitation of the "head" motive, the ascending third, here transposed up a fourth, first by the piano (measure 9), and then by the violin (measure 10). Then, in measure 11 and again in measure 12, the time between imitative entrances is shortened from one measure to one beat. This is clearly indicated on the score, but now we are faced with making decisions about how much of this to include in our graph. One solution is offered in Example 4.10. First, a decision was made to notate events as they sound, even if requiring numerous ledger lines, and second to indicate imitative statements by arrows. Turning our attention for a moment to the harmony, note that the subdominant, which is subsequently transformed into ii⁶ by the 5–6 motion above the bass, is prolonged throughout the phrase until it progresses to V supporting $\hat{2}$ in the fifth measure. The prolongation of the subdominant and D6 in the first three measures of the phrase is a clear imitation, modified and transposed, of the opening measures of the movement. What follows is analogous to what we found in the second theme from the first movement of Mozart's Piano Sonata

EXAMPLE 4.9 Schubert, Trout Quintet D. 667 (II), 1–19

EXAMPLE **4.9** *continued*

EXAMPLE 4.10 Graph of Schubert Trout Quintet (II), 1–19

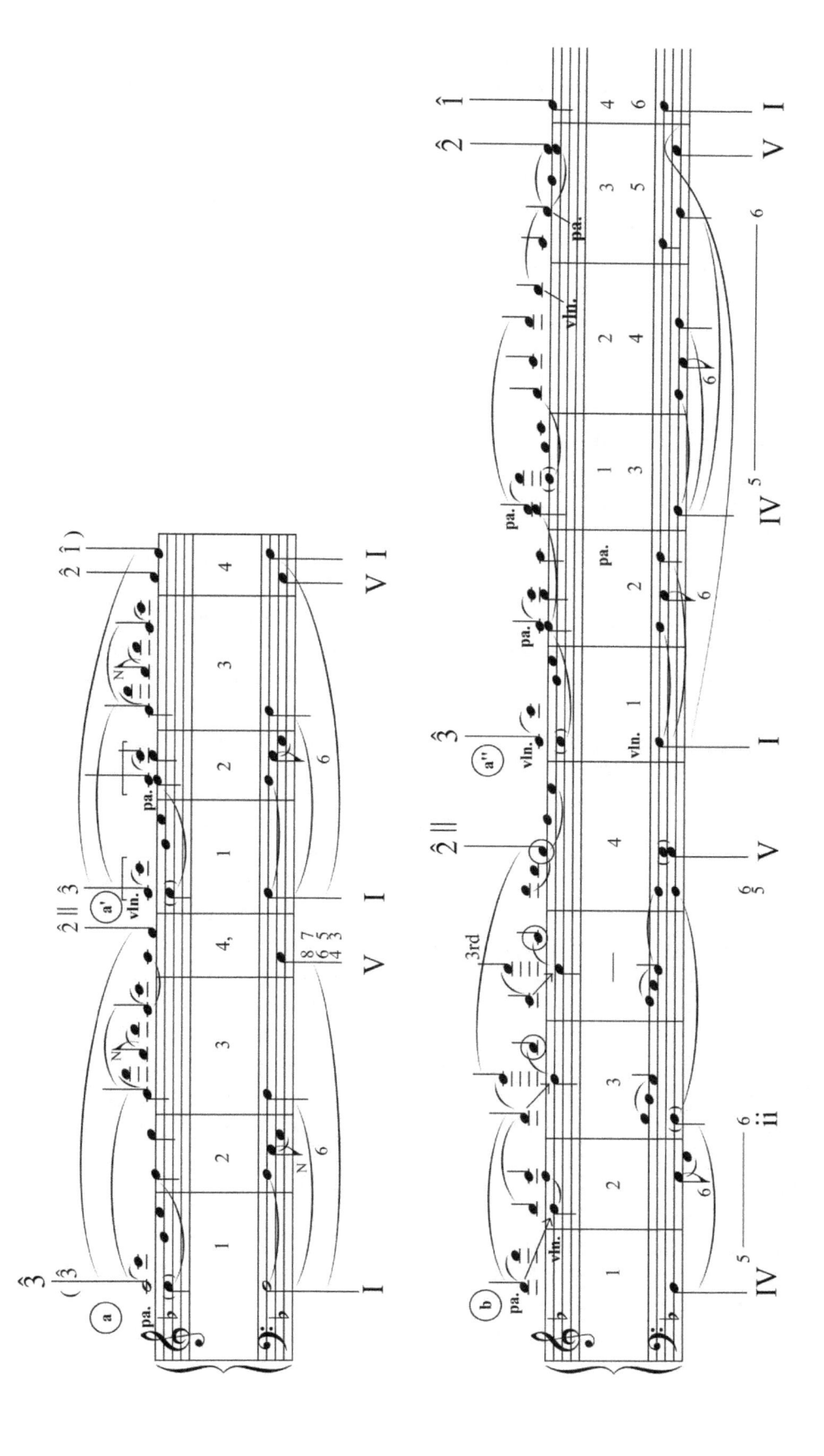

K. 310 (see Examples 3.7 and 3.8), where a passing tone is accorded a full measure in the repetition of an initial four-measure idea, thus expanding the phrase by one measure. This is another instance where there is a correlation between the number of elements and the number of measures.[1] Here the content of the third measure is stated a step lower in the following measure, providing support for the passing tone A6 within the descending third Bb6-A6-G5. This gesture is stated in two registers by two instruments. The higher of the two (piano), including the registral transfer, is indicated by a slur. The equivalent line in the violin part is indicated by the circled pitches.

The imitation between violin and piano in the final phrase results in the extension of this four-measure idea to six. The imitation of the opening third A5-C6 by the piano in the second measure of the phrase is exactly what happened in the second phrase. But this turns out to be a false start that anticipates the real imitation, which begins a measure later over subdominant harmony, recalling the b phrase. From this point on, the piano takes over the lead role. As noted earlier, the result of these competing hypermeters (indicated between the staves in Example 4.10) is an expansion of the phrase to six measures.[2] The final motion to closure, the descending third Bb5-A5-G5, is shared by violin and piano.

Our third and final example of this formal scheme is the opening theme from the first movement of Schubert's Piano Sonata in Bb, D. 960. The score is reproduced as Example 4.11 and a graph of the voice leading as Example 4.12.

The first two phrases, each nine measures in length, follow the normal pattern for an antecedent-consequent pair, and identification of the primary tone is perfectly clear right from the outset. It is D5 ($\hat{3}$). The first phrase opens with an ascent to $\hat{3}$, followed by an initial descent back to Bb4 on the downbeat of measure 4. D5 is subsequently re-established via its upper neighbor Eb5 and then prolonged until resolving to $\hat{2}$ and dominant harmony at the local interruption. What is unusual about this cadence is the arrival at scale degree 2 and a stable dominant in the middle of measure 7 rather than on the downbeat of measure 8. This is followed by a trill in the bass on Gb resolving to F, a detail that foreshadows events to come. The dominant is then extended for an additional measure, resulting in a nine-measure phrase. The first four measures of the consequent phrase are an exact repetition until the last quarter of the fourth measure, where the bass begins its chromatic descent to V supporting $\hat{2}$. Rather than resolve directly to $\hat{1}$ and tonic harmony in the next measure, the dominant is extended for an extra measure, the result being that this phrase too is nine measures in length with the goal harmony, delayed by a suspension, falling in an accented measure in the hypermetric scheme. There is something oddly unsettling about this opening section. On the one hand, it is very simple, following a predictable path to interruption, then local closure, and, except for some passing chords in measures 13–15, based on just two harmonies, I and V. What is unusual is the placement of goal harmonies in both phrases.

As shown in Example 4.12, the extended b phrase is preceded by an upbeat measure. The key is Gb major (bVI), Schubert's initial expansion of the trill in measure 8. In fact, if we look ahead we see that this entire passage is built on a Gb pedal that eventually becomes unstable as part of the augmented sixth chord in measures 34–35 leading back to F. That is, this entire phrase is built on an extended upper neighbor of F (V). As happens so frequently with these "contrasting" phrases, this one is derived from earlier material. Here the opening eight measures of the melody are really a recomposition of the initial phrase in a new key. It

EXAMPLE 4.11 Schubert, Piano Sonata D. 960 (I), 1–45

EXAMPLE **4.11** *continued*

EXAMPLE 4.12 Graph of Schubert Piano Sonata D. 960 (I), 1–38

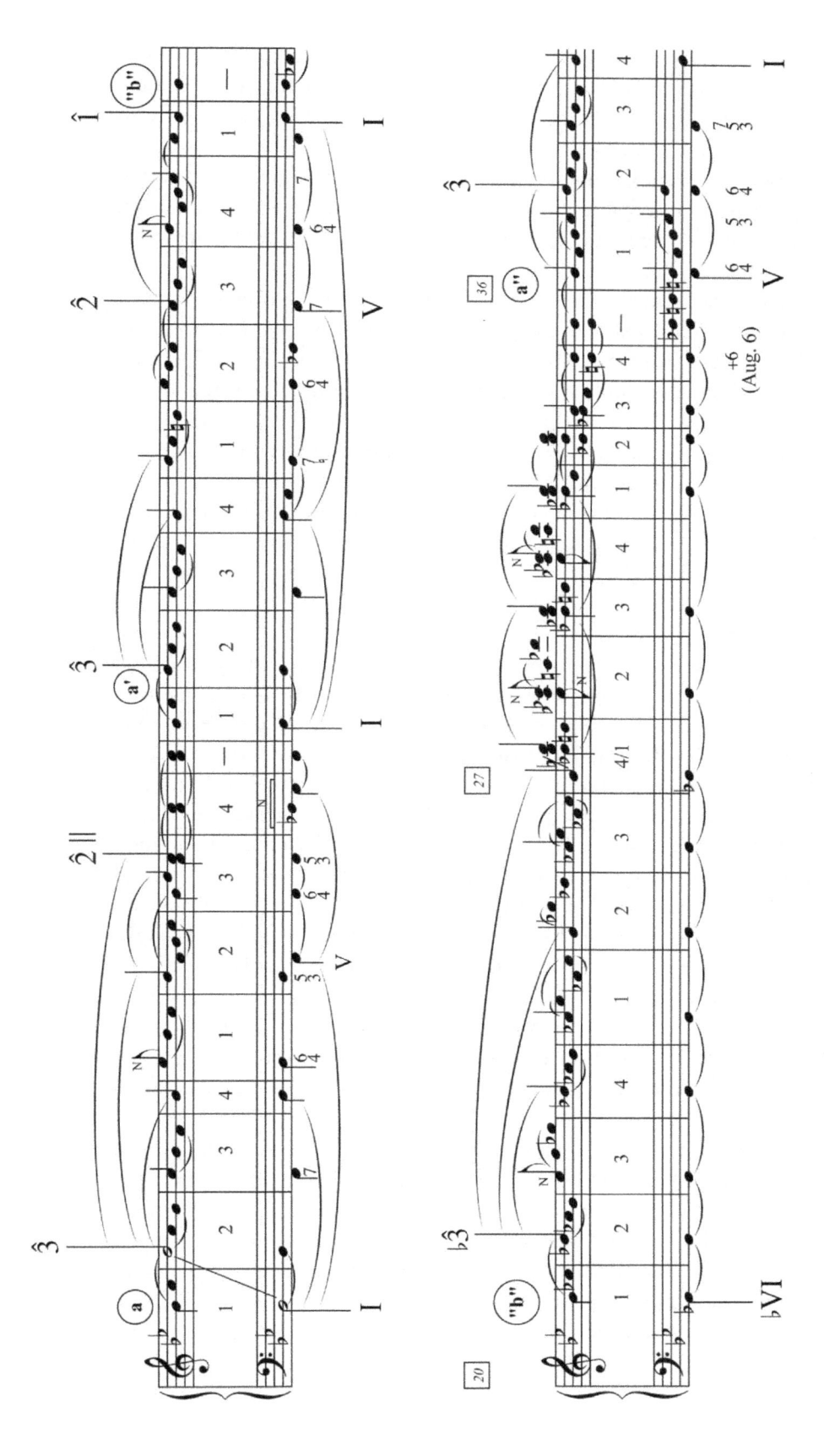

opens with an ascent to scale degree 3, now D♭5 ($\flat\hat{3}$), which is subsequently prolonged by its upper neighbor before descending twice to B♭4. As indicated in Example 4.12, measure 27 is both a point of arrival and the point of departure for the following excursion into the upper octave and acceleration of surface motion leading to the augmented sixth chord, where Schubert now slows the motion in preparation for the return. The graph of measures 27–31 notates the arpeggiations as vertical chords to save space. It shows the prolongation of B♭5 by its upper neighbor C♭6 before the transfer to B♭4 in preparation for the return of the opening idea in that octave.

What is different about the return is that the opening measures occur over a dominant pedal. Example 4.12 shows the return of $\hat{3}$ in measure 37, but tonic harmony is not reached until two measures later. In fact, we never do get a statement of D5 in direct association with a stable tonic chord, though certainly it is implied by context and by our memory of the opening. And this phrase does not close, but instead is led by Schubert to the second theme in F♯ minor, a further expansion of the G♭-F relationship introduced in measure 8. The eventual goal of the exposition is F major. Thus, from a motivic perspective, we can understand this movement as a series of ever increasing expansions of the neighbor-note relationship F-G♭/F♯-F.

Formal Type: a b a′

The primary topic of this chapter has been the incorporation of "contrasting" material into extended phrases or periods, and some of the examples examined have involved phrase expansions of various types—a logical extension of the previous chapter. Along the way, some of the commentary has dealt with notational issues, since it is imperative that we learn to communicate accurately and as clearly as possible our interpretation of the voice leading. That is what is at the core of Schenkerian analysis. If we are talking about preparing a written presentation, then there are really two types of analytic sketches or graphs: (1) those that show considerable amount of detail and include bar lines to aid in reading; and (2) middleground graphs, often involving a certain amount of "normalization" to facilitate communication, that are designed to show longer-range connections.[3] Almost all graphs in this book are of the first type. However, neither of these types is particularly useful in communicating to an audience, whether in class/seminar or at a theory conference, since those listening must shuffle back and forth between score and graph, which can lessen the effect of what otherwise might have been an excellent presentation. It is this thought that prompts me to present a very different type of analytic graph that is superimposed on a simplification of the score.

The passage that is the subject of this experiment is the A section from the second movement of Schubert's String Quartet in G Major (D 887), the score of which is provided in Example 4.13. The form of this section is ternary (a b a′), but the initial phrase is repeated (written out) as are the b and a′ phrases. Each of the phrases is eight measures in length, divisible into four plus four. The initial phrase is preceded by a two-measure introduction (an extended upbeat) and the b phrase is extended by five measures, three extending the dominant plus a repeat of the two-measure introduction in preparation for the return of the opening idea.

Example 4.13 Schubert, String Quartet in G Major D. 887 (II), 1–39

EXAMPLE 4.14 Interpretation of Schubert String Quartet D. 887 (II), 1–39

A simplification of the score, where note values indicate relative duration, not structural significance, with an interpretation of the voice leading superimposed on it is provided in Example 4.14. The structure is interesting. We know that the primary tone is G4 ($\hat{3}$) almost immediately by implication—that is, by virtue of the opening leap to the seventh of the dominant, yet $\hat{3}$ is never stated in conjunction with a tonic triad. The only clear statements of G4 come first in the b phrase above a sustained submediant harmony and later as part of a G⁷ chord. Otherwise its function is passing within another harmony, usually the dominant, sometimes only by implication. Example 4.14 requires little amplification. The first four measures of the first phrase support a motion from the seventh to the fifth over a dominant pedal, and the second half of the phrase completes the motion to local closure with a standard cadential pattern, the one noticeable omission being $\hat{3}$. The b phrase sustains the submediant harmony, which at the very end gives way to the dominant. By implication this dominant supports $\hat{2}$, though statement of $\hat{2}$ here would have resulted in clearly audible fifths. The main change in the final phrase is the use of F♮, a seeming reference to the b phrase, which is "corrected" in the final descent to closure. Note the interpretation of the harmony and voice leading at the approach to the final cadence. The motion to the C major chord, second quarter of the penultimate measure, is shown as an extension of the underlying subdominant harmony.

SUGGESTED ASSIGNMENTS

1. Mozart, Piano Concerto in C Minor, K. 491 (II), 1–19. Here the a phrase is closed and the b phrase is expanded from four to seven measures. Show in your graph how this is accomplished.

2. Beethoven, Piano Sonata Op. 2, No. 2 (II), 1–19. Here the last phrase is expanded from four to seven measures. Show in your graph how this is brought about.

3. Beethoven, Piano Sonata Op. 7 (II), 1–24. The form of this A section is ternary: a (8)-b(6)-a′ (10). The brief b section can be shown as an expansion of four measures and the a′ as an expansion of six. Show this in your graph. In preparing your sketch, pay particular attention to the voice leading in measures 17–18.

4. Beethoven, Piano Sonata Op. 14, No. 1 (II), 1–51. All but the last phrase beginning in measure 41 are eight measures in length. What is being prolonged in this last phrase and by what techniques?

NOTES

1. Nevertheless, like the Mozart example, I have chosen to indicate this as an expansion of an underlying unit of four.

2. So we have seen a slow growth over the span of this theme from phrases of four measures to five and finally to six.

3. In addition, there are metric representations of the voice leading, often done as a preparatory step to developing an analytic graph.

5 Ternary (Rounded Binary) Form

Structure vs. Formal Design

How different writers describe musical forms can be an area of considerable confusion to students grappling with this matter for the first time. This is particularly true of the form we are dealing with in this chapter, which traditionally has been labeled "rounded binary" form. It is designated as follows: ||: a : ||: b a′ : ||. It is "binary" because it consists of two parts, each of which is repeated. It is "rounded" because the second part contains a return to the opening material simultaneously with a return to tonic harmony, a feature that distinguishes it from most binary movements of the baroque. Rounded binary form is typical, for example, of minuet and scherzo movements of the classical period, and, on a grander scale, it is the form of early classical sonata form, where a is the exposition, b the development and a′ the recapitulation. While "rounded binary" is accurate as a description of the formal design, the underlying pattern of events is ternary: a b a′. At least that is the case when considering voice-leading structure, which can cross formal boundaries and does not take repeats into account. For this reason, Schenker labels this and all other forms that have a recapitulation as ternary. While it may be confusing at first to have two different designations for the same formal scheme, it is important to understand what gives rise to the difference in terminology. One is a description of the formal design and the other view expresses its underlying pattern, which is exactly how we deal with this formal design when considering voice-leading connections, particularly those at "deeper" or more remote levels. At the same time we must make a clear distinction between this ternary form and regular ternary form (A B A′)—for example, the form of the second movement from Mendelssohn's Piano Trio in D Minor, which we will examine in Chapter 7. To make this distinction as clear as possible, we will refer in this text to ternary (rounded binary) form and the other simply as ternary form without any further qualification.

The first section of this formal scheme[1] is either "closed", by which is meant that it ends on the tonic, or "open", normally leading to a cadence on III (minor mode) or V (major mode). The first type is normally found in relatively short works—for example, a theme used as the basis for variation—whereas the second occurs in more substantial movements, including those in sonata (allegro) form. In the first type (closed), the b section normally progresses to the dominant, which may function locally or at the deep middleground level—for example, to provide support for the upper neighbor of the primary tone (to which it returns at the beginning of the a′ section)—or it is structural, supporting an interruption of the fundamental line. In the first instance, the interaction of formal design and structure might be represented as in Figure 5.1 (where the mode is major and the primary tone is $\hat{3}$).

```
a        b        a'
^3       N        ^3   ^2   ^1

I        V7       I    V    I
```

FIGURE 5.1 Ternary Formal Design without Interruption

Figure 5.2, however, represents the interaction of formal design and voice-leading structure when the dominant supports an interruption of the fundamental line (where the primary tone is once again $\hat{3}$).

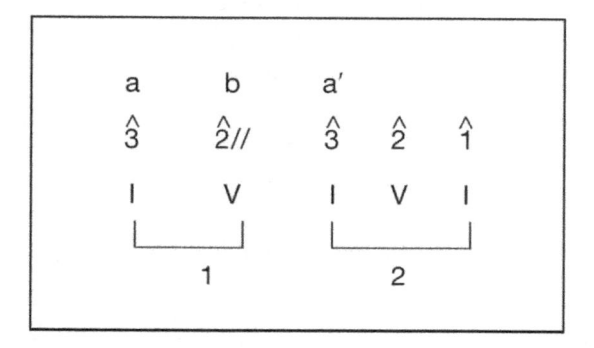

FIGURE 5.2 Ternary Formal Design with Interruption

This latter situation illustrates an important feature inherent in the interaction between the design and the voice-leading structure of this formal scheme. From a Schenkerian perspective, the design is ternary, but the voice-leading structure falls into two parts, indicated in Figure 5.2 by the brackets and the numerals 1 and 2. That is, the voice leading of the first part of the structure leading to the interruption incorporates both the a and b sections of the formal design, while the second part corresponds to the a' section (the restatement or recapitulation). Understanding this distinction is crucial to understanding Schenker's concept of voice leading in relation to this formal design, whether small in scope (rounded binary [ternary]) or large (sonata form). The voice-leading progressing to the interruption spans the formal boundary between the a and b sections. The overall voice-leading pattern created by the interruption should be familiar to you; it is the same one we have encountered numerous times with antecedent-consequent phrase pairs in Chapters 2–3, but now on a larger scale. To illustrate, consider the following scenario, where the a section consists of two phrases, the first leading to local interruption and the second leading to local closure. This is then followed by a b section leading once again to an interruption, now at a deeper level,

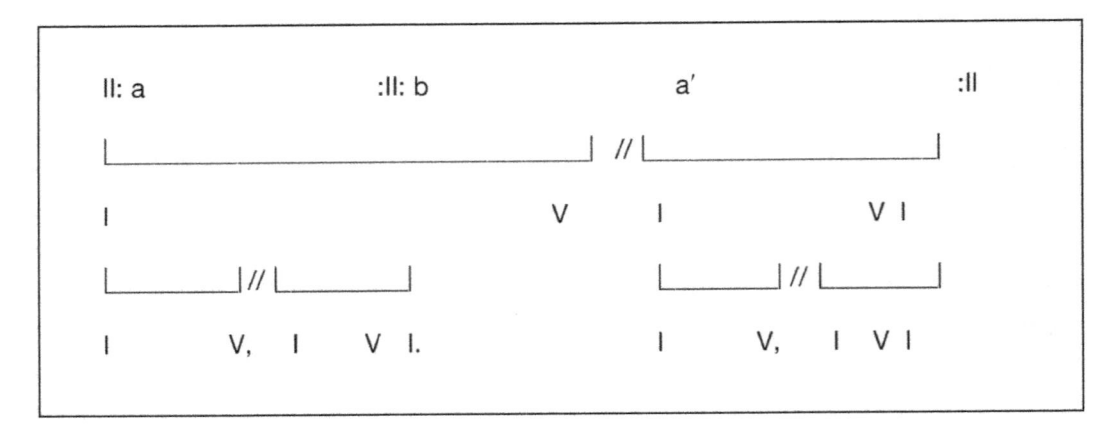

FIGURE 5.3 Detail of Sectional Design with Interruption

followed by a varied repetition of the opening section. This means that the voice-leading pattern of the a and a′ sections is replicated at a higher (deeper) level, where the first part leading to the interruption incorporates both the a and b sections. This situation is outlined in Figure 5.3, where the different levels are represented by brackets of different lengths and corresponding harmonies. In a musical graph, the different levels would be represented by the use of different note values combined with slurs.

A potential obstacle to understanding this important concept is the terminology associated with it, so I will summarize what has been stated earlier. Depending upon one's perspective, the formal scheme is referred to as "rounded binary" or ternary. On the one hand, it is binary because it falls into two parts that are repeated, but on the other hand, it is inherently ternary because of the simultaneous return to the opening material and tonic harmony. Once the repeats are removed from consideration, as one does in considering long-range voice-leading connections, then we are left with a ternary design. This is the perspective of Schenkerian analysis, which is concerned with voice-leading structure at multiple levels. So, from this perspective the design is ternary, but, as demonstrated earlier,

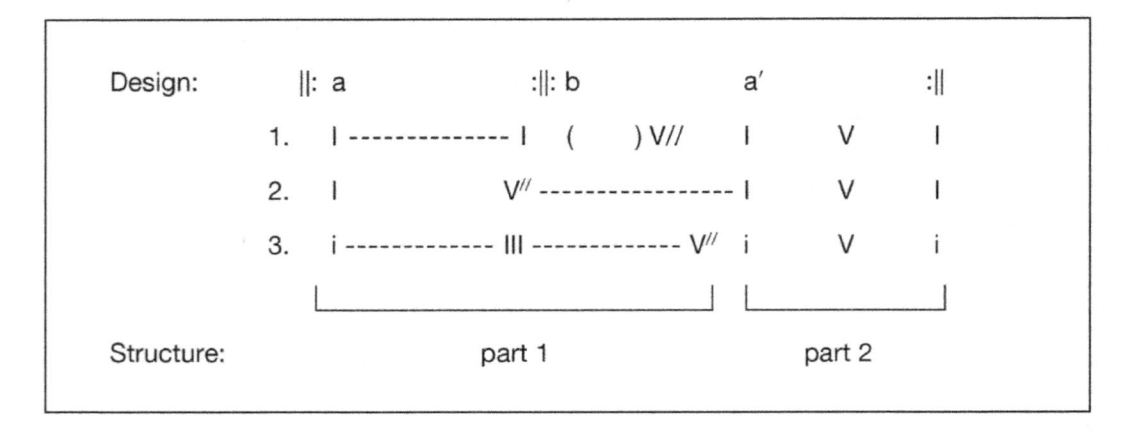

FIGURE 5.4 Design vs. Structure in Ternary (Rounded Binary) Form

the voice-leading structure itself falls into two parts when the b section leads to interruption of the fundamental line. That is, the design is ternary, but the underlying structure is binary (!), though in a very different sense than the description of the form as "rounded binary".[2] This dichotomy is demonstrated in Figure 5.4.

The first scenario shows an initial section that is closed, followed by a digression (represented by the parentheses) and then the interruption. In this situation, it is also possible that the dominant functions at a more local level and that there is no interruption. The second one shows a first part that ends in the dominant key and a prolongation of the dominant through the b section. And the third one represents a typical movement in the minor mode, where the first part ends in the key of the mediant (the relative major) and progresses to V at the end of the b section. In all three cases, the first part of the structure includes both a and b. The second part of the structure corresponds to the restatement of the opening material, now ending in the tonic.

Analyses

Haydn, St. Anthony Chorale

The first three works we will examine have closed first parts. The first of these is the St. Anthony Chorale, a work reportedly borrowed by Haydn and made famous by Brahms's Haydn Variations, Op. 56. The music is reproduced as Example 5.1. The a section consists of an antecedent-consequent pair of phrases, each five measures in length. One of the first matters we must deal with as a preliminary step to preparing a graph is to decide how these five-measure phrases naturally divide, and, in fact, if they are to be understood as expansions of a four-measure norm. It is interesting to note in this regard that the eight-measure b section is clearly divided into two four-measure subphrases.

What evidence is there for us to make an informed decision about the natural division of the opening phrase? If we look at the harmony alone, one might make a logical case for either three plus two or two plus three, but when we look at the melodic line, which, following the prolongation of D5 by its harmonized upper neighbor in measure 2, descends a third D5-C5-B♭4, then the only possibility—without destroying the linear motion—is three plus two. The motion is directed beyond measure 3 to the ii⁶ chord on the downbeat of measure 4, which we hear as a strong measure in the hypermetric scheme. This decision will have a direct impact on our graph. If B♭4 is the melodic goal of the opening three-measure gesture, then so is its support, vi, and, as we shall see, this chord is part of the progression I-vi-ii⁶ associated with the descending bass arpeggiation B♭-G-E♭, which joins the two parts of the phrase. Regarding the other question—whether the five-measure phrase is based on a four-measure norm—the only way to accomplish this would be to eliminate the second measure, which is possible, but, in doing so, would destroy the character and dynamic tension of the phrase. With these basic *musical* decisions behind us, we are prepared to develop a voice-leading graph. See Example 5.2.[3]

The primary tone is clearly D5 ($\hat{3}$), which is initially decorated in measure 1 by its upper neighbor, a relationship that is immediately developed in measure 2 as the upper neighbor is harmonized by IV. As already noted, the melodic line then descends through C5 to B♭4, this last note harmonized by vi, which is the middle member in the descending

EXAMPLE 5.1 Haydn, St. Anthony Chorale

EXAMPLE 5.2 Graph of Haydn, St. Anthony Chorale

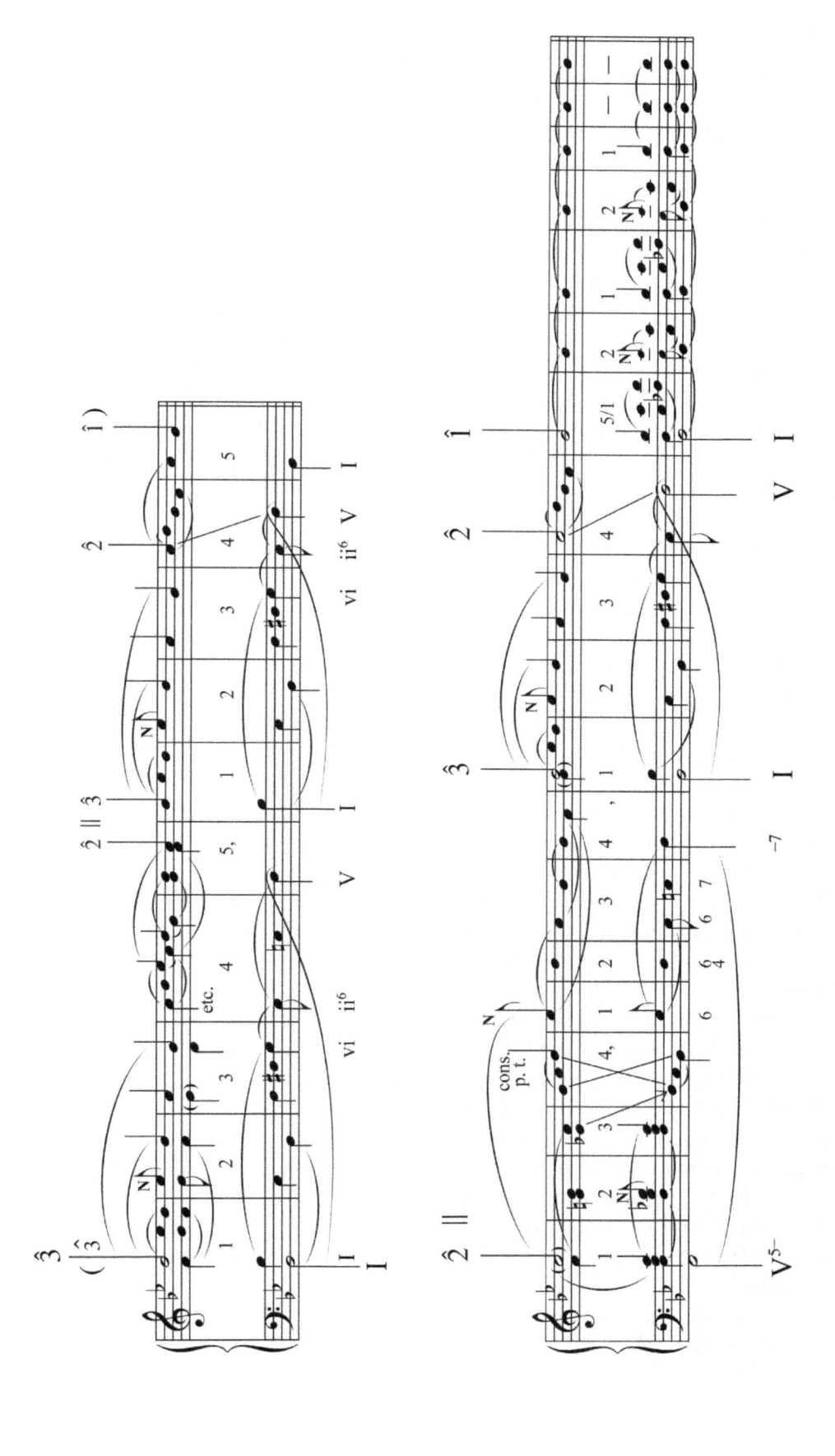

arpeggiation to ii⁶. This ii⁶ is preparation for the dominant, the goal of the phrase. This means that the dominant chord on the downbeat of measure 3 offers consonant support for the passing tone C5, and is thus of lower status in the hierarchy than the following harmony, vi, which supports the goal of this initial descent, B♭4. You might try an experiment here by rewriting the third measure so the support for B♭4 is a tonic harmony, perhaps with the third in the bass so it doesn't sound too final. This shows the function of the dominant, but the result is certainly less successful than what we have in directing the motion on to ii⁶. The next matter to decide is how to interpret the melodic contents of measures 4–5. If the initial descent of a third prolongs D5, then a natural reaction may be to take the C5, harmonized by ii, as the next step in the structural descent, which is subsequently prolonged by its own third at the cadence. But if we look ahead, we see that the goal of the phrase, C5, falls on the second half of measure 5, and that this note is approached by a descending third from E♭5. So the best solution is the one provided by Schenker—namely, that the C5 on the downbeat of measure 4 belongs to an inner voice, and that the descending third of measures 1–3, D5-C5-B♭4, is answered in measures 4–5 by the descending third E♭5-D5-C5. When we look ahead to the consequent phrase, we see that the C5 on the downbeat of the fourth measure is not a member of an inner voice, but $\hat{2}$ on its way to local closure. This is not an inconsistency. As stated earlier, interpretation is based on context, and here the context, the continuation, is different from the preceding phrase, requiring a different interpretation.

The b section, which is divided into two four-measure subphrases, prolongs the dominant. The first four-measure group begins from the inner voice tone F4 and progresses by step to D5 supported by tonic harmony. (Details of the voice leading are shown in Example 5.2.) Schenker provides this example in *Free Composition* to illustrate motion from an inner voice to reach back to the primary voice. But how are we to interpret the return to D5 and tonic harmony in the middle of a section controlled by the dominant? Schenker's graph is of no help in this regard. The one thing this event cannot represent is a reinstatement of the primary tone and tonic harmony. Why not? The answer is very simple. This tonic chord exists within a prolongation of the dominant. So we must look for another explanation. If we look to the remainder of the phrase, we see that this D5 reaches up to E♭5, which initially is provided consonant support by the IV chord and then becomes the dissonant seventh in relation to the dominant harmony at the end of the phrase. The resolution of this dissonant seventh comes at the beginning of the final phrase with the return to D5 ($\hat{3}$) and tonic harmony. There can be no doubt then that this reaching up to E♭5, the upper neighbor of the primary tone, is the focal point of this b section. But we still do not have a cogent explanation for the consonant support for D5 in the preceding measure. The most logical explanation is that it is a consonant passing tone between the fifth and seventh of the dominant. The fifth ($\hat{2}$) is not present in this register, but it is a prominent note in an inner part, where it is prolonged by its chromatic upper neighbor. The main difference between Example 5.2 and Schenker's graph in *Free Composition* is the inclusion in the former of C5 ($\hat{2}$) in parentheses. Example 5.2 posits an interruption with the return to D5 approached from E♭5, the seventh. The inclusion of C5 provides an explanation for the following events within the context of a dominant prolongation.[4]

The final phrase requires little comment. Because it is the final phrase, the notation reflects the structural descent of the fundamental line to closure. Once closure is achieved, the phrase is extended for several measures, with the final measure of the phrase proper being reinterpreted metrically as the first measure of the extension. Internal to this extension, reference is made twice in an inner voice to E♭ as neighbor note to D. By its repetition at many structural levels, the neighbor-note pattern D–E♭–D assumes a motivic role.

Chopin, Mazurka Op. 7, No. 2, 1–32

The second work is Chopin's Mazurka in A Minor, Op. 7, No. 2, a section. The score is provided in Example 5.3 and a graph of its voice leading in Example 5.4. The a section consists of two eight-measure phrases, an antecedent leading to V and a consequent leading to local closure. The b section, also eight measures in length, does not lead to the dominant,[5] but rather to the subdominant to overlap with the final phrase, a slightly varied repetition of the consequent phrase from the first part. The hypermeter is duple/quadruple throughout.

The Mazurka opens—as many of Chopin's pieces do—with a neighboring harmony, here providing support for the upper neighbor of the primary tone E5 ($\hat{5}$). I have chosen to indicate the opening pitch as $\hat{5}$, but it would be equally as logical to indicate the E5 on the third beat of measure 2 as $\hat{5}$, where it is associated for the first time with tonic harmony. (The diagonal line in Example 5.4 provides this association.) The melodic line begins its descent through D5, harmonized by V⁷, to C5 supported by tonic harmony in measure 4. The second half of the phrase is heard in relation to the key of the dominant, which at the cadence is changed to a major chord. The next step in the melodic descent, B4, is introduced first in measure 6 and restated in the next measure over the cadential six-four. This pitch is implied at the cadence on V in measure 8, so I have supplied it in parentheses. A different notational solution that conveys the same information would be to draw a diagonal line in the graph from the B4 in measure 7 to the bass note in measure 8, similar to my solution at the beginning.

The consequent phrase progresses exactly the same as the antecedent until the fourth measure, where C5 is supported by the submediant rather than tonic harmony. In the next measure ♭7 (E♭) is added to this chord, directing the harmony in the next measure to ♭II. The B♭4 in the seventh measure is shown to be a member of an inner voice, which subsequently progresses through A4 to G♯4 over the dominant. This G♯ substitutes for B♮4, scale degree 2, which has been added in parentheses in Example 5.4.

The b phrase opens with a two-measure idea based on the opening gesture introducing $\hat{5}$ by its upper neighbor, here a step lower. The E♭5–D5 is harmonized by the German augmented sixth chord leading to V in C minor (iii). Repetition of this idea is reharmonized leading to a B♭ seventh chord in four-two position, which prepares the following sequential progression leading to F5 supported by the subdominant in measure 25, overlapping with the beginning of the final phrase. Here, for the first time, the upper neighbor introducing $\hat{5}$ is given consonant support. The outer voices of the progression leading to F5 and iv proceed in parallel tenths, the top line descending a fourth from B♭5 to F5 on successive downbeats while the inner voice progresses from the previously introduced D5 to A4. Note how Chopin's slurs counter the overlapping of the phrases. Finally, regarding the final phrase, we have indicated the descent as if it were the structural motion to closure, since we are treating this initial portion of the Mazurka as if it were the complete piece.

Example 5.3 Chopin, Mazurka Op. 7, No. 2, 1–32

EXAMPLE 5.4 Graph of Chopin Mazurka Op. 7, No. 2, 1–32

Schubert, Impromptu Op. 142, No. 2, 1–46

The third work is Schubert's Impromptu, Op. 142, No. 2, the a section only. (The Impromptu is a composite ternary form: Allegretto-Trio-Allegretto.) The a section consists of two eight-measure closed phrases, the second of which is a varied repetition of the first an octave higher. This same scheme is followed in the a′ section as well. The b section consists of metric groups of four (I) plus four (IV) plus six, the last leading to the dominant. This is a complex passage that will require our careful attention. The score is provided in Example 5.5.

The first phrase is divided into subphrases of four measures, the first of which is an elaborated version of the common paradigm where the melodic line and supporting bass exchange patterns. That is, the initial prolongation of A♭4 by its lower neighbor, A♭4-G4-A♭4, is supported by the ascending third in the bass, A♭-B♭-C, and the following melodic ascent from A♭4 through B♭4 to the primary tone C5 (3̂) is supported by the bass motion A♭-G-A♭. Stated somewhat differently, the outer parts exchange passing and neighboring functions. In the second half of the phrase, the primary tone is prolonged first by a voice exchange with the bass and then by its upper neighbor D♭5 as part of the descending third E♭5-D♭5-C5. These comments describe the underlying voice leading, but you should also examine its elaboration carefully. The B♭4 in measure 1 is an escape tone or incomplete neighbor, depending on what terminology you use, and the A♭4 on the next downbeat is an accented passing tone leading to G4. This establishes a descending third pattern that is repeated in measures 5–6 and 6–7 as D♭5-C5-B♭5 and C5-B♭4-A♭4, respectively; in all three cases, the middle member is an accented passing tone. Because this idea is repeated, its occurrences have been marked in Example 5.6 by brackets.[6]

The variations of the opening phrase require little comment, except to note their slightly different treatment in the second subphrase leading to closure. In the first phrase, the primary tone is prolonged first by a voice exchange with the bass and then by its upper neighbor, as noted earlier. In the second phrase C6 is first extended by a descending third in parallel tenths with the bass (I − [V$_3^4$] − vi) before progressing to local closure. In both phrases of the a′ section, this passage is harmonized differently. The outer voices still progress in parallel tenths, with chromatic inflection in the bass recalling the modal mixture of the b section, but now with harmony directed toward the supertonic (in six-four position) as preparation for the following cadence and completion of the motion to closure. This is indicated clearly in Example 5.6.

The graph of the b section is presented at two levels: the lower one providing detail and the upper one a simplification to show the underlying connections more clearly. The first four-measure subphrase prolongs tonic harmony supporting first the arpeggiation E♭5-C5-A♭4 in parallel tenths with the bass and then a descent through D♭5 to C5. The second four measures prolong F5, the upper neighbor of E♭5, and subdominant harmony, first by the answering arpeggiation down to A♭4 and then by its own upper neighbor G♭5, harmonized by the minor subdominant of the subdominant, the G♭ minor chord. This passage introduces the modal inflection that extends into the last part of this middle section, which takes the minor subdominant of IV in six-three position as the point of departure. With the chromatic alteration of the G♭ to G♮ and the introduction of F♭ in

EXAMPLE 5.5 Schubert, Impromptu Op. 142, No. 2, 1–46

the top part, we might expect this augmented sixth chord to resolve to the cadential six-four in Db minor. Instead, Schubert skips directly to a Db harmony with Fb in the bass and with the position of the top two parts reversed—that is, with Db as an inner voice rather than on top. This switch of positions makes it more difficult to identify the underlying voice-leading connection. This minor subdominant harmony in six–three position is subsequently altered, becoming an augmented sixth chord, this time leading to the cadential six-four and its resolution to the dominant. In the process, the top two parts switch positions again, restoring the original order, but now an octave lower in preparation for the return to the beginning.

The lower level of the graph preserves events in the registers as written, but care has been taken to indicate top versus inner part, even while reversed, by direction of stems. Also included in brackets is the "missing" resolution of the augmented sixth chord in measure 26, which Schubert omitted, skipping instead directly to the minor subdominant harmony in first inversion. (The symbol above the insertion indicates that it has been omitted.) This addition suggests that this final six-measure group of the b section may be considered a contraction of eight rather than an expansion of four.

The upper level of the graph normalizes the registral placement of events in this complex passage. Now the underlying voice leading becomes clearer. Following the initial four-measure prolongation of the tonic, the voice leading is "controlled" by a chromatic voice exchange prolonging the subdominant harmony from measure 21 until its resolution to the dominant in measure 29. The return to the primary tone in the final section (measure 34) is prepared by its upper neighbor, similar to what occurs in the St. Anthony Chorale. However, you will note that an interruption has not been indicated here. The difference is that the b section of the St. Anthony Chorale prolongs the dominant, whereas in this work it is the subdominant that is prolonged, with the dominant assuming a more local function.

Haydn, Symphony No. 103, Menuet

The remaining two works we will examine in this chapter are longer, and they present some interesting analytic challenges. The first of these is the Menuet from Haydn's Symphony No. 103. The score is provided in Example 5.7. The a section consists of one phrase divided into two contrasting subphrases. The first is "boisterous" and is characterized by its Lombard rhythm ("Scotch snap") and wide leaps, while the second is much "tamer" rhythmically and combines stepwise motion with small leaps until the final gesture, which returns to the Lombard rhythm with the reiterated fifth. The first subphrase, which is four measures in length, is closed, and the second, which is extended by the two measures (echoing the fifth), ends on the dominant. As we shall see, this harmony functions as a divider. The b section consists of two phrases, the first of which is legato. It begins in the minor tonic and modulates to its mediant (Gb major). The second, also in the minor tonic, returns to the Lombard rhythm of the beginning. It is canonic, with first violins and flutes answered by the other strings at the third and fifth below. This phrase leads to the dominant, which is extended for several measures before the return. Again we have a contrast between the two phrases of this section, as there certainly is between the first two sections. If one might characterize the first as lively and boisterous, the second is somber, imitating the old "learned" style. The

Example 5.6 Graph of Schubert Op. 142, No. 2, 1–46

EXAMPLE **5.7 Haydn, Symphony No. 103, Menuet**

EXAMPLE 5.7 *continued*

EXAMPLE 5.7 *continued*

EXAMPLE 5.7 *continued*

final section then returns to the opening idea, the main change being the last-minute delay of closure, which extends the phrase by nine measures.

The "melody" of the first four measures is characterized mostly by leaps, the only connection by step being F4 (measures 2–3) to E♭4 in measure 4. Example 5.8 shows the origin of the F4 as an implied G4 in the first measure, though one might argue convincingly that this F4 is the upper neighbor of E♭4. The G4 has been placed in parentheses because it is not present in the main part, though it is stated by the second oboe and clarinet. The role of B♭4 and E♭5 as members of an arpeggiation to the primary tone G5 ($\hat{3}$) becomes clear when we arrive at the second half of the phrase. Here G5 is immediately prolonged by its upper neighbor A♭5 and then by a voice exchange with the bass, after which it is reinstated again by its upper neighbor. This leads directly to F5 supported by V in measure 8, and the melodic fifth is then restated an octave lower, and then an octave higher, extending the phrase by two measures. Looking ahead, we see that subsequent events are controlled by the minor tonic, so we know that this dominant is not prolonged through the b section, but rather functions here as a divider.

The b section opens with the introduction of the minor tonic and corresponding inflection of the primary tone (♭$\hat{3}$), which is immediately followed by a modulation to the upper third (G♭), thus prolonging ♭$\hat{3}$. The fifth and sixth measures of the phrase are repeated, confirming the modulation and rounding out the eight measures. This is followed immediately by the canonic passage, again in the minor tonic. How, then, are we to interpret the modulation to G♭? Potentially this might be part of a large-scale arpeggiation to the dominant, but the immediate return to the tonic negates that possibility. It is the upper third of the tonic that it prolongs. The canonic passage itself is difficult to sketch because of the crossing of voices resulting from the large leaps, and for this reason the viola part, which doubles the celli and basses at the octave, has been omitted. Despite the crossing of parts, it is possible to keep track of the individual voices, as shown in Example 5.8. Of particular interest is the descending line of the top part from B♭5, which leads to F5 ($\hat{2}$) supported by the dominant in the seventh measure of the phrase. This point of arrival represents the interruption of the structure. (Again I suggest you refer to Figure 5.4. What occurs in this piece is similar to paradigm 1, except that the first section is not closed, but ends on a dividing dominant.) The sixth and seventh measures of this canonic phrase are then repeated, and in the following measure the seventh of the dominant is introduced in preparation for the return to the primary tone several measures later. The following lead-in to the a′ section extends the phrase.

The final section proceeds like the opening phrase, but with fuller orchestration, until the seventh measure, where, following the voice exchange, the motion is directed to closure through a standard cadential progression supporting $\hat{2}$. The melodic line does lead to scale degree 1, but its deceptive harmonization by an incomplete diminished seventh chord sets in motion a parenthetical insertion delaying closure (the expected eighth measure of the phrase) by nine measures.

EXAMPLE 5.8 Graph of Haydn Symphony No. 103, Menuet

Haydn, String Quartet Op. 74, No. 1, Menuetto

Our final example in this chapter is the Menuetto from Haydn's String Quartet Op. 74, No. 1. The music is reproduced in Example 5.9, and a graph of its voice-leading structure follows in Example 5.10. Close examination reveals a movement that exhibits some interesting and perhaps unique characteristics in both its phrase organization and its voice leading. The movement begins in a normal fashion with a four-bar group containing the melodic progression E4-F4-G4-C5. In the following measures the melodic line progresses to D5, first supported by ii⁶, and then V. The clear implication is that the melodic line will continue to E5 supported by I, but Haydn suddenly aborts and begins again, this time directing the motion to the dominant. The last four measures of the phrase extend the goal harmony, and, as shown in Example 5.10 by the brackets, the repeated triplet figure in these measures creates a duple pattern against the triple meter. This a section is fourteen measures in length, an expansion of an underlying eight-bar idea created by the "false start" (measures 5–7) and extension of the goal harmony. There is a strong suggestion that the melodic line is headed toward E5, but instead we find ourselves stalled at D5.

The b section explores sonorities related to the parallel minor, beginning with A♭ (♭VI), from which point the bass progresses up by step through B♭ to C (i) before returning to A♭, this time supporting an augmented sixth chord. Up to this point Haydn has limited melodic motion to the lower octave, but in measure 26 the melodic line moves to E♭5 and by implication this resolves to D5 over the dominant, though statement of D5 is delayed until later to avoid direct fifths. Overall the b phrase prolongs both the dominant and D5 by their upper neighbors, A♭ in the bass and E♭5 in the top part. Above the system I have provided a registral simplification of measures 15–27, which shows the return to D5/V from the covering tone G5. Here we are on D5 again, at least by implication. Curious. There has been motion, but we haven't made any progress. Once the dominant has been reached in measure 27 it is extended for several measures, and it is motion from an inner voice that leads us back to E4 and tonic harmony to start over again.

The a′ section begins as before, progressing in the opening four-bar group to C5/I. In the beginning the appearance of a three-bar group was an anomaly, but here Haydn exploits this feature, first prolonging C5 by its upper neighbor, and then by its chromatic upper neighbor, once again returning us to an A♭ sonority (♭VI) in measure 42, at which point the top voice leaps up to A♭5 to approach G5, supported by an E♭ chord (♭III) in measure 43, from above. This initiates a motion in parallel tenths with the bass to B5 supported by the dominant in measure 45. Temporarily the hypermeter has become triple, but at this point— arrival at the dominant—the hypermeter reverts to quadruple as the top voice progresses to F6, the seventh of the dominant, in measure 48. After scrupulously avoiding a stable E up to this point, the primary tone E6 ($\hat{3}$) is finally introduced in measure 49! The final portion of this section is an expanded eight-bar phrase. First the primary tone is moved to the lower octave (E5), and then it is led to D5 ($\hat{2}$), first supported by ii⁶, then V. Arrival at $\hat{1}$ (C5) and tonic harmony is delayed by a three-bar insertion[7] based on the material used to extend the goal harmony at the end of the a section.

Example 5.9 Haydn, String Quartet Op. 74, No. 1, Menuetto

EXAMPLE 5.9 *continued*

Fine

EXAMPLE 5.10 Graph of Haydn, String Quartet Op. 74, No. 1, Menuetto

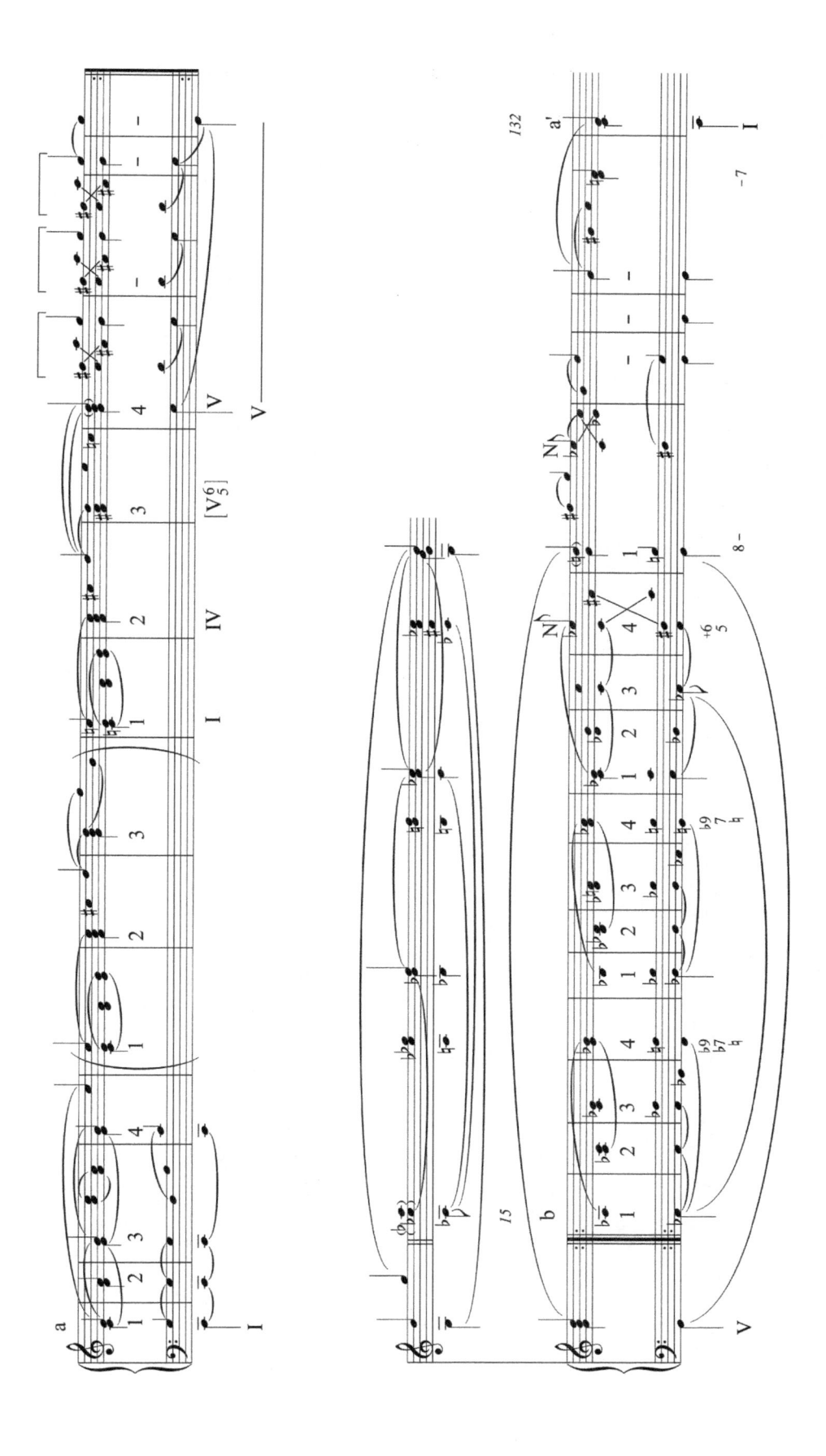

EXAMPLE 5.10 *continued*

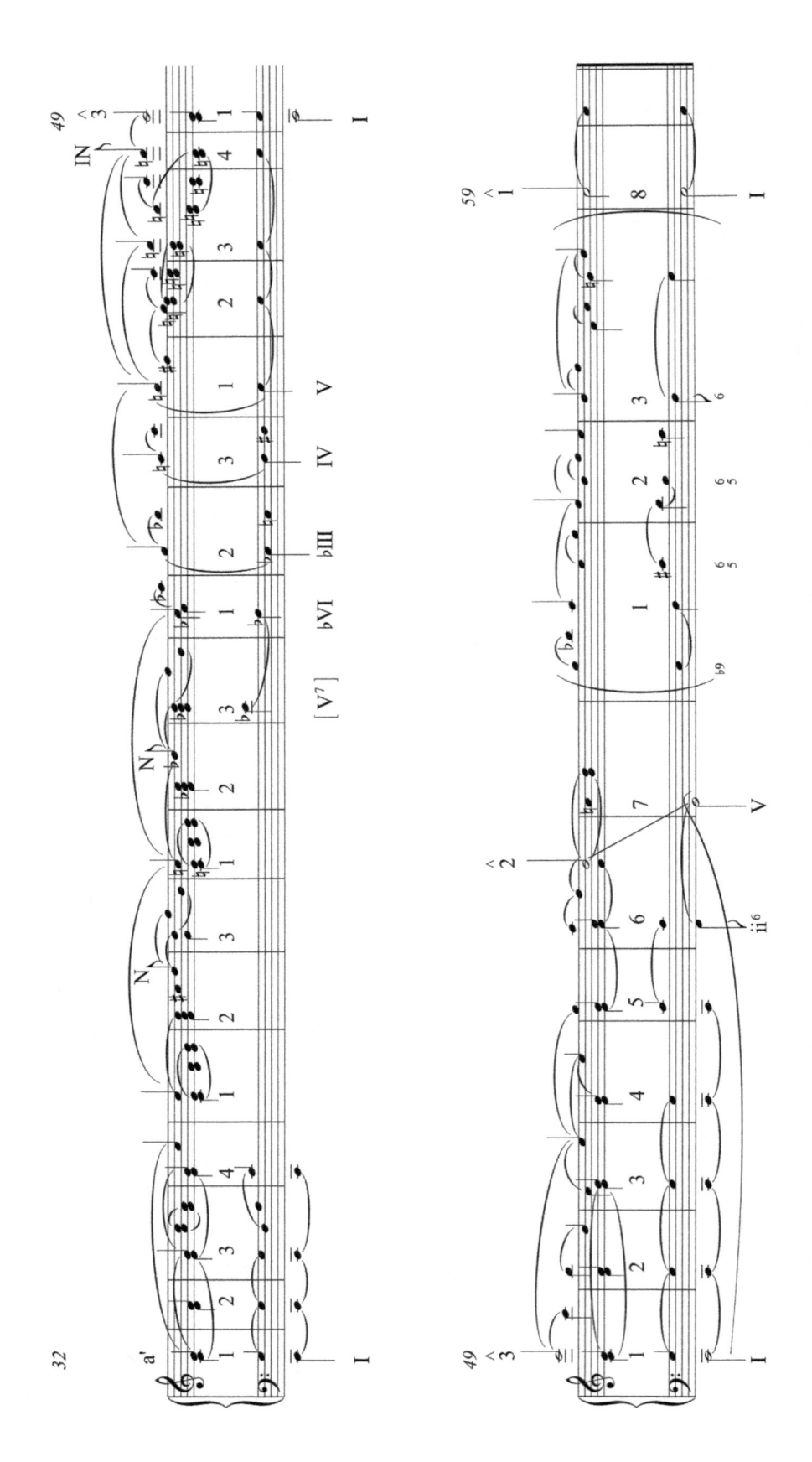

SUGGESTED ASSIGNMENTS

1. Mozart, Piano Sonata K. 331 (III), 1–24. This is relatively simple, but a good place to start. You can compare your solution to Schenker's in *Free Composition* (Figures 35.2 and 139).

2. Mozart, Piano Sonata K. 545 (II), 1–32. The first part consists of an antecedent-consequent pair, closed in the tonic. How do you interpret the C5, the seventh of the dominant, on the downbeat of measure 5? Where is its resolution? In your analysis of the b section, consider its possible derivation from the opening section.

3. Mozart, Piano Sonata K. 331 (II), trio. This trio has an unusual structure resulting from a change Mozart makes in the second measure of the a′ section (measure 38). What is the result of that change? Do not read an interruption in this movement. You can check your solution against Schenker's in *Free Composition* (Figure 20.4). While you are having fun with the piece, check to see how the first section might be considered an expansion of an underlying eight-measure phrase.

4. Schubert, Impromptu, Op. 142, No. 2, trio. This is the trio of the Allegretto portion we examined earlier (see Examples 5.5 and 5.6 and accompanying discussion). Although the formal design is the same as the one outlined in Figure 5.4, the structure is not. The first part is closed, and the second part begins in the minor tonic. The dominant at the end of the b section functions locally to bring about the return; thus there is no interruption. In this regard, the trio follows the same pattern as the Allegretto. One issue you must resolve is the meaning of A major within the context of D♭ major/minor!

5. Mozart, String Quartet K. 421, Menuetto. The a section of this movement is closed. The salient features of the melodic content of this opening phrase are the arpeggiation to A5 and the following descent, which eventually leads to local closure. Your initial reaction is probably to take A5 ($\hat{5}$) as the primary tone, which is a reasonable conclusion, but beware! Can you see/hear how this descent from A5 functions within a larger context? Read the entire b section, which consists of two overlapping phrases, as a prolongation of $\hat{2}$ / V reaching up to the seventh in preparation for the return.

6. Additional Suggestions

   a. Haydn, String Quartet Op. 74, No. 3 (II), 1–22.

   b. Haydn, String Quartet Op. 76, No. 4 (Menuetto). The structural descent to closure involves a transfer to the bass.

   c. Mozart, String Quartet K. 575 (Menuetto).

SUMMARY AND REVIEW

A preliminary listing of terms and definitions associated with Schenker's concept of structural levels is provided at the end of Chapter 1. The following provides a more extensive review of concepts and terminology, in which reference will be made primarily to works examined in this chapter but also occasionally to works discussed in earlier chapters.

Structural Levels

Basic to Schenker's conception of musical structure is the idea that voice leading is multidimensional, consisting of three structural levels: *background, middleground* and *foreground*. While it is difficult to define the exact boundaries between successive strata, Schenker does provide concrete information in his final work, *Free Composition*.[8] The deepest level of organization is the *fundamental structure*, which consists of the *fundamental line* and its harmonic support, all variants of the bass arpeggiation I–V–I. The *fundamental line* itself has three possible forms, $\hat{3}\hat{2}\hat{1}$, $\hat{5}\hat{4}\hat{3}\hat{2}\hat{1}$ and rarely $\hat{8}\hat{7}\hat{6}\hat{5}\hat{4}\hat{3}\hat{2}\hat{1}$. Coincidentally, four of the works examined in this chapter exhibit structural descents from $\hat{3}$: the St. Anthony Chorale; Schubert's Impromptu, Op. 142, No. 2; the Menuet from Haydn's Symphony No. 103; and the Menuetto from Haydn's String Quartet, Op. 74, No. 1. The other work, the Chopin Mazurka, has a fundamental line from $\hat{5}$.

The initial tone of the fundamental line is called the *primary tone*. In some instances, the primary tone is articulated clearly at the outset, but there are also instances where it is not established for several measures; in these latter cases, a line is drawn in the analytic graph to show the association between the initial tonic (bass) and the primary tone. In rare instances statement of the primary tone is delayed until much later, as we have just witnessed in the Menuetto movement from Haydn's String Quartet, Op. 74, No. 1. Schenker indicates two ways in which the delayed primary tone is established: (1) by an *initial ascent*, a harmonized linear progression; and (2) by *arpeggiation*. Both are middleground progressions. An example of an *initial ascent* to the primary tone $\hat{3}$ occurs in the opening four measures of the Schubert Impromptu (see Examples 5.5 and 5.6). An example of *arpeggiation* to the primary tone is found in the opening measures of the Menuet from Haydn's Symphony No. 103 (see Examples 5.7 and 5.8).

There are instances where the *primary tone* is covered by another pitch that in the immediate context may become the focus of melodic activity, thus temporarily obscuring the primary tone. This is referred to appropriately as a *covering tone*. See the discussions of the initial sections from the second movements of Beethoven's Piano Sonata Op. 2, No. 1, and Schubert's Trout Quintet in Chapter 4.

A concept basic to Schenker's idea of fundamental structure is that of *closure*, the simultaneous and conclusive arrival at scale degree 1 and tonic harmony. As we have witnessed on numerous occasions, this can occur at more immediate levels as well—for example, at the end of a section or theme, in which case we refer to this phenomenon as *local closure*. A related concept is that of *interruption*, where the motion to closure is stopped at $\hat{2}$ and dominant harmony, following which the primary tone is reinstated and the fundamental line then completes the descent to closure. As we have seen, *interruption*, like *closure*, exists at more immediate levels—for example, at the end of an antecedent phrase in a musical period consisting of an antecedent-consequent pair. Also pertinent here is the distinction made between a *structural* and a *dividing* dominant. A structural dominant supports $\hat{2}$ of the fundamental line, whether at an interruption or leading to closure. The dividing dominant, however, functions to articulate a major musical division—for example, the end of a section. It does not support a note of the fundamental line, but rather functions at a more immediate level. An example of a *dividing* dominant occurs at the end of the a section of the Menuet from Haydn's Symphony No. 103 (see Examples 5.7 and 5.8).

A primary feature of the middleground is the existence of *linear progressions*, harmonized stepwise motions that prolong elements of the background. Such progressions span consonant intervals and can be either ascending or descending. Linear progressions are identified in musical graphs by note heads with stems connected by slurs or sometimes by beams. Here is a list of some linear progressions in works examined in this chapter.

Haydn, St. Anthony Chorale	3 desc.	mm. 1–3
	6 asc.	mm. 11–14
Chopin, Mazurka	4 desc.	mm. 1–8, 21–25
	5 desc.	mm. 9–16, 27–33
Schubert, Impromptu	3 asc.	mm. 1–4
	3 desc.	mm. 13–15
Haydn, Minuet	4 desc.	mm. 19–25
Haydn, Menuetto	3 asc.	mm. 1–3, 32–34, 43–45

Specific Techniques of Voice Leading

Voice Exchange

We have observed this phenomenon on numerous occasions in the preceding chapters. This technique of prolongation involves the exchange of two notes from different statements of the same harmony. The exchange must be between the same two voices, an important requirement to keep in mind, because a common error made by beginners is to identify false voice exchanges involving three voices. Voice exchanges occur in the foreground and the middleground. They are most frequently diatonic, but at deeper levels they often involve chromatic alteration of one or occasionally both notes of the exchange. This is referred to as a *chromatic voice exchange*. A list of some of the voice exchanges encountered in this chapter is provided here.

Schubert, Impromptu	Examples 5.5 and 5.6	mm. 5–7
		mm. 21–27 (chromatic)
Haydn, Menuet, Symphony No. 103	Examples 5.7 and 5.8	mm. 4–7, 35–38

Substitution

We have also observed this phenomenon on numerous occasions. This term refers specifically to the substitution of the leading tone for scale degree 2 over the dominant at the cadence. When scale degree 2 occurs as part of the preceding harmony (e.g., ii⁶), a diagonal line is drawn in the graph connecting it to the dominant *or* the missing note is supplied in parentheses over the dominant. Examples of substitution at the cadence encountered in this chapter are as follows:

Chopin, Mazurka	Examples 5.3 and 5.4	mm. 15 and 31
Schubert, Impromptu	Examples 5.5 and 5.6	m. 45
Haydn, Menuetto	Examples 5.9 and 5.10	mm. 10–11, 54–55

Unfolding

This technique involves motion between two parts, often between the top and an inner part. Unfolding may occur between two notes of the same chord or between notes of two different chords. Quite often this phenomenon is notated graphically by adding an upward stem on the lower of the two notes, a downward stem on the upper of the two, and a beam connecting the two stems. Stems are often added in the opposite direction as well to identify the notes as part of a linear progression in a particular voice. Clear instances of unfolding and its notation are shown in the analysis of Bach's C Major Prelude (Example 1.7) and in the first movement of Schubert's String Quartet D. 804 (Example 3.10). An example of unfolding observed in this chapter is shown in the graph of the St. Anthony Chorale (Example 5.2).

Reaching Over[9]

This technique was introduced briefly in Chapter 4 in our analysis of the second theme from the first movement of Mozart's Piano Sonata K. 280—see Examples 4.1 and 4.2. This process results from an inner voice tone reaching across or above a note of the upper voice, either to maintain the same note or, more typically, to gain the next higher note. Continuation of this latter procedure results in an ascending line. Reaching over can occur directly (*superposition*) or consecutively. In either case, the note reaching over descends to introduce the next note in the top voice. In this chapter we observed this technique in the Menuetto from Haydn's String Quartet Op. 74, No. 1.

Linear Intervallic Patterns

On several occasions we have observed motion in parallel tenths between the outer voices. This is indicated in a graph either by the designation 10–10–10 between the staves or by lines connecting the voices, either curved when the parts are together or diagonal when they are not—see Example 5.6, mm. 13–16 and 35–36, and Example 5.10, mm. 43–45. There are many other possible patterns of alternating intervals, such as 10–7—see Example 2.4, a graph of the opening phrase of the Brahms Intermezzo Op. 117, No. 2.

Consonant Passing Tone

A dissonant passing tone on one level is made consonant at the level at which it is given consonant support. A simple example is found in the opening measures of the Schubert Impromptu, where the passing tone Bb4 in the initial ascent to $\hat{3}$ is given consonant support—see Examples 5.5 and 5.6. Also see Example 5.2, where D5 in measure 14, harmonized by a tonic chord, is interpreted as passing between the fifth and seventh of the dominant. In this instance, the seventh is first introduced as a consonance (IV⁶) before becoming the dissonant seventh in relation to V.

Elements of Formal Design

The smallest unit that gives rise to form is the motive. We spoke about this briefly at the beginning of Chapter 3, where we discussed Schoenberg's and Schenker's views of the opening phrase from Beethoven's Piano Sonata Op. 2, No. 1. Schenker's notion of motive is linked directly to his ideas on voice leading and structural levels. While a surface statement of a motive will have a particular rhythmic articulation, it is not the rhythm but the pitch/intervallic succession plus the fact that it is repeated that identifies it as a motive for Schenker. This is particularly true when an idea of this type is repeated at a deeper level in the voice-leading structure, in which case its rhythmic distribution will be different. Repetitions of motives, referred to as *parallelisms* in Schenker's writings, are frequently identified in analytic graphs by horizontal brackets, which can be of varying lengths depending on the repetition—see the brackets identifying repeated descending thirds in the graph of Schubert's Impromptu, Op. 142, No. 2 (Example 5.6). Particularly fascinating are instances of motivic *enlargement*, where a surface or foreground configuration is repeated at the middleground, thus operating at a more extensive level. We have already observed this phenomenon in the introductory chapter in our consideration of excerpts from Mozart's Piano Sonata in Bb, K. 333. Refer also to the discussion of the opening sections from the first movements of Beethoven's Piano Sonata Op. 57 in Chapter 2 and Schubert's Piano Sonata in Bb (D. 960) in Chapter 4. This topic will resurface several times in the following chapters.

Chapters 2–4 deal extensively with the phrase and the combination of phrases to form periods. Divisions of phrases have occasionally been referred to in this text as "segments" or, following the terminology adopted by William Rothstein in *Phrase Rhythm in Tonal Music*, as "subphrases". Considerable attention has been given to the matter of phrase expansion, a topic all but ignored in other texts on Schenkerian analysis, probably because it is not the main focus of his work. This is unfortunate, since this leads to the exclusion of many works from consideration or to the ignoring of an important feature of their organization. Examples of extensions (external expansions) encountered in this chapter can be found in the St. Anthony Chorale, mm. 23–29, the first measure of which is the last of the final phrase (*metric reinterpretation*), in the Menuet from Haydn's Symphony No. 103 (Examples 5.7 and 5.8), mm. 9–10 and 29–31, and in the Haydn Menuetto (Example 5.10), mm. 5–7 and especially mm. 56–58. Internal expansion also is found in the Haydn Symphony movement: mm. 26–27 (internal repetition) and mm. 39–47, a parenthetical insertion delaying closure, thus expanding the underlying eight-measure phrase.

Related to our study of musical phrases, especially when dealing with the matter of phrase expansion, is the important concept of *hypermeter*, the regular recurrence of strong and weak measures, most frequently in multiples of two. Of the movements studied in this chapter, the one exhibiting the greatest metric regularity is the Chopin Mazurka. The Schubert Impromptu exhibits a consistent quadruple hypermeter, the one exception occurring in the b section, where there appears to be a contraction of the second group of eight to six. The Haydn Symphony movement is also "regular", subject to the expansions outlined earlier. Finally, two of the movements examined in this chapter exhibit irregular or changing metric groups: the St. Anthony Chorale and the Haydn Menuetto.

NOTES

1. In this chapter we will concern ourselves only with movements that are rounded. In the next chapter we will deal with baroque binary forms.

2. Confusion of terminology is compounded by the terms "inner" and "outer" form to describe what I have referred to as structure (voice-leading structure) and design (formal design). See Felix Salzer, *Structural Hearing* (Dover, 1962) and William Rothstein, *Phrase Rhythm in Tonal Music* (Schirmer, 1989), where the use of this terminology is clarified.

3. Example 5.2 is based on Schenker's graph in *Free Composition* (Figure 42/2).

4. Assuming my assertion that the b section is controlled by the dominant, then the interpretation given here is the only logical explanation for the internal return to D5 supported by I.

5. In this regard, this example does not follow the paradigms outlined at the beginning of this chapter.

6. The author has written about this impromptu previously in "Modal Mixture and Schubert's Harmonic Practice," *Journal of Music Theory* 42/1 (Spring 1998), 73–100.

7. See Rothstein, *Phrase Rhythm in Tonal Music*, ex. 3.19.

8. A practical demonstration of these strata is provided in Schenker's analysis of the C Major Prelude by Bach in *Five Graphic Music Analyses*. See Chapter 1.

9. In a footnote to the passage in *Free Composition* where reaching over is discussed (p. 48), the editor/translator Ernst Oster distinguishes between two types, one where the main note generates the lower one, and the other where the superimposed inner voice tone introduces a note of the upper voice from above. We will focus here on the second type.

PART II

Applications

6 Baroque One-Part and Two-Part Forms (Bach)

The music of J. S. Bach presents some unique challenges to the analyst, due, in a general sense, to its contrapuntal complexity. Particularly challenging are his works for solo cello and violin. We will begin by examining two preludes from the first volume of *The Well-Tempered Clavier*. For the first time, we will encounter a work in which the fundamental line is an octave, a phenomenon that does not occur in classical music. Then we will examine two movements for solo instruments, the sarabande movement from the first Cello Suite and the sarabande movement from the first Partita for violin. Here we will encounter two specific issues. First, in dealing with music for a non-keyboard solo instrument, where lines by necessity are temporarily suspended, we must be acutely aware of their implied continuation. For that reason I will always begin with a voice-leading reduction, by which I mean a simplification of the score, eliminating notes of embellishment and rhythmic displacements, but including notes implied by the context. Many crucial decisions are made at this initial stage of the analytic process that will aid in preparing an analytic graph of the voice-leading structure. Second, there is an important difference between the designs of the typical late baroque and classical binary forms. The classical form is "rounded", which, as we know, means that there is a dual return to the tonic and to the opening material in the second part, frequently resulting in an interruption of the structure. With rare exceptions, baroque binary movements are not "rounded", and thus their voice-leading structures are continuous, not interrupted. We have encountered situations in rounded binary movements where the dominant at the end of the first part is a divider, but more typically it is structural. In baroque binary movements, this phenomenon (the dividing dominant) is more common. Part of the analytic process is understanding the possibilities; then comes the challenge—making informed choices. This chapter will end with an examination of the sarabande movement from the French Suite in E Major.

One-Part Form

Prelude in C Minor, WTC I

Before embarking on an analysis of this prelude, let's review the main features of the first prelude in C Major as presented in Chapter 1, since, as we shall discover, there are many parallels between the two. We began our analysis of the C Major Prelude by examining its formal, harmonic and metric organization. Like the preludes examined in this chapter, the C Major Prelude has a one-part form, which means that the motion is continuous from beginning to end and, from a Schenkerian perspective, there is no division (interruption) of the fundamental line. It is divided into two parts by the imperfect authentic cadence on I in measure 19, and this first part is further divided by the cadence on the dominant in measure 11. The second part consists of a four-measure bridge to the dominant, an eight-measure prolongation of V, and a final four measures extending the tonic. As occurs so frequently in Bach's preludes, arrival at the tonic is accompanied by the addition of ♭7, thus propelling the momentum forward to the final cadence. When we then examined the metric organization, it became apparent that the prelude exhibits consistent four-measure groups, the only exception occurring at the very beginning. And once we examined the pitch organization of these initial seven measures, we determined—indeed, following Schenker's lead—that they are an expanded group of four: 1 (– – –) 2 3 4. This is the organization of the opening seven measures of the C Minor Prelude as well.

Schenker's analysis of the C Major Prelude shows the prolongation of the primary tone E5 ($\hat{3}$) over the first nineteen measures by an embellished descending octave progression proceeding in parallel tenths with the bass. This octave is divided into a fourth, E5–B4, and a fifth, B4–E4, by the cadence on the dominant. The following transition leads to D4 ($\hat{2}$) and the dominant in measure 24, and the following extension involves the unfolding of the fifth to the seventh of the dominant, D4–F4. This is answered by the sixth E4–C5, completing the descent of the fundamental line to $\hat{1}$ in the original octave.

It is important to keep in mind that many of these preludes were originally written by Bach as teaching pieces—most likely compositional models as well as keyboard exercises—for his sons. The C Major Prelude is a minimally elaborated embellishment of a simple underlying model, and the following prelude is a more elaborate version of the same model, now in the minor mode. Though the characters of the two preludes are different, they both involve the repetition of a melodic-rhythmic pattern that is repeated every half measure. In the C Major Prelude, the repeated pattern persists until three measures from the end; in the C Minor Prelude the original pattern persists until three measures before the *Presto* passage in measure 28. In both preludes, the opening four measures function in the same way—to establish the tonic before digressing from it. If we now look at the overall organization of the C Minor Prelude, we see that there is a return to tonic harmony in measure 18, which is followed by a transition leading to the dominant, first in measure 25, and then in measure 28 (*Presto*). The dominant is subsequently prolonged over the next six measures leading to I♭⁷ in measure 34 (*Adagio*). The parallels to the first prelude couldn't be clearer, though the setting of this latter portion of the minor prelude is more elaborate and freer in style than the equivalent passage in its major counterpart.

An analysis of the harmony and of the hypermetric organization of the C Minor Prelude is provided on the score (Example 6.1). The hypermetric organization is also indicated in Example 6.2, a detailed analytic graph of the voice-leading structure. This graph is divided into two parts, measures 1–28 and 28–38. The first part is modeled after Schenker's detailed graph of the C Major Prelude in *Five Graphic Music Analyses*; it presents a metric representation of the voice leading on which is superimposed an interpretation of its structure. The notation of the remainder is intentionally freer, aimed solely at explicating the essential voice leading.

EXAMPLE 6.1 Bach, Prelude in C Minor (WTC I)

EXAMPLE **6.1** *continued*

You might recall that the primary tone of the C Major Prelude was introduced right away, and then initially prolonged by its upper neighbor. Here the opening four measures function in a similar way to extend the tonic harmony, but the primary tone ($\hat{3}$) is not introduced until measure 5. From that point $\hat{3}$ is prolonged by a descending octave, here without any covering motions, progressing in parallel tenths with the bass (shown in Example 6.2 by the curved lines). In this instance, the octave is subdivided into a sixth, articulated by the internal cadence on III, and a third leading to E♭4 and tonic harmony in measure 18. Note that the metric unit leading to III consists of three, not four, measures. Bach could easily have extended this to four measures by employing suspensions, as he did at the end of the next unit leading back to the tonic, but he chose not to do so, possibly to avoid too strong an emphasis on III. Except for the minor differences noted, the underlying structure is the same as the C Major Prelude. One can almost imagine Bach teaching his sons how to write another piece, now in the minor mode, based on the same model. The continuation follows in the same manner as in the first prelude, but in a more complicated way. The next two chords lead to the cadential six-four, which is extended for four measures before resolving to five-three in measure 25. This is followed by a coupling back to the original octave and a clear articulation of $\hat{2}$ supported by V in measure 28. The metric organization of these measures is complex. As suggested by the notation in Example 6.2, we might understand the organization occurring simultaneously at two levels, where the third and fourth measures of the underlying unit, indicated by the circled numbers, each support a lower-level unit of four measures.

The final portion of the prelude is a bit trickier to sketch. The best approach, I believe, is to look first at the large picture—the longer-range goals—and if we can determine what is happening at that level, then it is much easier to deal with the foreground details. This portion is divided into two parts, the *Presto*, which prolongs the dominant, and the *Adagio* and following *Allegro*, which prolong the tonic. As occurs so frequently in Bach's works, particularly those in the minor mode, the initial statement of the goal harmony is the major tonic chord with lowered seventh, which propels the music onward to end eventually with the major tonic. As shown in the upper level of the graph of these measures, the dominant of measures 28–33 supports the unfolding of D5($\hat{2}$) to F4, which is answered by the unfolding of E♮4 to C5($\hat{1}$) within the prolonged tonic. Again the similarity to the C Major Prelude is clear, though the details are different.

We can now begin to unravel the details of these final measures within the established framework. The figuration of measures 28–30 outlines a descending arpeggiation D5-B♮4-(G4) in parallel thirds, the first two members of which are decorated by their upper and lower neighbors. This is answered by the arpeggiation G5-E♭5-C5, the last supported by a tonic chord. The function of this chord is to support the passing tone C5 within the third D-C-B♮, where the final note is transferred to an inner voice. Thus $\hat{2}$ is prolonged not only by the unfolding D5-F4 but also by the third D5-C5-B♮3. Of particular interest in the final five measures is the articulation of the neighbor-note motive E♮4-F4 . . . F4-E♮4 in the inner voice highlighted by the broken bracket, a possible reference to the statement of E♭4-F4-F4-E♭4 in measures 1–4. The very same idea occurs in the same positions in the C Major Prelude. Here the inner voice motion is accompanied by the unfolding E♮4-C5 answered by F4-B♮4 resolving to the final C5 over E♮4.

EXAMPLE 6.2 Graph of Bach Prelude in C Minor

Prelude in A Minor, WTC I

The score of the A Minor Prelude is provided in Example 6.3. Like the preceding example, this prelude has a one-part structure, but the similarity ends there. It has a very different character and organization. This prelude is divided into two large phrases articulated by the cadence on III in measure 16. If we now examine the first sixteen measures, we see that they are clearly divided into four groups of four measures. The first of these involves statements of a four-note motive (initially stated on the first beat of measure 1) and its extension over a tonic pedal reaching up to A5. The next four-measure group involves an answer at the fifth with the original right-hand part now in the left-hand with new counterpoint added above. The third four-measure group begins as a sequence growing out of the previous material that leads us to III, and the final four-measure group confirms the modulation with statements of the motive returned to the right-hand part. The remainder of the prelude is less regular metrically. The pattern established in measures 17–19 sets up the expectation that measure 20 will be treated similarly to measure 18, completing the sequence, but instead we have a statement of the motive on iv in the left-hand, which is followed by a diminished seventh chord with D in the bass. This leads us to a statement of the motive (right-hand) at the original pitch level, a very clear reference to the beginning, this time, however, over C in the bass (i⁶). This initiates a complex motion to closure, which is achieved on the downbeat of measure 26, followed by a two-measure extension.

Having talked through the prelude, albeit very briefly, we are now ready to examine its voice-leading structure, a graph of which is provided in Example 6.4. There are two important voice-leading components in the opening four measures that I want to stress. The first is the neighbor-note motion E5-F5-E5 marked by a bracket, and the second is the covering motion G♯5-A5. Looking ahead we see that the top voice progresses from this A5, and thus it seems likely that we are dealing here with a fundamental line generated from $\hat{8}$.
[1] This assumption will prove to be correct, though, as we shall see, the path to closure is far from obvious. The second four-measure group progresses from G5 ($\hat{7}$). As shown in both Examples 6.3 and 6.4, the top voice descends a third G5-F♯5-E5, a motion to an inner voice prolonging G5, which is restated in measure 9. The notes of this descent are not immediately apparent because of their weak metric placement, so I have shown exactly where they occur on the score. The line then begins its descent once again from the G5 in measure 9, this time continuing a fifth to C5 in measure 13. Again this will turn out to be a motion to an inner voice prolonging G5; if we look ahead we see that there is a definitive arrival at E5 ($\hat{5}$) in measure 16 supported by the cadence on III. So where is $\hat{6}$ in the descent of the fundamental line? It must occur in the passage immediately preceding. If we examine these measures carefully, we see that there is a statement of the E-F-E neighboring motion distributed between inner and top voice, notated in Example 6.4 by the bracket broken into two segments. It is the transference of F4 to F5, the latter harmonized by the dominant of III, that brings the fundamental line to rest on $\hat{5}$.

If we now follow the top voice descent from E5 in measure 16, including implied tones (supplied in Example 6.4 in parentheses), the line progresses all the way to F4, an inner-voice tone, supported by subdominant harmony. Immediately following, F5, the upper neighbor, is stated, and in the following measure this is covered by G♯5 as part of the diminished seventh chord in four-three position. Instead of resolving to A5, as it had in the beginning, the

EXAMPLE 6.3 Bach, Prelude in A Minor (WTC I)

EXAMPLE 6.3 *continued*

EXAMPLE 6.4 Graph of Bach Prelude in A Minor

resolution is transferred to an inner voice, allowing Bach to state the opening motive at the original pitch level, this time over C in the bass. What we have, then, in addition to a clear statement of the opening motive and the covering G♯, is a clear reference once again to the neighboring figure, where the F5 is given temporary support: E5 (measure 16)-F5 (measure 20)-E5 (measure 22). All this is quite apparent, but the path to closure starting from this point is far from obvious. I suggest you first look at the "normalized" version I have provided below these measures. This shows how the continuation might proceed under "normalized" conditions. Now let's look at what Bach wrote. The E5 of measure 22 continues into the next measure, where it becomes the dissonant seventh, requiring its resolution to D5. This D5 occurs in the following measure as part of a descending arpeggiation in the right-hand part, and then at the last minute transferred to an inner voice, now as part of the dominant harmony. A "normal" resolution of this dissonant harmony would be to C5 supported by tonic harmony in root position, but instead the resolution has been transferred to the bass (3̂) on the downbeat of measure 25. Transfer of the resolution of the dissonant seventh is not uncommon, but in this instance it has occurred at a crucial point in the prelude as the top part begins its descent to closure. The result is a wide registral distribution of this portion of the fundamental line: E5-D5/D4-C2-B3-A3. Closure (measure 26) is followed by a two-measure extension that makes reference one final time to the neighboring motion F-E as well as the covering motion G♯5-A5. The final portion, beginning in measure 22, is complex, and I recommend that you play through these measures several times slowly to hear the underlying voice leading of the passage.

SUGGESTED ASSIGNMENTS

1. Little Prelude in D Minor (*BWV* 926). This not-so-little prelude presents some interesting analytic challenges. I suggest beginning with an examination of the harmony and hypermetric organization before tackling the voice leading. The opening eight measures establish the key and primary tone, which is subsequently prolonged by an octave descent. Measures 21–38 then prolong V. One issue you must resolve is what happens in the long run to the prolonged E5 in this passage. A related question: what is the function of the tonic "cadenza" in measures 39–42?

2. Prelude in B Major. This is a study in three-voice counterpoint, except at the end, where there are four parts. Keep track of the individual lines throughout. This prelude is divided into clearly articulated phrases: 1–6, 6–10, 10–15 and 15–19. Consider the voice leading of each phrase individually, then 1–10 as a unit, and then finally 1–15. The final measures complete the avoided closure on the downbeat of measure 15, where you can supply B4 in parentheses.

Binary Form

Cello Suite I, Sarabande

The score of this movement is provided in Example 6.5. It is divided into two parts, each containing eight measures, which are further divided into four plus four. The first division is articulated by arrival at the dominant (measure 4), and the first part ends with a perfect authentic cadence in the key of the dominant. The second part is divided by a cadence on vi, and the final phrase ends with a perfect authentic cadence on the tonic.

The first step in examining the voice leading of a movement like this is to prepare a reduction—a simplification—of the voice leading, eliminating notes of embellishment and rhythmic displacements, but being very careful to supply notes clearly implied by the context. Such reductions will differ slightly from one person to the next, depending upon the criteria chosen, the level of detail shown and so forth. That is, there isn't a single "correct" solution. Some choices can be said to be incorrect, but there are always slight variants that are valid. So I think the most useful step to take here is to talk through my reduction of this movement, which is provided at level a in Example 6.6, and to explain the choices I have made.

First, since the C4 of measure 1 is picked up in measure 2, I have shown this note as sustained from the second beat of measure 1 through the first beat of measure 2, while the inner voice ascends by step from D3 to G3. Though this G is not stated until the third beat, it is implied already on beat 2 because of the tonic harmony. I have eliminated the passing tone B3 at the end of measure 1, but if it had been included, it would be shown to pass on to the inner voice tone A3 in measure 2. Next, the D4 on the downbeat of measure 3 resolves by implication to C4 over the bass note E, and this implied C4 is sustained in my reduction until it is picked up in the next measure as a dissonant note resolving to B3 on the second eighth. This B3 is then understood to continue on to an implied A3 over the dominant, a clear instance of substitution of the leading tone for scale degree 2. The harmony on the first beat of measure 5 is the dominant with the seventh in the bass. I have indicated an implied G3 over the next bass note, B, though one could show the A3 sustained until the third beat. In the next measure, the B3 is restated in the top voice, and I have indicated an implied A3 on the second beat over the C♯. This A3 is not actually stated until the second sixteenth of the second beat of the next measure as G3, the seventh of the A major chord, finally resolves. I hear this G3 sustained all the way from measure 5 to this point. This is a complex passage that you should play several times at the piano to see if you agree with this interpretation of stated and implied notes. The remainder of the first part is clear. The top two parts descend in parallel thirds to the cadence on D.

The second part requires fewer implied tones. I have added an implied B2 in the lowest part on the downbeat of measure 12, but this is not necessary. However, my addition of an implied C3 in the lowest voice on the third beat of measure 15 is crucial to my interpretation of the voice leading. It provides an explanation for the B2 and the implied tonic chord earlier in the measure as passing within a locally prolonged supertonic harmony—initially stated on the second beat of measure 14—progressing to the dominant on the downbeat of measure 16.

EXAMPLE 6.5 Bach, Cello Suite I, Sarabande

As you can see, I have already made several analytic decisions in preparing the reduction, decisions that will aid in preparing a voice-leading graph. My solution is offered in Example 6.6b. The first four measures offer no real difficulties. The primary tone is clearly B3 (3̂), which is prolonged initially by its upper neighbor. The D4 on the downbeat of measure 3 prepares the restatement of the neighbor-note C4, which is suppressed until the next measure, but clearly implied already over the bass note E (IV⁶). This time C4 does not resolve back to a stable B3, but passes through it to an implied A3 over the dominant. This is a strong point of division in the phrase, and the slurs in my graph show this as a local point of arrival. The addition of the passing tone C3 in the bass on the first beat of the next measure leads to an implied tonic harmony in first inversion, and this leads to an E minor chord and a restatement of B3, the primary tone, on the downbeat of measure 6. This chord is the pivot in the modulation to the key of the dominant: vi becomes ii in the new key. We have already discussed the following implied A3 as well as the sustained G3, which is resolved on the second quarter of the next measure as the two voices progress in parallel thirds to closure in the dominant. Meanwhile, this is covered by C♯4-D4, which I have interpreted as a temporary projection of the bass above the main melodic voice. The top voice descent of a fifth leading to closure on the dominant prolongs A3, which has the potential to be 2̂. However, as we look forward, we see that this A3 is not prolonged until its resolution to closure at the very end. Instead B3 is restated by means of C♮4, and thus the dominant at the close of the first part must be interpreted at a lower level—that is, as a divider.

Immediately following the double bar, C4, the seventh, is added to the dominant, which resolves to the G major chord supporting B3 in measure 10. As tempting as this may be to interpret as a return to 3̂, the music pushes beyond this point to the dominant of vi in four-two position, which is then changed into the diminished seventh chord on the first beat of measure 11. The voice leading is a bit complex here. The C♮4 of measure 9 leads to the B3 in measure 10, which is retained over the change of harmony, finally leading on to A3 as part of the diminished seventh chord. That is, there is a descending third C♮4-B3-A3 from measure 9 to measure 11, a motion to an inner voice prolonging C♮4 until its resolution to B3 supported by the E minor chord (vi). Meanwhile the lowest-sounding voice has progressed from D to G to A (the four-two chord), which is then transferred up an octave to resolve to G3 as third of the E minor chord, while it is the upper bass that progresses from D3 to E3 via the chromatic passing tone D♯. Once the E minor chord is reached in measure 11, there is a descent of a fifth in the top voice from B3 to E3 at the cadence on vi. This cadence is an important point of arrival, and in my graph I have shown the association of this point with the opening tonic by means of slurs and the designation I⁵⁻⁶ below the staff. Following the cadence on vi, the harmony progresses to IV and ii, both supporting the upper neighbor C4, which, as occurred earlier, passes through B3 to A3 (2̂) and on to closure.

The graph in Example 6.6b incorporates many levels of structure. I have not offered a middleground graph, since I believe the notation at 6.6b delineates these levels sufficiently.

EXAMPLE 6.6 Reduction and graph of Sarabande from Cello Suite I

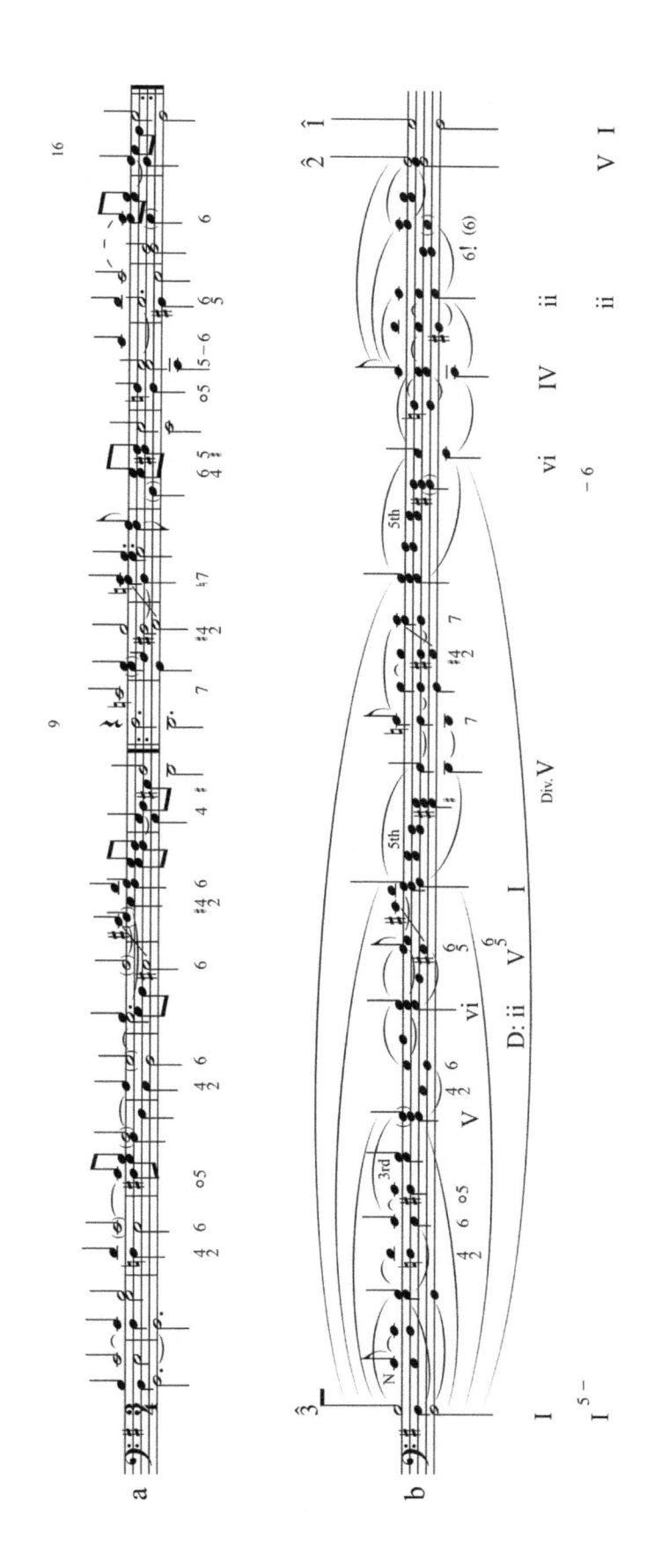

Violin Partita I, Sarabande

The score of this movement is provided in Example 6.7, and, following the procedure established with the preceding sarabande, the accompanying example (Example 6.8) is divided into two parts: a voice-leading reduction at level a, and a graph of the voice-leading structure at b.[2] The first part of this movement is eight measures long, progressing from i to V, divided by an internal cadence on V in measure 4. The second part is divided into three eight-measure phrases, the first leading to a cadence on iv, the second leading to a half cadence on V, and the last leading to closure. The reduction provided at Example 6.8a requires little comment. Twice I have supplied C♯ in parentheses, at the half cadences in measures 4 and 24. Both are instances of the leading tone substituting for scale degree 2. I have also supplied the third of the E minor chord at the cadence in measure 16 and the A4 as fifth of the D major chord two measures later. Both are clearly implied by the context.

As we found with the cello movement, the primary tone—here F♯5 ($\hat{5}$)—is clearly articulated from the very beginning. It is initially prolonged by its upper neighbor before descending by step to the implied C♯5 at the local cadence in measure 4. As occurred in our previous example, the addition of the seventh in the bass leads to a tonic chord in first inversion to initiate the second half of the phrase. Initially, the top voice continues its descent to G4, above which C♯5 is introduced (supported by VII) and then E5 is brought in above it as seventh of the dominant. This resolves to D5 and tonic harmony on the downbeat of measure 7, completing the voice exchange with the tonic chord on the downbeat of measure 5. From here the ascending line continues to F♯5, the final two notes of the ascent harmonized by iv⁶ leading to V♯.

The second part opens with a motion to B5, supported by tonic harmony in first inversion, which is the point of departure for a descending fifth progression leading to $\hat{4}$ supported by the cadence on iv in measure 16. Following the i⁶ harmony in measure 10, the A major chord (VII), which offers initial consonant support for A5 in this descent, is introduced by its dominant. As shown by the slur in the bass, this motion to A is understood as occurring within the chromatic inflection of D to D♯ leading to E supporting G5, the third of the descent. (This connection is highlighted by the dotted slur below Example 6.8a.) This is followed by the cadential pattern supporting the completion of the descending fifth to $\hat{4}$.

The next phrase opens with an A⁷ harmony leading to a D major chord involving a voice exchange leading to F♯5 over D4. This ascending third D5-E5-F♯5 is then answered by the descending third G5-F♯5-E5 with E5 supported by VII. To show the underlying counterpoint, I have added the bass note C♯4 below the A4, which prepares the following bass note, while the A4 is chromatically altered to A♯4 leading to the B minor chord supporting D5. The bass motion to this point in the phrase, beginning from the cadence on iv, is the descending fourth E4-D4-C♯4-B3 supporting a melodic motion from E5 to D5 with the latter introduced by the descending third F♯5-E5-D5. From there the line leads to C♯5 supported by V at the cadence with the progression from D5 and tonic harmony to C♯5 over the dominant elaborated by thirds as shown in the graph. This dominant is an important point of arrival, and potentially it could offer support for $\hat{2}$ of the fundamental line, in which case $\hat{3}$ would occur over the tonic harmony on the downbeat of measure 22. But, if we look ahead, we see that completion of the fundamental line occurs at the end of the next phrase.

Example 6.7 Bach, Violin Partita I, Sarabande

EXAMPLE 6.8 Reduction and graph of Sarabande from Violin Partita I

The final phrase opens with a tonic harmony in first inversion that leads to D5 ($\hat{3}$) and tonic harmony on the third quarter of measure 30. The relationship between these two points is a large-scale voice exchange, which I have not attempted to superimpose on the graph. The space between these poles is filled in as follows. First the B4 over D4 (measure 25) is extended by a voice exchange, and the D5 is subsequently harmonized as the dissonant seventh of an E major chord. This leads to the middle step in the ascending third of the top voice, C♯5 over E4, which is treated parallel to the initial step. This time the dissonant seventh, E5, is not resolved directly, but rather it is extended first by the covering motion to B5 and then the descent back to it as the bass leads down by step in parallel motion. Once D5 ($\hat{3}$) is finally reached, the line continues directly to closure.

SUGGESTED ASSIGNMENTS

1. Cello Suite I, Minuetto I. Following the procedure I have established, first prepare a careful reduction, and then a graph of the voice leading. In what ways is this movement similar to, as well as different from, the sarabande?

2. Violin Partita III, Menuet I. This is one of a few binary movements from the Bach Suites and Partitas that is "rounded". What effect, if any, does this have on the structure? Be careful with your reduction, particularly measures 18–26.

French Suite VI, Sarabande

The final movement by Bach we will examine is the sarabande movement from the French Suite in E Major. The score, with annotations, is provided in Example 6.9. Like the other sarabande movements we have examined, the phrase lengths are uniform, and the hypermeter is consistently quadruple/duple throughout. The first part consists of an eight-measure phrase, divided into four plus four, that modulates to the dominant. The second part consists of two eight-measure phrases, the first modulating to ii. The second, divided at the midpoint by a cadence on V, leads to closure. Unlike the previous two examples, there is no need in this instance to provide a reduction of the voice leading; all the information is there before us, though, of course, it requires interpretation. The harmony is simple, though elegant, and an examination, even a cursory one, reveals the repetition of a descending third motive. Statements of this idea have been highlighted on the score by brackets.

The choice of primary tone was not an issue with any of the works examined so far in this chapter, but the choice is perhaps not so clear here, so I think it is well worth our time to consider the possibilities and to sift through the evidence. This is a situation you will face repeatedly as you learn more about Schenkerian analysis and study more and more pieces on your own. This is, of course, only one aspect of Schenker's theory of structural levels, and some would argue not the most important aspect at that, yet this is a matter we must all grapple with. Let's begin with $\hat{3}$. The movement opens from $\hat{3}$, and, looking ahead, we see that there is strong emphasis on $\hat{2}$ beginning with the cadence on ii in measure 16 and later in relation to the dominant in measure 20, though $\hat{2}$ is not actually stated at the final cadence. Substitution of the leading tone for $\hat{2}$ at the cadence, as happens here, is quite common. If this were a classical piece in rounded binary form, we would expect $\hat{3}$ to lead to $\hat{2}$ and dominant harmony, which would then be prolonged by a descending fifth leading to the cadence at the end of Part I. That does not occur here, but this fact does not discount $\hat{3}$ as a possible primary tone. What it does tell us is that, under this scenario, the dominant in measure 8 is not structural but a dividing dominant. So $\hat{3}$ is a distinct possibility. What about $\hat{5}$? There is a perfect authentic cadence on $\hat{5}$ supported by V in measure 8, and it is certainly possible that a primary tone can be introduced well after the opening, possibly even after modulating to the dominant. If we look ahead, there is an initial descent from A5 to F♯5 leading to the cadence in measure 16 and then a more convincing descent from $\hat{4}$ to $\hat{1}$ in the final four measures. So, I believe a case could be made for $\hat{5}$ as primary tone, though it seems we should consider this option only if the evidence seems to negate $\hat{3}$ as a possibility or the evidence overwhelmingly supports $\hat{5}$. I do not believe it does. While we are doing mental gymnastics, what about $\hat{8}$? There is no $\hat{8}$, so I think we can discount that possibility. However, if one projects an implied E5 in measure 1, then it is possible to trace an entire octave descent across the course of the movement.[3] So the best choice, I believe, is $\hat{3}$, and in this case we must consider some other explanation than a primary tone of $\hat{5}$ for the motion to B4 in measure 8. As we shall see, this motion can be explained as a projection of the primary motive, indeed of the fundamental line itself.

A detailed interpretation of the structure of this movement is provided in Example 6.10. Earlier it was noted that an important idea that permeates this movement is the descending third, statements of which are marked on the graph as well as on the score by brackets. Statements of this idea in the opening six measures create an ascending line from G♯4. ($\hat{3}$) to

EXAMPLE 6.9 Bach, French Suite VI, Sarabande

EXAMPLE 6.10 Graph of Sarabande from French Suite VI

D♯5, from which point the line descends another third to B4, which I have marked as $\hat{3}$ $\hat{2}$ $\hat{1}$ in the key of the dominant, a motivic projection—a motivic parallelism—of the fundamental line. The arrow from A4 (measure 3) to G♯3 (measure 5) indicates the transfer of the resolution of the dissonant seventh to the bass. Technically, then, it is the A4 of the previous measure that participates in the ascending line.

There is a direct motivic link between the cadence in measures 7–8 and the opening of the next phrase—namely, the repetition of the descending third at the same pitch level, but with B4 altered to B♯4. This initiates a sequence that takes us to the F♯ minor chord with A5 in the top part (measure 13). From there the line begins its descent, but the chord on the third beat of measure 13 does not function as a local dominant as expected, but turns out to be passing within a voice exchange extending the supertonic harmony in F♯ minor, which then leads to the local dominant in four-two position and on to the local tonic chord on the downbeat of measure 15. Meanwhile, A5 has been prolonged by its upper neighbor and now descends a third to F♯5 at the cadence in measure 16, locally $\hat{3}$ $\hat{2}$ $\hat{1}$ in F♯ minor (ii).

The final phrase begins from the inner voice tone C♯5, from which point the line ascends back to F♯5, now harmonized by the dominant. Potentially this is $\hat{2}$ in the fundamental line, and though I have marked it so in parentheses, it would be perfectly logical to notate it as $\hat{2}$ with an open note head. In essence, this dominant is headed for closure, but first Bach leads the line up to A5, now supported by the subdominant, for one more statement of the descending third motive leading back to an implied F♯5 ($\hat{2}$) and closure in the upper octave. I have interpreted this final statement as embedded within a prolongation of V.

SUGGESTED ASSIGNMENT

There are a large number of movements from the keyboard suites and partitas, the "easiest" generally being the sarabandes and, where they exist, the minuets. One suggestion is the sarabande from the B♭ Partita (*BWV* 825). Try two readings, one from $\hat{5}$ and one from $\hat{3}$. Both seem feasible. Which seems to fit better?

NOTES

1. A different interpretation of the underlying structure of this prelude was given by this author in "The Fundamental Line From Scale Degree 8: Criteria for Evaluation," *Journal of Music Theory* 32/2 (1988), 271–294.

2. A different interpretation of the voice leading of this movement was given in *Aspects of Unity in J.S. Bach's Partitas and Suites* (University of Rochester Press, 2005), Fig. 4.5.

3. In *Aspects of Unity in J.S. Bach's Partitas and Suites* (University of Rochester Press, 2005), I made a case for a reading from $\hat{8}$ (see Figure 6.7, p. 78). The octave does play some abstract role here, but not at this level. There are instances where a note of the fundamental line is "missing"—for example, $\hat{2}$ at the final cadence, as here—but I am not aware of Schenker ever reading a suppressed primary tone.

7 Ternary Form

This chapter picks up where we left off at the end of Chapter 5, which is an introduction to ternary (rounded binary) form. You should review the opening paragraphs of that chapter, which explain the difference between what in this text we are calling ternary (rounded binary) and (extended) ternary form (A B A′). The introductory section of that chapter outlines the distinction between the formal design and underlying voice-leading structure of rounded binary or sonata form. This is an important distinction to keep in mind as we proceed with this and the following two chapters. In this chapter, we will first examine two examples of ternary (rounded binary) form that are longer and more complex than those examined in Chapter 5: the second movement of Mozart's Piano Sonata in F, K. 280, and the Menuetto movement from Schubert's Quartet in A Minor, D. 804. We will then examine two works in extended ternary form: the second movement of Beethoven's Piano Sonata Op. 7, and the second movement of Mendelssohn's Piano Trio in D Minor.

Extended Rounded Binary

Mozart, Piano Sonata K. 280 (II)[1]

The score of this movement is provided in Example 7.1. Let's begin by taking a brief look at its formal design. The first part consists of three phrases, the first a closed statement in the tonic (F minor), and the second, which begins in an unusual manner on a six-four chord (measure 9), leading to a cadence on the mediant (measure 21). The final four measures, divided two plus two by the repetition in the lower register, confirm the new key while summarizing many of the features of the preceding material. The b section—the equivalent of a development section—opens with an eight-measure-long phrase leading from III to V of v. This is followed by a four-measure phrase with the opening material stated in the key of the dominant, a phenomenon often referred to as a "false recapitulation". At the last moment the minor dominant is changed to the major dominant to introduce the real restatement of the opening idea in the tonic, beginning in measure 37. The final section (a′) parallels the opening, but with important differences. The first phrase is shortened from eight to six measures, and the second phrase, which leads to closure on the downbeat of measure 57, opens with a tonic harmony, not a six-four. The final four measures, which are once again divided into two plus two, confirm closure.

EXAMPLE 7.1 Mozart, Piano Sonata K. 280 (II)

EXAMPLE **7.1** *continued*

EXAMPLE 7.1 *continued*

A detailed sketch of the voice leading of the first phrase is provided in Example 7.2a. The primary tone is identified as C5 ($\hat{5}$), which is decorated in the opening measures by its upper neighbor D♭5, first in measure 1 itself and then harmonized in measure 2 as part of the descending fourth F5-E♭5-D♭5-C5, which is marked by a bracket because of its importance later in the movement. The neighbor-note idea is developed immediately. The dotted rhythmic pattern of measure 1 (top voice) is answered a fourth below in measure 2 (middle voice) and at the original pitch level but an octave lower in measure 3 (lowest voice), which has the effect of different instruments answering in imitation. More important, perhaps, is the use of D♭ to prolong the dominant in measures 4–7. The contents of these measures are interesting. Though one might hear a descent from C5 (measure 3) to F4 (measure 8), this occurs only at a superficial level. As shown both at a and b of Example 7.2, the motion in thirds B♭4/G4 to G4/E♮4, which occurs twice, is an extension of G4/E♮4 in measure 3. The sketch at Example 7.2b shows that the motion to F4 is generated from A♭4,[2] an inner voice tone, and thus we can understand measures 4–7 as prolonging measure 3 until its resolution in measure 8. Stated somewhat differently, this eight-measure phrase can be understood as an expansion of an underlying four-measure idea, as indicated by the Arabic numerals between the staves in both sketches.

EXAMPLE 7.2 Graph of K. 280 (II), 1–8

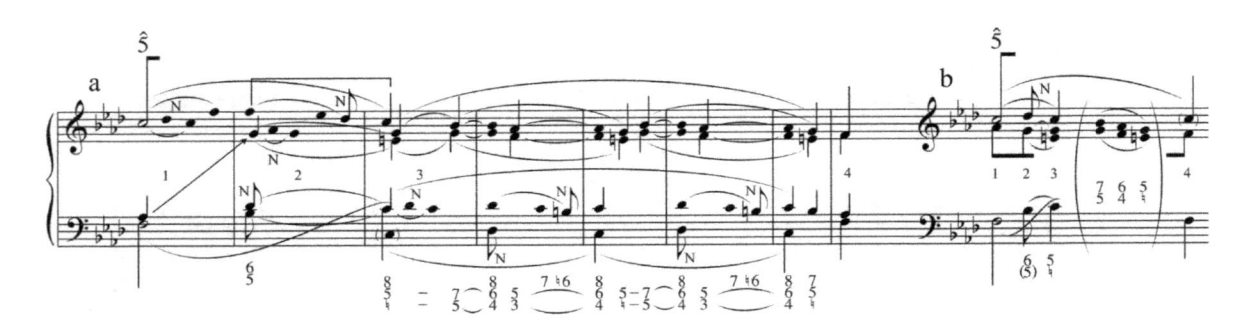

A graph of the voice leading of the second phrase is provided in Example 7.3. The first thing one must deal with is the meaning of the opening six-four. Though Mozart begins with a new idea in measure 9, the meaning of the six-four in terms of the voice leading is dependent on its connection to the preceding phrase, a situation we have encountered elsewhere. That is, we must understand the bass note E♭ in relation to its origin, the preceding F. Careful examination of the harmony shows that the six-four in the first half of measure 9 leads eventually to the five-three on the second half of measure 12. What about the five-three on the second half of measure 9? It is not a resolution of the six-four, but is passing between two six-fours, offering consonant support for the passing tone B♭4 connecting the inner voice tone A♭4 and the top voice tone C5—in other words, re-establishing the third C5/A♭4 of the initial phrase, now over the bass note E♭. In the next measure, our bass note E♭ is prolonged by its upper neighbor F, supporting the harmony IV⁶ in the key of the mediant, and then its lower neighbor, supporting the harmony ♮II⁶ (V⁶ of V)

in the new key, which leads back to the six-four and finally to its resolution to five-three. This process occupies four measures, which coincides with the hypermetric organization of the movement. In the next four measures, our bass note E♭ is further prolonged by its chromatic upper neighbor F♭, supporting an augmented sixth chord, and then, following its reinstatement and subsequent registral transfer, E♭ passes through D♮ to D♭, supporting the dominant of III in four-two position, leading on to C, supporting III⁶ (I⁶ in the new key) on the downbeat of measure 17. This point of arrival coincides with a change of surface articulation in the right-hand part. If we now look at the bass line of these eight measures in relation to the preceding F, we see that it outlines a descending tetrachord F (m.8)-E♭ (mm.9–15)-D♭ (m.16)-C (m.17), the same tetrachord marked by a bracket in measures 2–3. It would appear that the bass line may well have been written first and the upper part then added above it.[3] Regardless of whether this supposition is correct, one thing is clear: it is much easier to make sense of the upper parts with their incomplete lines and registral changes once we have an understanding of the bass line.

EXAMPLE 7.3 Graph of K. 280 (II), 9–24

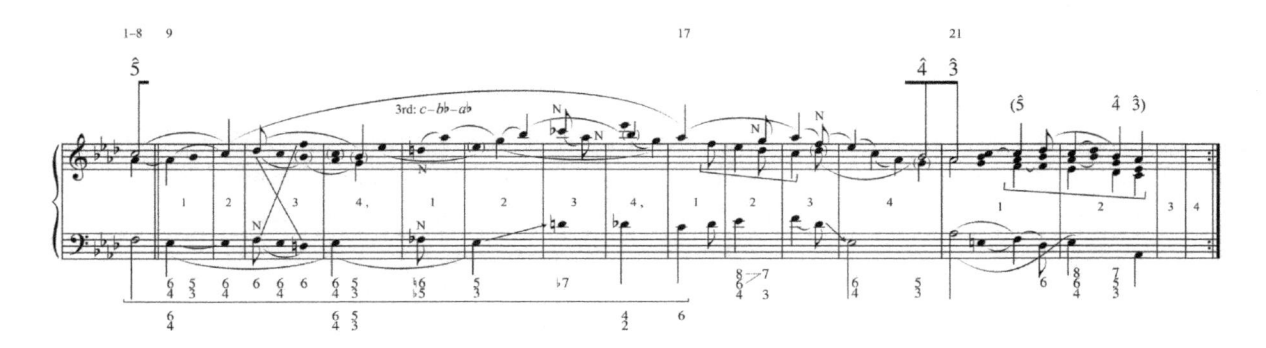

We have already noted that the opening melodic gesture reinstates the third A♭4-C5, the inner and outer voice tones associated with the tonic triad in the initial phrase. What we must do now is to follow the progress of the two lines leading from these two notes, supplying where necessary pitches implied by context but not stated in that register. If the resolution of the six-four with C5 over A♭4 is to five-three in measure 12, then C5 leads to B♭4, while A♭4 leads to G4. This is clear in the left-hand part, but in the right-hand the B♭4 is not stated. It is supplied in parentheses. If we examine measure 11 in detail, we see that the F5 on the second half of the measure, which can be understood as resulting from a voice exchange with the bass, displaces an implied B♭4, which fills in the gap between inner and outer voice tones. While D♭5 can be understood to continue on to an inner voice, as shown in Example 7.3, it can also be understood as the upper third of the implied B♭4 at the five-three in measure 12. This is a complex passage that requires careful attention to detail, including supplying implied tones, to arrive at an understanding of the voice leading. This process applies to the next four measures as well. The D♮5 in measure 13 must lead to E♭5 in measure 14, which is supplied in parentheses, above which the notes of the five-three, including the previously missing fifth, are now stated in the upper register. The notes of this third are then prolonged by their upper neighbors C♭6-A♭5 in measure 15, harmonized by the diminished seventh chord of V in the new key, and in the following measure E♭6 displaces the implied resolution of C♭6 to B♭5. The contents of these eight measures (measures 9–16), while complex in some respects, elaborate a very simple underlying pattern over a single prolonged harmony, V in the key of the mediant. The six-four resolves to five-three, which is subsequently transferred to the upper register, and then decorated by a neighboring harmony before being reinstated once again and finally resolved to A♭5 over the bass note C4, I⁶ in the key of the mediant. Overall, then, the melodic content of these measures leading to the downbeat of measure 17 is a descending third C-B♭-A♭ with a shift to the upper register. Resolution to the lower register will come at the end of the phrase.

The next four measures lead to a cadence in A♭ (III) on the downbeat of measure 21, which signals the descent of the fundamental line from C5 ($\hat{5}$), measures 1–8, through B♭4 ($\hat{4}$) in measure 20 to A♭4 ($\hat{3}$). Thus the descent of this same third, but with a shift to the upper register in measures 9–17, is to be understood as embedded within the encompassing descent of the fundamental line. But what about the content of measures 17–20? The late Ernst Oster had a remarkable insight into this passage. He pointed out that there is yet another statement of the descending tetrachord F5-E♭5-D♭5-C5 embedded in the passage, obscured by the fact that the line moves from the right-hand to inner part of the left-hand. This statement of the tetrachord motive is indicated in Example 7.1 as well as the graph of Example 7.3 so you will not miss it. But once you know it is there, it seems obvious! Note that the final note of the tetrachord motive, C5, is harmonized by an F minor chord, here functioning as vi in the key of the mediant, but still, it would seem, as a reference to the original association of this motive from the beginning. Meanwhile, A♭5 is reinstated above this C5, resolving the preceding augmented fourth G5/D♭5, and from this point the top-sounding part arpeggiates down to F5, which leads to E♭5 on the downbeat of measure 20. This E♭5, which covers the main line, prepares the introduction of that note at the beginning of the b section, following the double bar.

Let us summarize what we have discovered so far about this remarkable little movement regarding its motivic organization. The descending tetrachord F5-E♭5-D♭5-C5 first identified in measures 2–3 becomes the controlling bass uniting the first phrase with its continuation leading to measure 17, an important point of articulation within the longer-range motion to A♭ in measure 21. Immediately following the completion of the tetrachord in the bass in measure 17, we have yet another statement of this idea (at the original pitch level) split between the right- and left-hand parts. This is followed by the cadence leading to A♭ and descent of the fundamental line to $\hat{3}$. The continuation is no less remarkable. In two measures Mozart manages to summarize the main features of all that has come before. First C5 is restated over an F minor chord, and then decorated by D♭5 before the line descends to A♭4, imitating the descent of the fundamental line. Meanwhile an inner line articulates the tetrachord F4-E♭4-D♭4-C4.

A graph of the b section is provided in Example 7.4. As already noted, this section begins melodically from E♭5, the covering pitch introduced at the approach to the cadence in measures 20–21. The implied harmony underneath is A♭ (III). This pitch is prolonged by a voice exchange with the lowest-sounding voice, which introduces G♭5, a covering note, preparing its return in that same register three measures later. Meanwhile the voice

EXAMPLE 7.4 Graph of K. 280 (II), 25–37

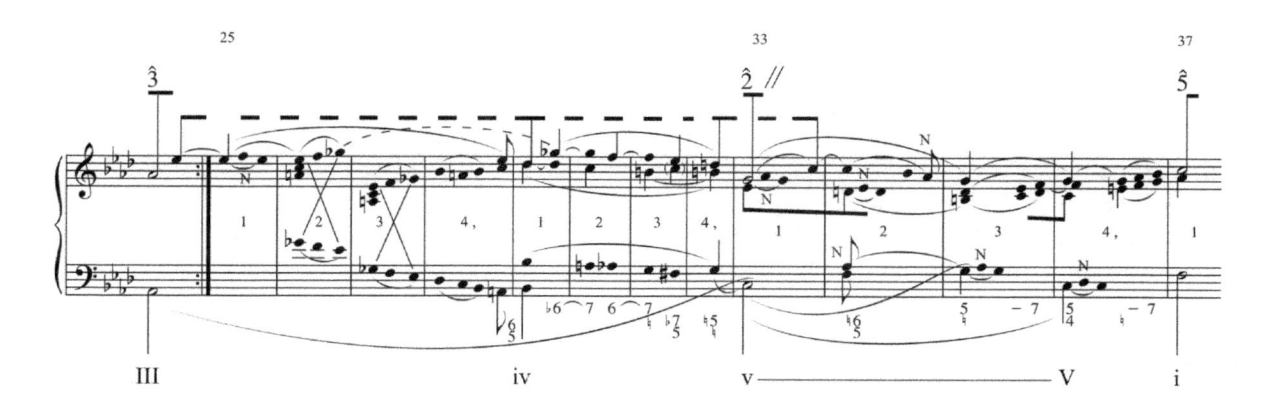

exchange is repeated an octave lower before E♭5 is once again introduced in measure 28 as the dissonant seventh of the secondary dominant of the subdominant. Thus the overall motion of these measures is E♭5, first supported by (A♭), then reinstated as the bass moves chromatically through A♮ to B♭ the latter supporting D♭5, the resolution of the dissonant seventh. This D♭5 continues its descent to the inner voice tone B♮4 over a chromatic descending bass line leading to V of the dominant. Above this descent, the prepared G♭5 is picked up, and this covering line descends to D♮5. This leads us to the "false recapitulation" on the dominant beginning in measure 33. Overall the motion is from III to v through an intervening B♭ (iv). This progression supports a melodic descent from E♭5 to D♭5, which continues on to an inner voice while the covering line generated from G♭5 descends to D♮5 on its way to C5 over v, which covers the clear statement of G4 ($\hat{2}$), completing the descent generated from the opening C5 to the interruption of the fundamental line. The subsequent four measures change the minor dominant to major in preparation for the real return. But what of the covering line from E♭5 leading to C5 in measure 33 as preparation for the return of $\hat{5}$? If one understands the E♭5 as related to the covering F5 in measure 1, then it appears that this line, which covers the fundamental line, is a greatly expanded statement of the descending tetrachord encompassing all of parts a and b, measures 1–36.

A middleground graph showing the main tonal and motivic components up to the interruption and restatement of $\hat{5}$ is provided in Example 7.5. Registral changes have been made in measures 9–17 to show more clearly the underlying voice leading of the descending third. Here one can see the overall plan, the progress of the fundamental line, and how the statements of the descending tetrachord, marked by brackets, fit into this scheme.

A graph of the voice leading of the final section is provided in Example 7.6. Missing from that graph is the initial phrase, which has been shortened from eight to six measures by omission of measures 5–6 from the original. So, we will begin our discussion from the second phrase, measures 43–51. The first obvious change to note is that the phrase does not begin on a six-four, as it did before, but on a tonic harmony in root position. Based on our experience with the equivalent phrase in the opening section, we would be wise to begin our investigation with the bass line. The first four measures in the bass are an elaboration

Example 7.5 Middleground graph of K. 280 (II), 1–37

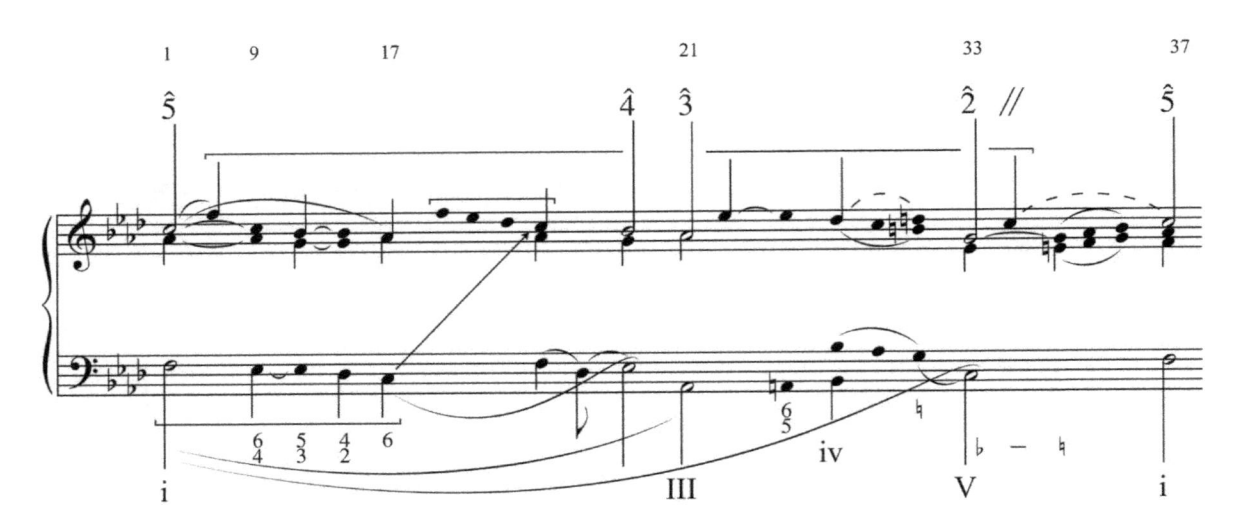

of the descending tetrachord F-E♭-D♭-C, where D♭ is extended by a motion to its lower third B♭. Harmonically the progression leads from tonic to dominant supporting a descent from C5 ($\hat{5}$) to G4. As before, the A♭4 and G4, the 6 and 5 of the six-four and five-three, are missing in that register, though clearly implied. The next four measures prolong the dominant leading to the i⁶ harmony on the downbeat of measure 51. Above this, G is introduced in the upper register (G5), and then prolonged by its upper neighbor before resolving to F5 supported by i⁶, completing the descending fifth (with octave transfer) in measure 43. As before, notes implied by context are supplied in parentheses. Overall, then, the tonal contents of measures 43–51 are controlled by a descending sixth in the bass, i to i⁶, supporting a descending fifth prolonging C5 ($\hat{5}$).

As we begin our investigation of the next phrase (measures 51–57), a prudent thing to look (and listen) for—at least from a Schenkerian perspective—is the path to melodic closure. Scale degrees 2 and 1 of the structural descent are perfectly clear, and if we trace the line from this point backward we see that A♭4 is part of the extended six-four of measures 54–56. But where is $\hat{4}$? The only possibility open to us is the B♭ in measure 52, where it appears as the seventh of the dominant. You might recall that this is the exact spot where Oster had pointed out a "hidden" statement of the descending tetrachord motive in the equivalent passage in the first section. Here the motive is transposed to begin on D♭5, which leads to C5 (rh), then B♭4 (lh), but then, instead of resolving to A♭4 in the inner voice, the resolution is transferred to the bass. This A♭ is then transferred back to inner voice as part of the six-four in measure 54, which eventually leads on to five-three and closure in measures 56–57. It is this extension of the six-four that results in the internal expansion of this metric group by two measures. So $\hat{4}$ and $\hat{3}$ of the fundamental line occur in conjunction with the transposed statement of this "hidden" motive. This is the second instance where we have witnessed transfer of resolution in conjunction with progression of the fundamental line.[4] The first occurred in the A Minor Prelude by Bach examined in the preceding chapter— thus the reading presented in Example 7.6. A subsequent reduction would "normalize" the register, showing $\hat{3}$ as an inner voice (A♭4) over F in the bass. A further abstraction would

EXAMPLE 7.6 Graph of K. 280 (II), 43–57

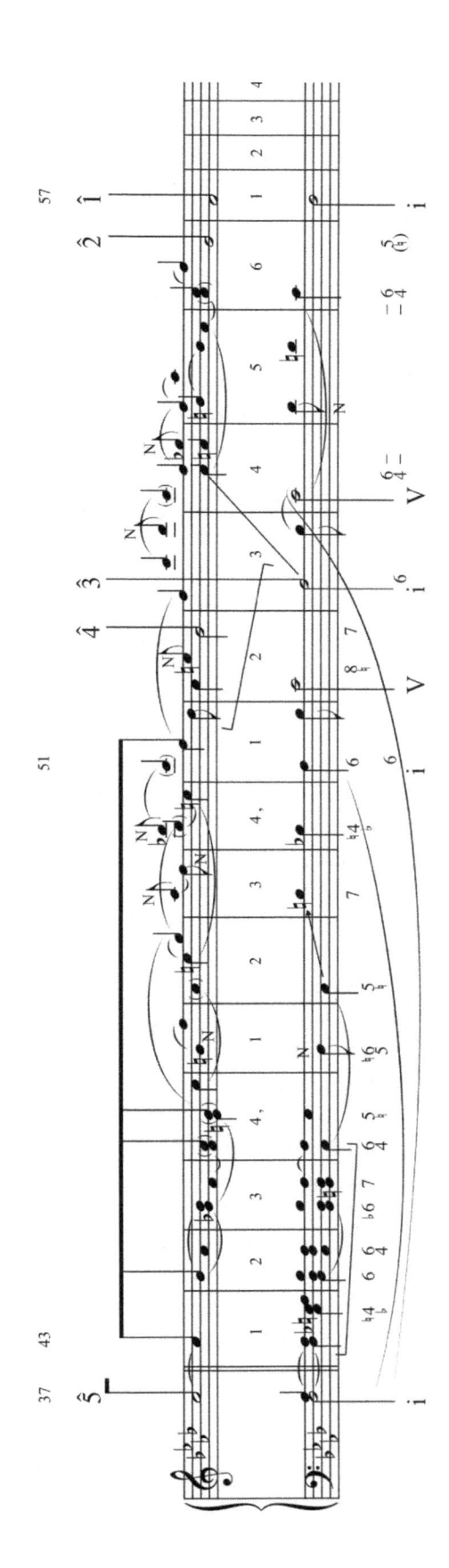

show the entire structural descent in the top part. These levels of "normalization" are fine as long as the actual musical presentation has been made clear.

The final phrase makes reference to the descending tetrachord from D♭5, identified in the score (Example 7.1). Both times D♭5, the important upper neighbor of $\hat{5}$ from the very beginning, is isolated registrally, and continuation of the idea is transferred to an inner voice.

Schubert, String Quartet in A Minor (D. 804), Menuetto

The score of this Schubert movement is provided in Example 7.7. The first part of the movement is divided into two phrases, the first initially establishing the tonic key of A minor (measures 1–8), followed immediately by four measures modulating to III. The second phrase (measures 12–20) confirms the modulation. The b section also consists of two phrases, the first leading from III (C) down a major third to A♭ (measure 28), and the second leading to the dominant in measure 35. The important harmonic pillars in this progression are the points of departure and arrival, III and V. The intervening goal (A♭) divides the space into two descending major thirds, a progression used by Schubert in several of his works, allowing him to inject considerable harmonic color into an underlying diatonic framework. Arrival at the dominant is immediately followed by the a′ section. Instead of extending the dominant, Schubert surprises us by stating a variant of the opening phrase in the key of C♯ minor! This is followed by a brief transition leading back to the tonic and immediate closure, all of which is repeated before the closing phrase. What are we to make of this modulation to C♯ minor? It appears as if Schubert has once again divided the space between V and I into two thirds, this time thirds of unequal size, minor third E-C♯ and major third C♯-A. The end points are once again diatonic, V and I, as we would find in the music of Mozart and Beethoven, for example, but the path in between is decidedly Schubertian. An outline of the harmonic scheme of this movement from III is provided in Example 7.8. A graph of the voice leading of the entire movement is provided in Example 7.9.

The movement opens with the low E2 in the cello part decorated by its lower neighbor. The dotted rhythmic figure of this opening gesture occurs throughout much of the movement, later shifted from its initial upbeat position to downbeat. This opening gesture is answered by the upper strings with E5 in the top voice (violin 1) as part of a six-four chord over the sustained E. This sound is continued until measures 6–7, where the top part descends by step to the inner voice tone B4, a motion doubled a tenth below by the viola, as the six-four finally resolves to five-three (V), followed immediately by tonic harmony in measure 8. The fact that the tonic harmony occurs with C5 in the top voice immediately brings into question the supremacy of E5. Is E5 the primary tone or is it a covering tone above $\hat{3}$? The answer comes immediately when the cello gesture of measure 8 is repeated two octaves higher (violin 1) reinstating E5, now as a dissonant seventh above the bass note F. It is this E5 that leads to D5 (measures 10–11) and on to C5 (measure 12) as the harmony progresses to III. Example 7.9 shows the primary tone as E5 ($\hat{5}$), which descends to $\hat{3}$ at the cadence on III in measure 12.[5] The remainder of the a section confirms the modulation to III, but within these eight measures E5 is twice reinstated via its upper neighbor F5 before the section ends very clearly on C5 in measure 20. The cadences on C5 in measure 12 and again in measure 20 establish it as the fundamental note of these measures, and thus

EXAMPLE 7.7 Schubert, Quartet in A Minor (D 804), Menuetto

EXAMPLE **7.7** *continued*

Example 7.8 Harmonic scheme of Menuetto, Part II

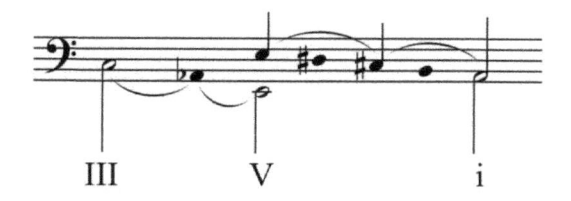

the return to E5 is heard in this context as covering, indeed a recollection of the original primary tone, but now in a subordinate role.

The first phrase of the b section prolongs C5 while the harmony progresses from C to A♭. The top voice first ascends by step to E♭5 as part of a six-four chord over E♭. The passing tone D is harmonized by a diminished seventh chord with F in the bass, and the subsequent resolution of F down to E♭ might be heard as an enlargement of the F5-E5 motion heard twice previously in the closing phrase of the a section. The E♭5 of measure 24 returns to C5 via the passing tone D♭5, itself elaborated by the third progression F5-E♭5-D♭5. The next phrase reinstates E♭5 in the top part with A♭5 projected above it. This A♭5 becomes G♯5 as the harmony shifts down a major third to E, the dominant. The prolonged C5 of the preceding phrase has all but disappeared, becoming an inner voice tone (C4) in measures 29 ff. (not shown in Example 7.9). Nevertheless we must understand this C5 to lead conceptually to B4 ($\hat{2}$) over the dominant, completing the motion to interruption of the fundamental line. This implied B4 ($\hat{2}$) is shown in parentheses in the graph.

The a′ section begins by extending the low E, this time decorated by its lower neighbor D♯, not D♮ as before, a subtle clue that a change is imminent. Indeed this D♯ passes down to C♯ for an altered statement of the opening phrase in C♯ minor, a key that adds a mysterious and dark quality to the movement. The G♯ of the dominant harmony now becomes the fifth of this new key. The first six measures of the phrase imitate measures 1–8, though here over a local tonic rather than dominant pedal. The top part descends from G♯4 to the inner voice tone D♯4 before leading on to E4 in measure 46. As before, the local primary note—here G♯4—is reinstated, now as dissonant seventh, but this time the line descends a fifth, not a third, to local closure (measure 51) in C♯ minor. This is followed by a brief retransition to the tonic through a passing six-four introduced by the diminished seventh chord A♯-C♯-E-G♮, a gesture that is repeated (and thus not shown in the graph). The return to the tonic is not to a root position harmony, but i⁶ (measure 56), which supports E5 and initiates a descent from there to closure. These nine measures[6] are then repeated, coming to rest for the last time on $\hat{1}$ in measure 69. This is followed by the closing phrase confirming the tonic and recalling the primary tone, twice introduced by its upper neighbor F5 as earlier, but now covered by G♯5-A5. The final measures, not shown in Example 7.9, end on A5 decorated by its lower neighbor G♯5, articulated by the dotted rhythmic figure that pervades the movement.

A middleground graph of the Menuetto is provided in Example 7.10, which clearly shows the interruption and subsequent completion of the fundamental structure to closure. It also reveals the function of Schubert's excursions to the distant keys of A♭ major and later C♯ minor. These excursions may at first seem difficult to explain, but in fact they fit quite logically into a larger well-established pattern. These colorful harmonic motions are a hallmark of Schubert's instrumental style.

EXAMPLE 7.9 Graph of Menuetto

EXAMPLE 7.10 Middleground graph of Menuetto

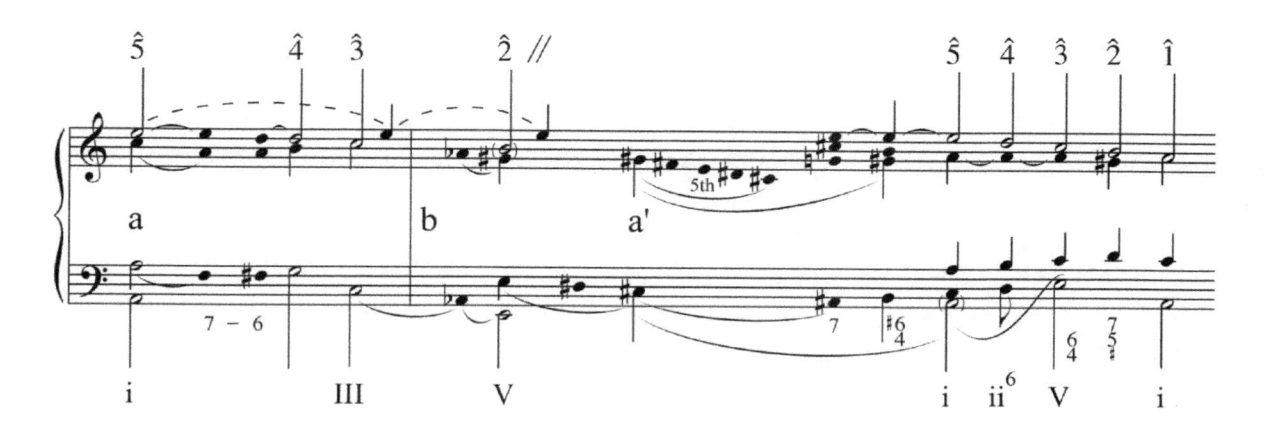

SUGGESTED ASSIGNMENTS

1. Mozart, Divertimento K. 563 (II): I suggest you prepare three separate sketches, as follows.

    a. Measures 1–18. This initial phrase leads to local closure in the lower register. What is the primary tone and when is it introduced?

    b. Measures 18–44. This second phrase consists of two parts, measures 18–25 and 25–44, the latter including a six-measure parenthetical expansion. Initially you may want to sketch these subphrases separately, but eventually you must show the long-range linear progression that unites the two.

    c. Measures 45 ff. (the b and a′ sections up to the reintroduction of the primary tone). How is the dominant prolonged and by means of what voice-leading paradigm is the primary tone reintroduced?

2. Schubert, Piano Sonata in A Minor, Op. 42 (D. 845), Scherzo. The a section modulates from i (A Minor) to III (C major), standard procedure for a classical movement in the minor mode. The primary tone is C5 ($\hat{3}$). Note that establishment of III involves a descending fifth to C5, where the fifth, G5, is introduced first by A5, then by A♭5 supported by an A♭ chord in first inversion (♭VI⁶ in the local key), a detail Schubert will exploit in the b section. We can predict that the goal of the b section will be the dominant, and indeed, if we look ahead beyond Schubert's digression into A♭ major/minor, we see that he does arrive at the dominant, first E minor and then an E major harmony, before the return to the opening material. Furthermore, the dominant supports $\hat{2}$, so at this level the structure is standard. The first part, which prolongs $\hat{3}$, progresses from I to III, and the eventual goal of this motion is V supporting $\hat{2}$.

    The eight-measure transition to the b section transforms the potential function of the C major chord to dominant, setting up the expectation of F minor, which is never realized. The real reason for this passage seems to be to introduce D♭, which becomes the seventh of the dominant leading to A♭. We can understand this as an expansion of the earlier reference to that harmony in the context of C major (III), or conversely the earlier reference as anticipating or foreshadowing its use here. But how do we interpret its place in the movement? In answering this question, I suggest you recall our interpretation of the Menuetto movement just examined.

A B A′

Beethoven, Piano Sonata Op. 7 (II)

This Beethoven movement, with its elegant simplicity, provides an interesting contrast to the preceding Schubert movement. The formal scheme is ternary: A B A′ plus coda. Each of the sections has a ternary design as well, and the B section is followed by an extended retransition. The score is provided in Example 7.11, and a graph of the voice-leading structure of the A section is provided in Example 7.12.

The primary tone of this movement is E4 ($\hat{3}$), clearly stated at the very beginning of the initial phrase (a), measures 1–8. The top voice progresses to local closure over the course of this phrase, harmonized by the progression I-ii⁶-V-I. Internal to this progression, E4 is initially prolonged by its upper neighbor, and E4 and tonic harmony are subsequently prolonged by a voice exchange (outer voices, measure 1 to the downbeat of measure 5), which is immediately answered by a second voice exchange reinstating E4 supported by I before the cadential pattern leading to local closure. The b phrase, which is six measures in length, is shown to be an underlying four-measure idea expanded by internal repetition. It consists of a secondary dominant seventh chord in four-three position leading to V supporting D5 ($\hat{2}$), which in the last measure is extended to the seventh of the dominant, initially stated as F5 but then transferred to the lower register for restatement of the opening idea. At a local level, there is an interruption with $\hat{2}$ in the upper register, where the return to $\hat{3}$ is prepared by the addition of the seventh to the dominant.

The a′ phrase is more complex, but as a result more interesting, particularly following the simplicity of the b phrase. It contains a four-measure parenthetical insertion delaying closure. This insertion could be omitted without significant effect, except to eliminate the tension created by delay of the completion of the phrase. Thus I have indicated the metric grouping as follows: 1 2 3 4 5 (1 2 3 4) 6. It is also possible to view the third and fourth measures as expanding the phrase internally, though in a much less obvious way. The phrase begins exactly like the opening two measures of the movement with prolongation of E4 by its upper neighbor. This is followed by an ascending progression in parallel tenths between outer voices, where each step in the upper line is approached from above. This is accompanied by an inner voice progressing in a series of 5–6 motions above the bass. The melodic goal of this ascending line is C5, but at the last minute the incomplete neighbor-note motion F5-E5 is superimposed, thus expanding the neighbor-note relationship of the first two measures while integrating the upper octave, which to this point had been isolated, into the phrase as a whole. Thus these measures play an important role not only within this phrase but also in the section as a whole. Finally, note the introduction of G4 by its upper neighbor covering $\hat{2}$ and dominant harmony as the phrase heads toward local closure. This covering tone prepares the following section, which prolongs A♭4, the chromatic upper neighbor.

A graph of the B section and the retransition is provided in Example 7.13. The B section proper consists of three four-measure phrases, where the last is a transposed variant of the first. The first phrase is a closed progression in A♭ (♭VI) in which A♭4 is prolonged by its upper neighbor B♭4. The third chord, the diminished seventh chord of ii⁶ in six–five position, is a chromatic substitute for I⁶, and thus the first three chords have been grouped together by slurs in the graph. The second phrase opens with the dominant of F minor (iv) supporting C5, and this is followed by a bass motion to A♭ supporting i⁶ in F minor, above which C5 is prolonged locally by its upper neighbor while F5 is introduced above it by E♮5. The slurs connecting

EXAMPLE **7.11** Beethoven, Piano Sonata Op. 7 (II)

EXAMPLE 7.11 *continued*

EXAMPLE 7.11 *continued*

this point to the opening of the first phrase show the arpeggiation A♭4-C5-F5 above A♭, a motion also indicated below by the extended 5–6. This is followed by a cadential progression in F minor supporting the motion to closure in that key. Overall, then, the first two phrases are united by a progression from ♭VI to iv supporting the descent A♭4-G4-F4, internal to which there is a covering motion to F5. I have indicated by the A♭4 in parentheses in measure 32 that the descending third is to be understood as prolonging the initiating tone A♭4.

The third phrase begins in D♭ (♭II) with a transposed repetition of the opening phrase of this section. The repetition is exact until the end of the third measure, where the E♮5 leads to F5 over the bass note A♭—that is, to iv⁶ instead of the expected dominant in the local key. The result of this change is a voice exchange between A♭4/F (measure 32) and F5/A♭ (measure 36). We might expect the upper line to continue its ascent to F♯5 and G5, but instead this motion occurs only in the lower octave, preparing the return to the opening, which, however, will be delayed for several measures. To this point the movement is very compact, the only significant digression being the parenthetical insertion in the a′ phrase of the first section. Now, with this transition, Beethoven will allow the piece to "breathe"— that is, to expand both in space and in time.

Overall the retransition prolongs the dominant. Beethoven begins by embellishing the open G octaves by the diminished seventh chord of V with the seventh E♭6 in the expanded upper octave. After stating this idea twice, he lowers the bass note to F♮, creating the dominant seventh of B♭, which is followed by a brief reference to the opening idea in that key in this upper register. This digression ends with a C minor chord, heard locally as ii in B♭.[7] This prepares the following descending arpeggiation begun in parallel tenths initiated from E♭6, which in the top-sounding part leads to A♭5 while the lower part continues to B♮. This diminished seventh chord reintroduces A♭, the chromatic upper neighbor of G, and this A♭ is eventually transferred to the bass, where it is extended to F♯ to reintroduce G. Above this G4 is stated once again, this time introduced by A♮4, a reference to the covering motion in the a′ phrase of the first section, and from there the line descends through F♮4 to E4 ($\hat{3}$) supported by I.

A middleground graph showing the role of the B section in relation to its surroundings is provided in Example 7.14. The role of A♭ (♭VI) at the outset of the B section is shown to be part of a descending arpeggiation (I-♭VI-iv), which introduces V leading back to I. This progression supports the prolongation of the covering tone G4 by its chromatic upper neighbor A♭4. Above the prolonged dominant, first A♭4 is reintroduced and then "corrected" to A♮4 as the upper line descends back to E4 and tonic harmony for the varied repeat of the A section.

The A′ section is a slightly modified restatement of the opening section. The one significant change comes at the end, where closure is completed in the upper octave (C5), realizing the potential suggested by the statement of D5 in the b phrase. This is followed by a coda that utilizes all three melodic registers, though significantly it closes in the lowest of the three where the movement began. A graph of the coda is provided in Example 7.15. This passage opens with a very clear example of the voice-leading technique of *reaching over* created by the superposition of tones above the preceding ones, whose resolutions are transferred to the bass or, in the case of the final one, to an inner voice. The goal of this motion, which is generated from the covering tone G5, is D6 supported by the dominant. I have indicated this goal as falling on a hypermetric downbeat, and though the following material grows out of this measure, I hear it as beginning from another accented measure— thus the indication of successive downbeat measures in my graph. This passage involves the exchange of parts and voice exchange between the outer voices reinstating $\hat{3}$ and tonic harmony in two registers. This is followed by a statement in octaves of A-A♭-G, a clear

EXAMPLE 7.12 Graph of Op. 7 (II), 1–24

EXAMPLE 7.13 Graph of Op. 7 (II), 25–51

EXAMPLE 7.14 Middleground graph of Op. 7 (II), 1–51

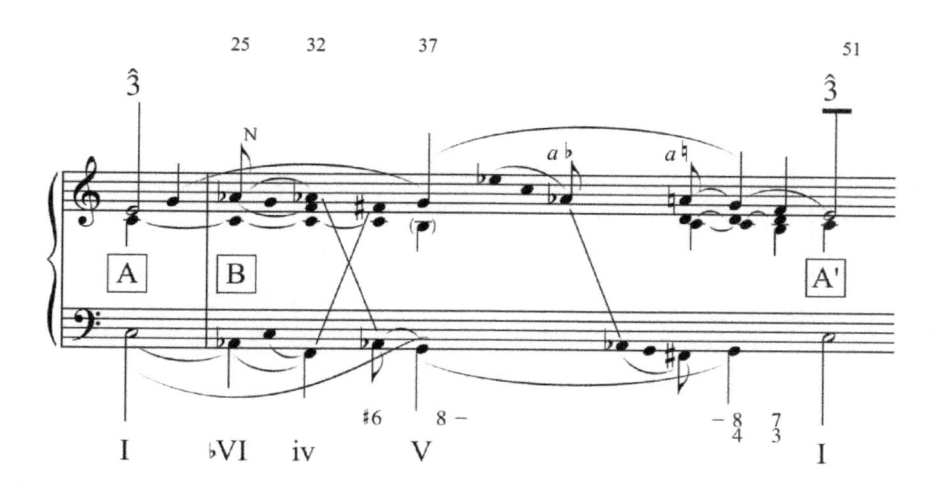

reference to the retransition passage and, in fact, all the way back to the very beginning (measure 7), where we first heard this idea. This passage leads to closure once again on C5 (measure 84), followed immediately by $\hat{3}\,\hat{2}\,\hat{1}$, stated twice in the uppermost octave (E6-D6-C6). The final statement of $\hat{3}\,\hat{2}\,\hat{1}$, with E4 once again decorated by its upper neighbor, occurs in the lower register over a chromatic descending bass.

Mendelssohn, Piano Trio No. 1 (II)

This beautiful slow movement from the D Minor Piano Trio is deceptive, straight-forward in some respects, particularly in its formal design and metric organization, but somewhat challenging in representing its voice-leading structure accurately in graphic form. The music is reproduced in Example 7.16, and graphs of the A and A′ sections are provided in Example 7.17. The A section consists of two contrasting phrases (marked a and b on the graph), each repeated with different instrumentation; the first leads to interruption and the second to local closure. Example 7.17 shows the introduction of the primary tone D5 ($\hat{3}$) in measure 4 via a stepwise ascent. What this graph does not reveal is the importance of the inner-voice tone F4, a pitch that becomes prominent in the B section, and the introduction of the passing tone C5 in measure 1 and the E♭5 in measure 3 by their upper appoggiaturas, a salient feature of the theme. The notational problem that arises is how best to represent the function of this E♭5. An initial reaction might be to mark it as an upper neighbor to the preceding and following D5s, but this makes little sense musically. This is why I have slurred it only to the following D5, the goal of this opening gesture. The remainder of the phrase also presents some notational challenges. I have used the unfolding notation to show the melodic motion G5-C♯5 in measures 5–6; here G5 is a temporary projection of the inner voice, to which it returns immediately, and the C♯5 prolongs D5 as the harmony changes from I to iii prior to the cadential progression leading to the dominant. C5 at the cadence is implied by the context but not stated and is thus placed in parentheses above F4, the important inner-voice tone from the beginning of the phrase.

The relationship of F4 (inner voice) to D5 (primary tone) is more clearly articulated in the opening of the answering phrase. Here D5 is prolonged while the supporting harmony is

EXAMPLE 7.15 Graph of Op. 7 (II), coda

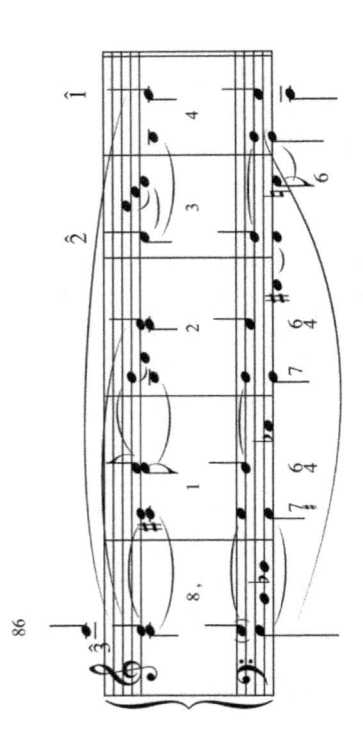

Example 7.16 Mendelssohn, Piano Trio No. 1 (II)

EXAMPLE **7.16** *continued*

EXAMPLE 7.16 *continued*

EXAMPLE 7.16 *continued*

EXAMPLE **7.16** *continued*

EXAMPLE 7.16 *continued*

EXAMPLE 7.16 *continued*

transformed into V⁷ of IV. The resolution of the tritone D5 over A♭4 is to E♭5 over G4, but, as shown in the graph, the inner-voice resolution is temporarily transferred to G5 at the climax of the phrase as the subdominant harmony is introduced. This harmony is prolonged by a 5–6 motion across three measures supporting the melodic descent of a third E♭5-D5-C5, internal to which the passing tone D5 is provided consonant support by a G minor chord (vi). My notation of the melodic line at this point shows the unfolding E♭5-A4 answered by B♭4-D5 supported by the G minor chord, below which an additional voice enters: F♯4-G5. It is this added line that continues as the inner voice while the top part continues to local closure.

A partial graph of the A′ section is provided below that of A in Example 7.17. I have not written out my interpretation of the a phrase, which is stated an octave higher than in the beginning, but not repeated. This time the melody is divided between violin (4 measures) and piano (4 measures), and the accompaniment is more elaborate than before. The main change comes in the b phrase, where closure—the eighth measure—is delayed by a ten-measure insertion, in which the structural descent is mimicked, but without proper harmonic support. Closure is achieved in measure 87 in the original octave, after which the tonic is extended by a motion to the minor subdominant, recalling the tonality of the B section.

A foreground graph of the B section is given in Example 7.18. This section, written in the key of B♭ minor, consists of two overlapping phrases, measures 33–47 and 47–61. The prominent pitch is F5, the important inner-voice tone from the beginning now stated an octave higher. The first phrase opens with an octave progression, F5-F4, a microcosm of things to come. This is answered by the unfolding E♭5 to A4, and though one can find a resolution of the dissonant E♭ in an inner voice, the V-like symbol indicates that the resolution is missing in the same octave. A repeat of the melody begins an octave lower (cello) in the fifth measure, but this is interrupted by the violin entrance on G♭5, the seventh of an Ab harmony, two measures later, which is repeated two additional measures later before being resolved an octave lower to a D♭ harmony (♭III). This four-bar unit has been expanded to six measures by the repetition of a two-measure segment beginning with the sudden entrance of the A♭⁷ chord with the prominent G♭5, the upper neighbor of F5. Resolution of the G♭ in the lower octave creates an octave coupling, and the remainder of the phrase reaches back up to F5. The voice leading of these last four measures of the phrase is most unusual. The progression of chords is D♭⁷-E♭⁷-F⁷ (V) leading to i. Though the dissonant sevenths are doubled and resolved properly in inner voices, as shown in the graph, the effect of their statements by the piano on successive downbeats is one of a series of sevenths progressing upward by step.

The second phrase begins as a varied repetition of the first, and once again we have the sudden introduction of G♭5 by the violin in the third measure of the unit, which is repeated two measures later, once again expanding the phrase by two measures, as shown by the notation 1 2 (3 4) 3 4. This time the resolution of the dissonant G♭ is transferred to the bass, after which the focus is shifted to D♭5, which introduces C5 ($\hat{2}$) over the dominant in measure 56.

Example 7.19 provides an overview of the movement. As noted earlier, the A section presents its own interruption/closure structure: $\hat{3}$ $\hat{2}$ // $\hat{3}$ $\hat{2}$ $\hat{1}$. The main pitch of the B section is F5, a registral transfer of the important inner-voice tone F4 from A. Because the A′ section begins an octave higher than originally, this F5 then becomes the inner voice at the return of the a phrase. Meanwhile C5 supported by the dominant has been introduced near the end of the B section. This is the point of interruption of the fundamental structure. The A′ section then repeats the middleground structure of A while at the same time bringing the fundamental structure to closure.

EXAMPLE 7.17 Mendelssohn, Graph of A and A′ sections

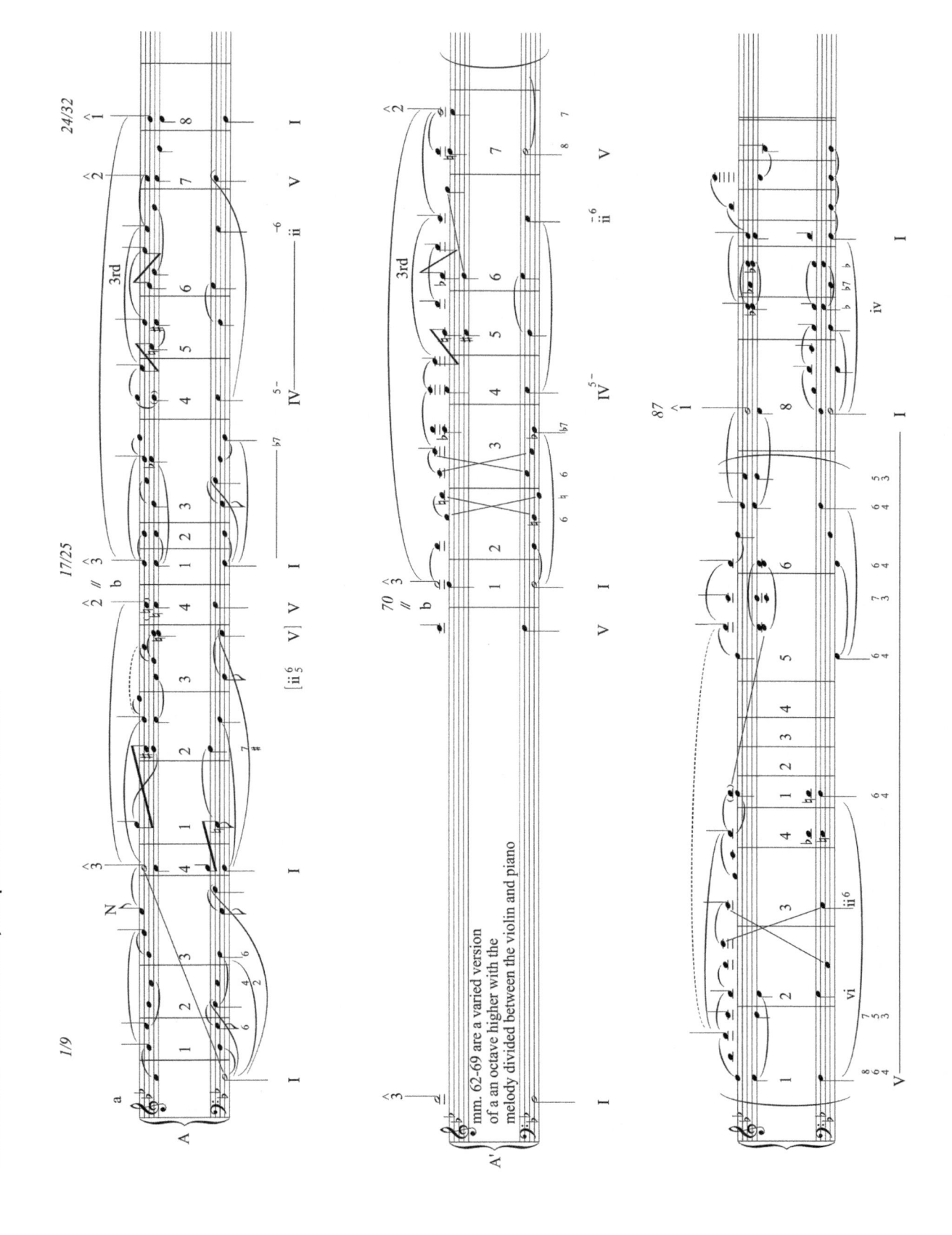

EXAMPLE 7.18 Mendelssohn, Graph of B section

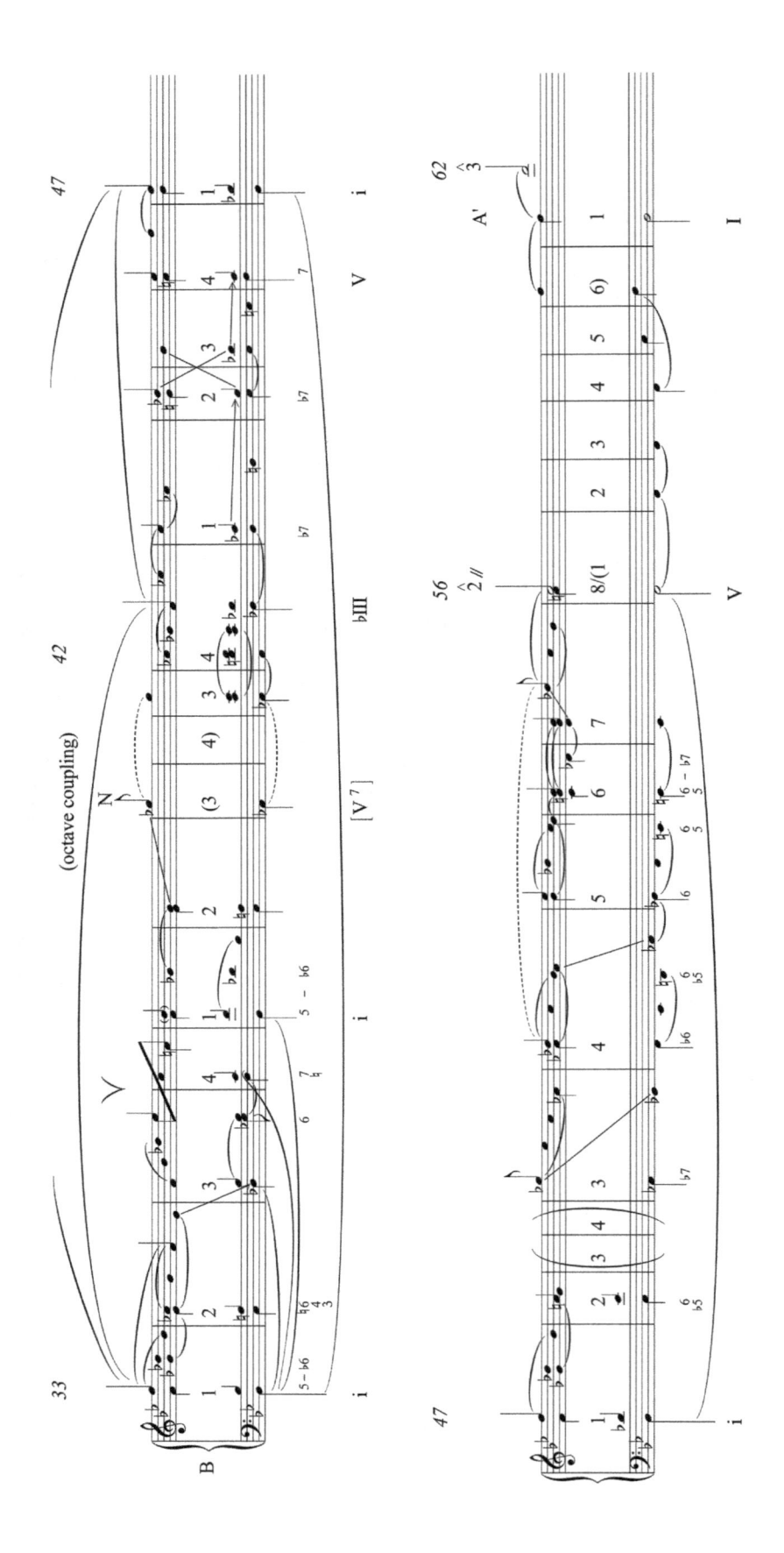

Example 7.19 Mendelssohn, middleground graph of Piano Trio No. 1 (II)

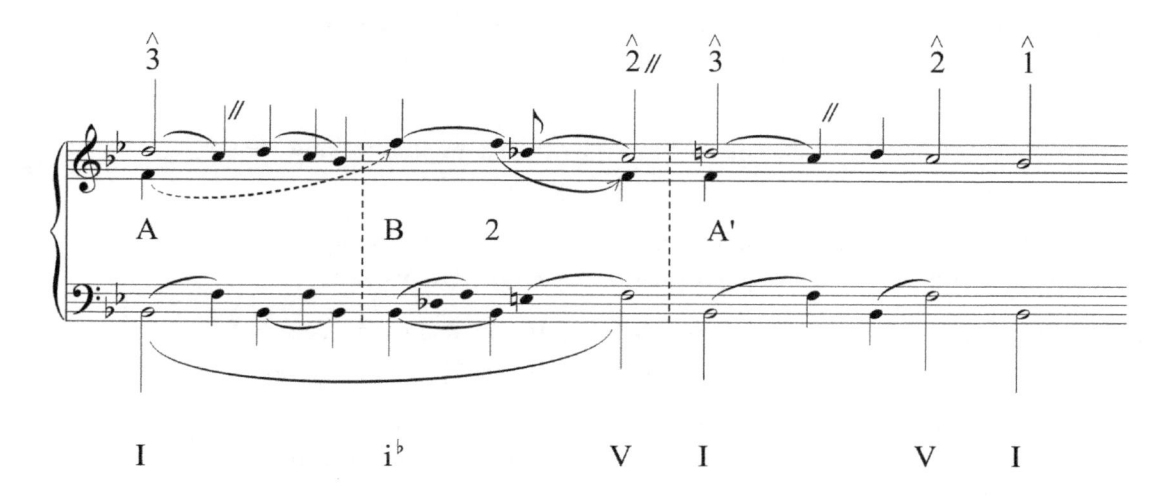

SUGGESTED ASSIGNMENTS

1. Beethoven, Piano Sonata Op. 10, No. 3 (II). This movement presents several issues to the analyst, not the least of which involves determining the primary tone. Assuming it to be $\hat{3}$, where is it established initially and where is it re-established in the A′ section? Also consider the role of B♭ in the movement and the source of the B section.

2. Schubert, Impromptu, Op. 90, No. 2. This is a long and complex work, so I recommend that you sketch only measure 1 to the downbeat of measure 59. This is most of the A section, which in itself has a ternary design.

1–8	a
9–16	a′
17–24	a″ (a′ repeated octave higher)
25–36	b¹
36–43	b²
44–51	Retransition
52–59	a′

As you can see, this formal scheme involves considerable repetition. All phrases but one (b¹) are eight measures in length. The b section involves modal mixture.

NOTES

1. I had an opportunity to study this movement many years ago with the late Ernst Oster, and many of the ideas expressed here, particularly those about motivic repetition, originate with him.

2. The purpose of the arrow in the first two measures of the detailed graph is to show that G4 (measure 2) is to be understood as coming from A♭3 (measure 1).

3. What I am suggesting is that the right-hand part may have been added, possibly improvised, over a figured-bass pattern, a procedure that was very familiar to Mozart.

4. This phenomenon is not as rare as one might expect. See Eric Wen, "Bass-Line Articulations of the *Urlinie*," *Schenker Studies* 2, eds. Carl Schachter and Hedi Siegel (Cambridge, 1999).

5. Questions raised in examining the opening of a movement can often be resolved by examining the a′ section. Here the choice of E5 as primary tone is confirmed by the clear descent of a fifth to closure in measures 56–60 and 65–69.

6. The hypermeter is regular (groups of four and eight) until the a′ section, where the metric groups become irregular, adding to the mysterious and perhaps unsettled character of this section.

7. The V-like notation indicated ahead in the harmonic analysis—likewise earlier below the graph of measures 35–36—indicates that the harmonic progression is left incomplete, at least in the immediate context. Also, note the use of the dotted slurs to indicate that specific pitches—in this case both E♭6 and the bass note F♯—are picked up later in the same octaves.

8 Sonata Form 1

Introduction

In this text I have used the term "ternary" (rounded binary) to describe the formal design $||:a:||:b\ a':||$. I have done so on purpose, despite the inherent contradiction, for two reasons. First, this form is described in different sources as either binary or ternary; and second, either is correct, depending on what is being described. A book on musical form is concerned with formal design, and from that perspective this is a binary form because it is divided into two parts that are repeated, at least theoretically if not always in practice. As explained in the opening of Chapter 5, it is called "rounded" binary because the second part contains a simultaneous return to the opening material and tonic harmony. However, when we are concerned with voice leading across formal boundaries—that is, throughout an entire movement—we do not take repeats into account. And once you remove repeats from the picture, the form is ternary. This is Schenker's perspective. He is interested in the voice-leading structure, not the design of the shell or outer mold. I have found it useful to make a distinction between formal *design* and *structure*, by which I mean voice-leading structure. Schenker does discuss form, but from a structural (voice leading) perspective, and from this perspective the form is ternary.

Sonata form is, in essence, an enlargement of this same design, where a is the exposition, b the development and a′ the recapitulation. This is simple enough to understand, but what are the characteristics of the voice leading associated with sonata form? Schenker describes the underlying structure as an interruption form exhibiting the same characteristics as a musical period consisting of an antecedent and a consequent phrase, except here the exposition and development together form the antecedent and the recapitulation is equivalent to the consequent. As we shall see, either the interruption occurs within the exposition, after which the structural dominant is prolonged through the development, or the interruption occurs at the end of the development. The first situation occurs in movements in the major mode, where the exposition modulates to the dominant, and the second occurs in the minor mode where the structural dominant is reached only at the end of the development. In either case, we are talking about a two-part (binary) division of the structure in contrast to a three-part (ternary) division of the design. It is crucial that you understand this distinction before reading any further.

Structural Prototypes

The next step in preparing you for structural analysis in relation to sonata form is to consider structural prototypes. It will be extremely helpful to you to know that there are a finite number of patterns at the deepest levels of structure and to know what they are. We know already that there are only two viable voice-leading paradigms at the level of the fundamental structure: $\hat{3}\ \hat{2}\ \hat{1}$ and $\hat{5}\ \hat{4}\ \hat{3}\ \hat{2}\ \hat{1}$, which divide into $\hat{3}\ \hat{2}\ \|\ \hat{3}\ \hat{2}\ \hat{1}$ and $\hat{5}\ \hat{4}\ \hat{3}\ \hat{2}\ \|\ \hat{5}\ \hat{4}\ \hat{3}\ \hat{2}\ \hat{1}$. But we can also predict a finite number of ways these prototypes may be prolonged at the next level as well. These are listed in Example 8.1.

The chart of structural prototypes provided in Example 8.1 is based on two premises: (1) that the archetypical exposition consists of two tonal areas, each containing a unique theme; and (2) that each theme progresses locally to closure. While it is true that the theme(s) in the second tonal area invariably do lead to local closure, this is not always the case with first themes. Consider, for example, the common situation where the consequent phrase in an antecedent-consequent pair becomes the transition to the second key area, a possibility not represented in our chart. So you must be cautious in interpreting the chart too literally or as representing all variants. It does not, but rather it is intentionally limited to the most basic paradigms against which one can understand the many variants.

Example 8.1 is organized into two parts: major key paradigms on the left and minor key paradigms on the right. Under each category musical events are aligned under the headings exposition, development and recapitulation, and the numbers 1 and 2 under exposition and recapitulation refer to first and second subject or tonal area. The rows marked a, b, c and d represent the four possible combinations of two tonal patterns, each shown as leading to local closure; the descending third and the descending fifth. A brief description of each is given ahead.

Major Keys

1. The situation outlined here represents a movement where the primary tone is $\hat{3}$ and where the melodic content of the second theme as well as the first is controlled by a descending third. In the exposition, the second theme is in the key of the dominant and it leads to local closure in that key. It prolongs $\hat{2}$, which I have placed in parentheses, since, in this circumstance, it may not be clearly stated. In the recapitulation, it is the second theme that will normally lead the fundamental line to closure. The development section is represented by an open parenthesis, and I have indicated the return to the primary tone by the addition of the seventh to the dominant, a common pattern. Note that the interruption occurs within the exposition and that the content of the development prolongs the dominant.

2. The difference here is that the second theme is controlled by a descending fifth, which in the exposition prolongs $\hat{2}$ and leads to closure in the key of the dominant. In the recapitulation, closure of the fundamental line from $\hat{3}$ occurs in conjunction with this middleground descent of a fifth associated with the second theme in the tonic key. This is a common paradigm.

EXAMPLE **8.1** Structural prototypes (sonata form)

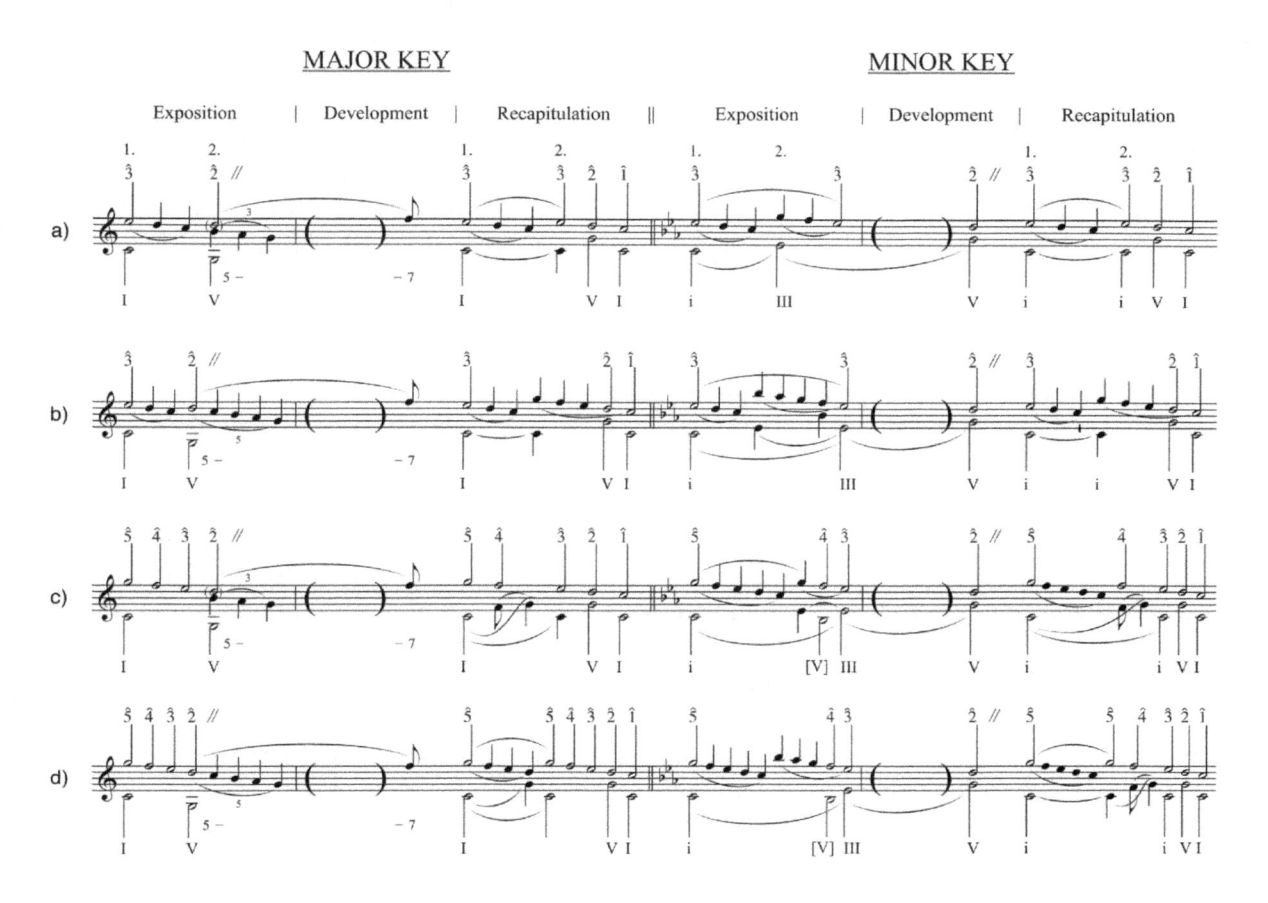

3. The situation here represents a movement in which the primary tone is $\hat{5}$, but the second theme is a descending third, a far less likely scenario than the situation shown at d. In this case, the descent of the fundamental line to $\hat{2}$ will occur within the first tonal area and transition to the second subject. In the recapitulation, the descent from $\hat{5}$ to $\hat{3}$ will occur in the first tonal area and transition, and the descent from $\hat{3}$ to $\hat{1}$ will then occur in the course of the second theme, now in the tonic key.

4. This paradigm, where the primary tone is $\hat{5}$ and the second theme or tonal area is characterized by a descending fifth, is common.

Minor Keys

In all cases, the normal situation in minor keys is to modulate to the relative major (III) for the second subject in the exposition and to reach the dominant only at the end of the development. In movements where the primary tone is $\hat{3}$ (a and b), this note is retained as the goal of local closure in III, and $\hat{2}$ (interruption) is reached only at the end of the development. In movements where the primary tone is $\hat{5}$ (c and d), the fundamental line progresses through $\hat{4}$ to $\hat{3}$ as the second subject leads to local closure in III at the end of the exposition.

The situations shown in Example 8.1 represent abstract norms, where the exposition contains two subjects and two tonal areas. There are always exceptions to be found, but we can recognize these as exceptions only if we understand the norms. We will not have an opportunity to examine an example of each prototype in this chapter, but we will encounter one exception. As you examine more music, you will also begin to see common procedures for transitions (the path to the second subject) and development sections, but for now I suggest you acquaint yourself with these structural prototypes. In doing so, keep in mind that these represent possibilities. Some are common, others less so.

Analyses

Mozart, Piano Sonata K. 280 (I)

The first movement of Mozart's Piano Sonata in F Major, K. 280, is a clear example of "standard" sonata form. The exposition contains two tonal areas, I and V. The first consists of theme 1 (measures 1–13), which is followed by a transition leading to the dominant. The second consists of two ideas: theme 2, which comprises two parts, the second leading to local closure in measure 43; and a closing phrase, repeated in varied form, confirming closure in V. The score of the entire movement is provided in Example 8.2, and a detailed sketch of the exposition is provided in Example 8.3.[1]

The opening gestures of the sonata—the descending arpeggiation of the tonic triad, both in the left- and right-hand parts, and the subsequent prolongation of C5 by its upper neighbor—strongly suggest $\hat{5}$ as the primary tone. The continuation supports our initial impression, and, as we shall see, this movement corresponds to prototype d (major key) in Example 8.1. I have shown the first six measures to be an expansion of four as part of an expanded eight-measure phrase, though this is not necessary, and perhaps not entirely clear. The logic behind this choice is that the second measure extends the first by repetition of the descending fifth motive (identified by the bracket) and that the fifth measure extends the upper neighbor of C5. These six measures could easily be rewritten as four, though, as always, something is lost in this process of normalization. These six measures are followed by a sudden leap to B♭5 (*forte*), harmonized as seventh of the dominant. The seventh is then introduced in the lower octave and resolved to A4, after which the descent is continued to G4 as if to close in this lower octave. Meanwhile this is covered by a varied repetition of the motion in measures 3–4 leading to D5, the upper neighbor of C5. (In this varied repetition, E♭5 is replaced by F5.) I have placed these three measures in parentheses because they are immediately repeated in varied form. There are two important changes in this repetition. First B♭, the dissonant seventh, is resolved in both octaves; and second, the descent in the lower register continues to completion on the downbeat of measure 13, the final measure of the phrase and the initiating point of the transition. While the descent in the lower octave continues to closure, the upper octave is temporarily abandoned after the resolution

EXAMPLE 8.2 Mozart, Piano Sonata K. 280 (I)

EXAMPLE **8.2** *continued*

EXAMPLE 8.2 *continued*

EXAMPLE **8.2** *continued*

EXAMPLE 8.2 *continued*

EXAMPLE 8.3 Graph of K. 280 (I), 1–48

of B♭5 ($\hat{4}$) to A5 ($\hat{3}$), which will be picked up in the transition and eventually lead to G5 ($\hat{2}$). The fundamental line, which began from C5 ($\hat{5}$), has been transferred to the upper octave to prepare the descent of a fifth from G5 ($\hat{2}$), thus ending in the same register as the opening.

The transition consists of two parts. The first consists of an ascending third in the lower octave, F4-G4-A4, where the G4 and A4 are introduced from above by the process of reaching over. Immediately after arrival at A4 in measure 17, A5 is introduced, picking up the A5 from measure 11. This introduces the second part of the transition, a chromatic descending passage prolonging the tonic harmony. This chromatic passage consists of a progression in parallel tenths between the outer voices leading from A5/F (I) to C5/A (I⁶), a motion within the voice exchange A5/F to F5/A. This leads to a ii⁶ harmony supporting G5 and G4, both elaborated by the fifth motive. The G5 prepares the fifth of the dominant ($\hat{2}$). Note, however, that Mozart has not modulated to the dominant. Rather than leading to V of V at the end of the transition, he has progressed to V in the tonic key, leaving the modulation to take place in the course of the second theme.

The second theme (measures 27–43) was discussed in Chapter 4, and thus it will be considered only briefly here. It consists of two contrasting phrases joined to make a single unit. The first consists of two four-measure subphrases, the first leading to the dominant and the second completing the motion to the local tonic. The first consists of the descending arpeggiation G5-E5-C5 and the following step progression C5-D5 harmonized by I-V in the key of the dominant. The answer begins from F5, the seventh of the dominant, and progresses to the inner voice tone D5. Both voices converge on E5 supported by I, completing the descent of a third from G5, a motion to an inner voice prolonging $\hat{5}$ in the local key, and the ascent initiated from C5. The two parts of the theme are connected by retention of G5 in the top part while the bass moves from the root (measure 27) to the third (measure 35) of the local tonic.

The second part of the theme involves more intricate voice leading. The bass progresses chromatically from E (I⁶) to A (vi), which I have shown to be the middle point in a descending arpeggiation from C (I) to A (vi) to F (ii⁶) leading to V-I. In the initial part of the phrase leading to vi, the inner voice progresses in parallel sixths above the bass elaborated by implied (5)-6 motions, where the 5 is replaced by 3. Above this the top part progresses by a series of overlappings (reaching over), where the octaves above the bass notes F, G and A are introduced from above. This progression predicts A5 over the bass note A, measure 40, which is temporarily delayed until the downbeat of measure 41, but supplied in parentheses in Example 8.3. This A5 leads to F5, harmonized by ii⁶, as the phrase begins its final push to local closure. We *hear* closure at the end of the phrase, though both E5 and D5 (the 6 and 5 of the six-four to five-three) are not actually stated in the top part. They are clearly implied by the context and are thus supplied in parentheses in the graph. You should play this passage several times, both as written and as supplying the implied notes, to hear for yourself that this is a variant of a common tonal convention. The following closing idea, which is repeated, leads even more convincingly to local closure on the downbeats of measures 48 and 54. This idea consists of a progression in parallel tenths between the outer voices leading to G5/E (I⁶) and the subsequent descent of a fifth to C5. The arrow from the top voice to the bass shows that the resolution of the dissonant F5 is taken by the bass, allowing the top part to continue its ascent to G5.

Let's review briefly what we have discovered about the progression of the top part throughout the exposition as it relates to line d in Example 8.1. The fundamental line progresses from C5 ($\hat{5}$) to B♭5 ($\hat{4}$) and A5 ($\hat{3}$) within the first theme itself. This then leads to G5 ($\hat{2}$) at the beginning of the second theme, anticipated by the G5 at the end of the transition. From this point we can expect a descending fifth leading to closure in the local key, which is precisely what follows, stated three times.

A graph of the recapitulation through the completion of the second theme is provided in Example 8.4. Since we have just examined the exposition in some detail, this seemed a good opportunity to provide a freer sketch, one without bar lines and containing less detail, of an equivalent passage of music. Though I have recommended that you begin with a detailed graph (like Example 8.3), eventually you must develop skill at producing middleground graphs of voice-leading structure as well. Example 8.4 provides a clear model.

The primary difference between the exposition and the recapitulation is that the second theme and closing phrases are in the tonic. We can predict in advance that closure will occur through the second theme and be confirmed by the closing phrase. There is an interesting issue associated with the background structure of the d prototype, where the fundamental line in the exposition descends to interruption by the beginning of the second tonal area and $\hat{2}$ is subsequently prolonged by a descending fifth leading to closure in the dominant key. Then, in the recapitulation, an equivalent descent through the transition will occur, as in this movement, followed by restatement of the primary tone and the subsequent descent of the fundamental line to closure. In other words, there is a second motion to interruption. The context has changed, so I have indicated this motion as a middleground progression within the encompassing descent of a fifth to closure.

There are two interesting changes in the recapitulation in addition to the obvious fact that the second theme and closing phrases are in the tonic key. The first occurs in the transition to the second theme. Because the transition in the exposition leads to the dominant rather than the dominant of the dominant, Mozart could have repeated the passage here exactly as it was earlier, so the changes he did make are clearly for the sake of variety. The surface pattern in this passage involves crossing of parts, though the underlying structure remains the same as before. This change creates a notational challenge as long as we retain the written octave placements. My solution is to indicate the crossing of parts by solid arrows and the underlying voice exchange by dotted lines. Otherwise the result would be a visual confusion of crossing lines. The second change is the expansion of the second theme by the insertion of a six-measure passage between its two parts. The most important outcome of this interpolation is transfer of the primary tone to the lower octave for completion in that register. Harmonically this passage is based on a progression by descending fifths supporting a descending fifth in the top part leading to the inner voice tone F4.[2]

A graph of the development section is provided in Example 8.5. This section opens with an eight-measure phrase extended to ten by repetition of the last two measures. It consists of a descending fifth in the top voice that involves a temporary transfer to an inner voice. This descending fifth prolongs G5, which is transformed into a dissonant seventh when the harmony changes from a C major to an A major chord with C♯ in the bass. The required resolution of the dissonant seventh is supplied in parentheses over the bass note D in measure 67, the point of departure for a descending fifth sequence supporting a variant of the common alternating 10–7 intervallic pattern in two parts above the bass. It

EXAMPLE 8.4 Graph of K. 280 (I), 83–131

is necessary to keep track of implied as well as written notes here to reveal the underlying pattern. The immediate goal of this sequence is the augmented sixth chord in measure 75, which is extended by a chromatic voice exchange transforming the augmented sixth chord into a diminished seventh chord of the following A major harmony. Here there is an abrupt transfer to the lower octave in preparation for the return to the opening. The A major chord is followed by a brief passage connecting it to the tonic harmony at the beginning of the recapitulation. Overall, then, the bass connecting the end of the exposition to the beginning of the recapitulation is the descending arpeggiation of the tonic triad, C-A-F, supporting the harmonies V-III♯-I. This may be considered an enlargement of the main motive of the movement, though we must be cautious in drawing this parallel, since Mozart uses this same progression in several other movements as a means of returning to tonic harmony at the beginning of the recapitulation. This bass progression supports a melodic motion from G5 to G♯5 (introduced from above) to A4, from which point the line continues its ascent to B♭4, the seventh of the passing dominant chord in four-three position. This B♭4 resolves to A4 over tonic harmony as C5 is introduced above it in preparation for the restatement of $\hat{5}$ at the beginning of the recapitulation.

EXAMPLE 8.5 Graph of K. 280 (I), 57–83

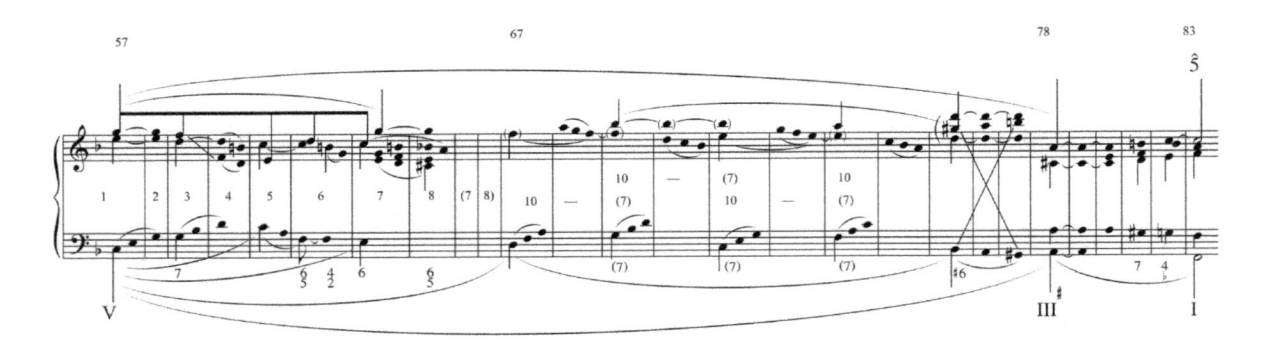

A middleground sketch showing the underlying voice leading from the beginning of the movement up to the beginning of the recapitulation is provided in Example 8.6. Following the foregoing discussion, this should require no additional commentary.

EXAMPLE 8.6 Middleground graph of K. 280 (I), 1–83

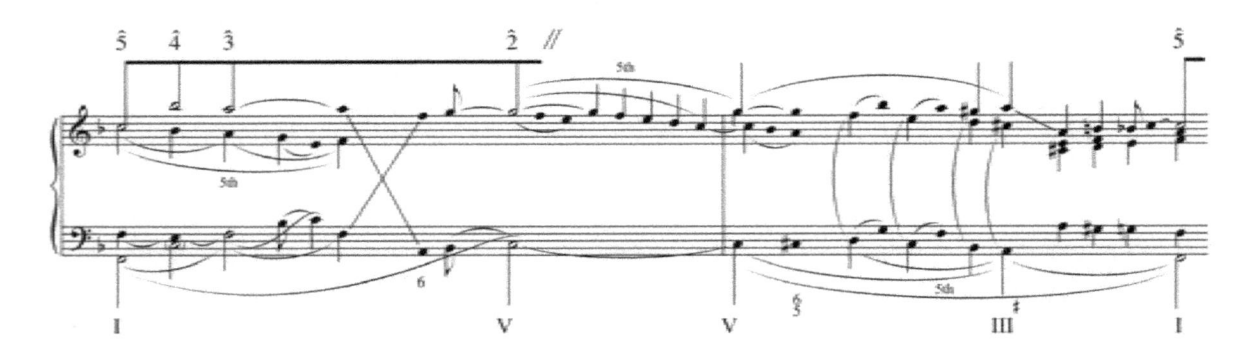

Mozart, Piano Sonata K. 280 (III)

It is always instructive to compare the outer movements of sonatas and other works where both movements are in sonata form. While we cannot expect correspondences beyond the obvious matter of key, sometimes we discover strong connections. Certainly that is the case with this sonata. The movements are very different in many respects, including character, but there are also strong motivic and structural connections between them, beginning with the descending arpeggiation motive of the tonic triad. The score of the third movement is provided in Example 8.7 and a detailed graph of the voice-leading structure of the exposition in Example 8.8.

The first theme, measures 1–16, consists of two eight-measure phrases in antecedent-consequent relationship. The antecedent phrase opens with the now familiar descending arpeggiation figure C6-A5-F5, which is followed by a melodic descent by step to F5 on the downbeat of measure 5. Overall there is a descent of a fifth, but there is a clear separation between the "head" motive and the harmonized descent from Bb5. I have marked the descending tetrachord Bb5-A5-G5-F5, scale degrees 4 3 2 1, with a bracket because this idea becomes a primary component of this movement. Look carefully at the relationships among these four chords and you will see there is potentially a voice exchange between the first and third as well as between the second and fourth chords. It can't be both, since overlapping prolongations are counter to the meaning of the term prolongation. So which one is correct? Neither. Instead there is an exchange between pairs of chords rather than a voice exchange. There is an important difference between exchange of voices and voice exchange. Think about it. This is followed by an elaborated arpeggiation F5-D5-Bb4 (measures 5–7), the last harmonized by ii. This is followed by an elaborated unfolding Bb4-E4, a dissonant interval requiring resolution. The following symbol indicates that the resolution does not follow. On the surface this phrase seems quite simple, but in fact there is much here requiring decisions about structure as well as notation.

The consequent phrase is the same, except an octave lower, until the fifth measure where C5 is restated over the goal of the preceding descent, F4. This C5 is led to D5 via the chromatic passing tone C#5, and though temporarily covered by a motion to C6, this D5 progresses to F5 by way of E5. In summary, then, this movement shares the same primary tone ($\hat{5}$) and surface motive with the first movement, but otherwise the voice leading is quite different. Still, based on our minimal experience, yet armed with our list of prototypes (Example 8.1), it is reasonable to expect a descent of the fundamental line to $\hat{2}$ over the course of the following transition preparing the descent of a fifth in the new key. This does not happen.

The transition, like the equivalent passage in the first movement, is divided into two parts. The first four measures are based on the descending tetrachord identified earlier as an important component, and the next four measures invert the top two parts, ending on A4. This is immediately followed by a transfer to the higher octave (A5), just as happened at this point in the first movement. From there the top voice descends to D5, harmonized by ii⁶ in the key of the dominant, which is extended to the inner voice tone Bb4 as we reach V in the new key, above which G5 is implied as resolution of the preceding A5. Overall, then, A5 has progressed to G5. What is missing is a connection between C6 ($\hat{5}$) and A5—that is, there is

EXAMPLE 8.7 Mozart, Piano Sonata K. 280 (III)

EXAMPLE 8.7 *continued*

EXAMPLE 8.7 *continued*

EXAMPLE **8.7** *continued*

EXAMPLE 8.7 *continued*

no $\hat{4}$ leading to an interruption. What we have is a variant of the d prototype where $\hat{5}$ is retained, below which an inner line progresses from $\hat{3}$ to $\hat{2}$.[3] There is no interruption from $\hat{5}$. Instead $\hat{5}$ is retained until it progresses to closure in the recapitulation.

Our expectation from the cadence on V in the new key (measures 32–37) is that the second theme will begin from G5 supported by tonic harmony, but once again our expectation is not realized. Not only has G5 never been stated, though it is clearly implied, but also the second theme begins from F5, scale degree 4 in C major, *unharmonized*. The melodic content of this second theme is a descending fourth, the tetrachord motive transposed to the local key. I have left measures 50–61 initially blank in the graph because they are a varied repetition of measures 38–49, delaying completion of the descending fourth to closure. We will discuss this varied repetition in a moment, but first we must deal with the unusual beginning of the second theme. What is the implied harmony supporting F5? I hear this F5 as the seventh of the preceding dominant despite the A5, the extension of F5—that is, the ninth of the dominant, which is not a normal part of Mozart's harmonic language. This seems the best solution to a puzzling spot, but still this means that the second theme begins as an extension of the preceding dominant: V. The term used by Schenker to describe this phenomenon—where the musical unit in question does not begin from a tonic harmony—is *auxiliary cadence*.

The varied repetition opens with F5 accompanied in parallel tenths below, hardly clarifying the underlying harmony. The primary change comes toward the end of the phrase, beginning in the sixth measure, where the descending fourth is stated once again and provided with a new harmonization, leading to closure on the downbeat of measure 62. However, the momentum carries beyond this point, leading to yet another statement of the descending fourth an octave lower, this time leading to a convincing close on the downbeat of measure 66.

The first twenty-four measures of the recapitulation—up to the second part of the transition to the second theme—is an exact repeat of the equivalent portion of the exposition, and for that reason only the opening descending fifth motive from $\hat{5}$ within these measures has been included in Example 8.9. The transition, beginning in measure 132, proceeds as before with a descending progression in parallel tenths. This progression continues for eight measures, but with a registral shift upward at the midpoint, resulting in the return to A5. Another result of this registral shift is to break the octave into disjunct tetrachords. The prolonged A5 then progresses to G5 harmonized by ii⁶-V at the cadence, again a motion from $\hat{3}$ to $\hat{2}$ in an inner voice prolonging $\hat{5}$. What follows is the descending tetrachord from B♭5, this time leading to closure of the fundamental line. As before, scale degree 4 is stated without harmonic support, which I hear as V despite the ninth (D6). In the exposition, the F5 was not connected to a prior G5 harmonized by the local tonic, but only to an implied G5 harmonized by the local dominant. Here, however, the B♭5 can be related to the C6 ($\hat{5}$) and tonic harmony at the opening of the recapitulation. A lot has happened between these points, but this way the gesture opening the second theme makes more sense than it did before. Earlier it was noted that the opening figure (C6-A5-F5) and the continuation, the descending tetrachord completing the initial descending fifth, are differentiated by their articulations. In a sense, the fundamental structure of the recapitulation may be understood as an enlargement of this opening idea, where the initial gesture is separated in time as well

EXAMPLE 8.8 Graph of K. 280 (III), 1–66

EXAMPLE 8.9 Graph of K. 280 (III), 108–173

as articulation from its continuation. It is perhaps significant that the disparate parts involve unharmonized material. The sketch of the second theme requires no additional commentary. With one exception it follows the statement of theme 2 in the exposition transposed to the tonic key. The one exception is that the varied repetition, beginning in measure 161, is stated an octave lower, resulting in closure in the lower octave, the octave of the first movement.

Let me play devil's advocate for a moment regarding the interpretation of B♭5 in measures 149–152. One might argue (somewhat convincingly) that this B♭5 is really the upper neighbor of A5 and thus not part of the fundamental descent from $\hat{5}$. This would leave us with two choices—either to reconsider the primary tone or to find another path for the descent to closure. Though a logical case could probably be made for a reading from $\hat{3}$, the interpretation provided here makes more sense musically to me given the prominence of $\hat{5}$ from the very beginning. The only other place where one might hear a structural descent from $\hat{5}$ is the final gesture leading to closure (measures 169–173), which is why I have placed the symbols $\hat{4}$ $\hat{3}$ $\hat{2}$ $\hat{1}$ above these measures in the graph. While this interpretation is theoretically sound, the explanation given earlier seems far better for several reasons, including the registral connection between C6 ($\hat{5}$) and B♭5 ($\hat{4}$).

A two-level graph of the development section is provided in Example 8.10. Let's begin with the large picture. The eventual goal of this section is the A major chord (III♯), after which Mozart proceeds directly to the recapitulation without a connecting dominant. Thus the overall bass progression is C-A-F, the descending fifth motive, supporting the harmonies V-III♯-I, the same as in the first movement. Furthermore, the path between V and III♯ is divided in both movements by an intervening motion to vi (D), thus providing aural logic to the motion to III♯, which has the potential to function as V of vi, a function, however, that is never realized and thus has not been labeled as such. You should compare Examples 8.5 and 8.10 in terms of their underlying structures. The differences are at more immediate levels resulting from the development of motivic components unique to each movement. This development opens with the unharmonized head motive from theme 2 on C5, followed by a statement of a descending fourth from C6 to G5 harmonized by V-i in G minor (ii). The next phrase begins like the preceding one a step lower, from B♭4. This establishes an important connection between C5 and B♭4, foreshadowing the connection between C6 ($\hat{5}$) and B♭5 ($\hat{4}$) in the recapitulation. From this beginning we might expect the continuation to proceed with a descending fourth from B♭5 in the next four measures. Indeed, this fourth does follow, but drawn out over eight measures rather than four due to the exchange of voices between the left- and right-hand parts. The result in the bass is the descending fourth, broken into two disjunct step progressions, leading to the D in measure 95, and in the top part we have the descending tetrachord B♭5-A5-G5-F5 that plays such an important role in this movement. This is followed by a voice exchange between outer voices leading to the augmented sixth chord that introduces the A major chord supporting C♯6 in the top part, the chromatic upper neighbor of the following C♮6 ($\hat{5}$).

A middleground graph of the movement through the beginning of the recapitulation is provided at b in Example 8.11. This requires no additional commentary. At a I have provided a representation of the underlying structure of the exposition, where $\hat{5}$ is prolonged while an inner voice progresses from $\hat{3}$ to $\hat{2}$.

EXAMPLE 8.10 Graph of K. 280 (III), 78–108

EXAMPLE 8.11 Middleground graph of K. 280 (III), 1–108

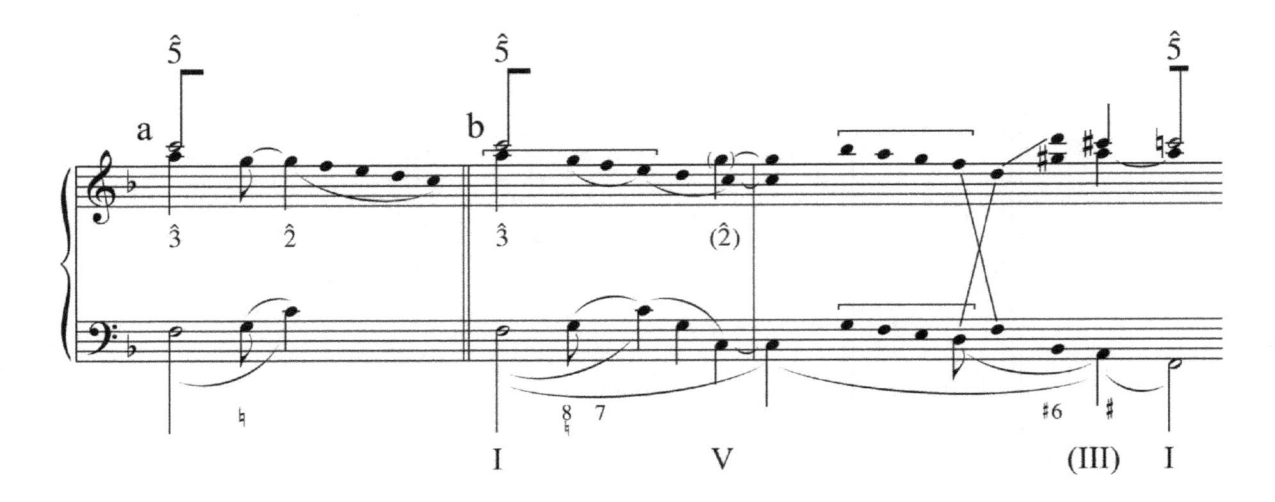

Beethoven, Piano Trio Op. 1, No. 3 (I), Exposition

As a final example in this chapter, I want to examine a work in a minor key, the opening movement from Beethoven's Piano Trio in C Minor, Op. 1, No. 3. We will examine the exposition only, the score of which is reproduced in Example 8.12. A detailed graph of this portion of the movement is provided in Example 8.13, and I have added a middleground graph of the exposition together with the development to indicate the underlying structure up to the point of interruption. As we shall see, the movement corresponds to prototype b (minor key) in Example 8.1.[4]

One of the first issues we must resolve is determining the function of measures 1–10. It has the character of an introduction, but as we progress through the movement we realize it plays an integral part in the movement's organization. This idea reappears at the outset of the consequent phrase beginning in measure 31, at the beginning of the development, leading eventually to the subdominant, and at the beginning of the recapitulation. I have labeled this idea 1a and the following idea 1b, which implies the two are equal. They are not: 1a is introductory and 1b is the "real" first theme, the point of departure for the movement's tonal structure. Taken by itself, 1a suggests a primary tone of $\hat{5}$ because of its emphasis on G and its upper neighbor A♭. Measures 5–6 foreshadow the opening of the consequent phrase, but I admit to some indecision regarding how best to indicate the hypermeter here. The first four and last four measures of the phrase form clear four-bar units. So what is the metric function of measures 5–6? Potentially they could be removed without disturbing the progress of the phrase to its close, so I have placed them in parentheses.

The formal organization of the first theme (mm. 1–58) can be described in two ways. At the macro level this section consists of two large phrases, an antecedent (mm. 1–30) and a modulating consequent (mm. 31–58). The formal organization of 1b (mm. 11–30) can be described as a musical sentence: presentation (basic idea, tonic version-basic idea, dominant version)-continuation. From a tonal perspective, the primary tone, E♭5 ($\hat{3}$), is introduced at the head of the phrase by the basic idea, an important motivic component that is marked by a bracket. The primary tone is subsequently prolonged in measures 10–18 by its upper neighbor F5. At the arrival at V, which is extended until the end of the phrase, the important covering tone G5, first stated in measure 10, is reintroduced. I have indicated this important pitch on the graph (Example 8.13) by the extended stems connected by the broken beam. The hypermeter throughout this section and the remainder of theme 1 is clearly quadruple.

The consequent phrase opens with the introductory idea (1a) on an A♭ chord (a motion anticipated in measures 5–6), which becomes the pivot in the modulation to E♭ (III). In the seventh measure of this phrase, F5 is introduced, decorated by its chromatic upper neighbor, and then restated in measure 39 supported by the dominant in the new key. The remainder of this passage—some nineteen measurers—extends this dominant and F5 until its resolution to the local tonic and E♭5 in measure 59. The prolongation of the dominant involves multiple statements of the motive first introduced in measures 10–11, as indicated by the brackets in Example 8.13. The graph shows a descent of a third from the covering tone G5 through F5 (m. 39) to E♭5 (m.59). A legitimate question that could be raised at this point is why I have not interpreted G5 as the primary tone, which is then prolonged within the first theme by this descending third, a common paradigm for sonata forms in the minor mode. One reason is based on how I have interpreted the opening phrase. As stated earlier, I hear it as introductory and the following phrase, initiated by the important motivic idea marked by the bracket, as the real point of departure for the movement. A second reason, looking ahead, is that G5 is missing from the statement of the first theme in the recapitulation.

The remainder of the exposition is divided into two parts, theme 2 (mm. 59–98) and a closing section (mm. 98–124 and 124–137). The hypermetric organization of the transition preceding the second theme leads to a hypermetric downbeat at measure 58, which is followed immediately by another downbeat measure, a clear illustration of this metric phenomenon. The second theme opens with a four-measure idea consisting of a descending third, distributed over two octaves and progressing in parallel tenths with the bass, from the covering tone B♭5. This idea is repeated, and then transposed to the subdominant, where the descending third is generated from E♭5. The following measures, which prolong the subdominant and lead to the dominant, involve modal change, first of the local tonic, and then its subdominant. The ensuing prolongation of the dominant, stated $f\!f$ by all three instruments, prolongs the leading tone by means of a descending third D5-C5-B♭5, below which one can trace a descending fifth B♭4-E♭4. Overall this theme progresses I⁶-IV⁶-V-I supporting a descending fifth, missing, however, the second scale degree in the key. This missing element will finally be supplied in the following section.

The initial closing phrase leading to local closure can be divided into two parts, measures 98–110 and 110–124. The top melodic line in the first part (violin) involves sequential treatment of the opening gesture from 1a, resulting in an ascending line from E♭5 to C6, the upper neighbor of the local covering tone B♭5. The resolution to B♭5 in that octave is not stated here, but I have supplied it in parentheses. Meanwhile the piano part has shadowed the violin an octave lower, though it continues its ascent beyond C5 through D5 to E♭5, completing an octave. The connection from the beginning of the phrase is from I to I⁶, divided by the arrival in the top part at C6, supported by vi, which

EXAMPLE 8.12 Beethoven, Piano Trio Op. 1, No. 3 (I), 1–59

EXAMPLE 8.12 *continued*

EXAMPLE 8.12 *continued*

EXAMPLE 8.12 *continued*

EXAMPLE **8.12** *continued*

EXAMPLE 8.13 Graph of Beethoven Op. 1, No. 3 (I), 1–59

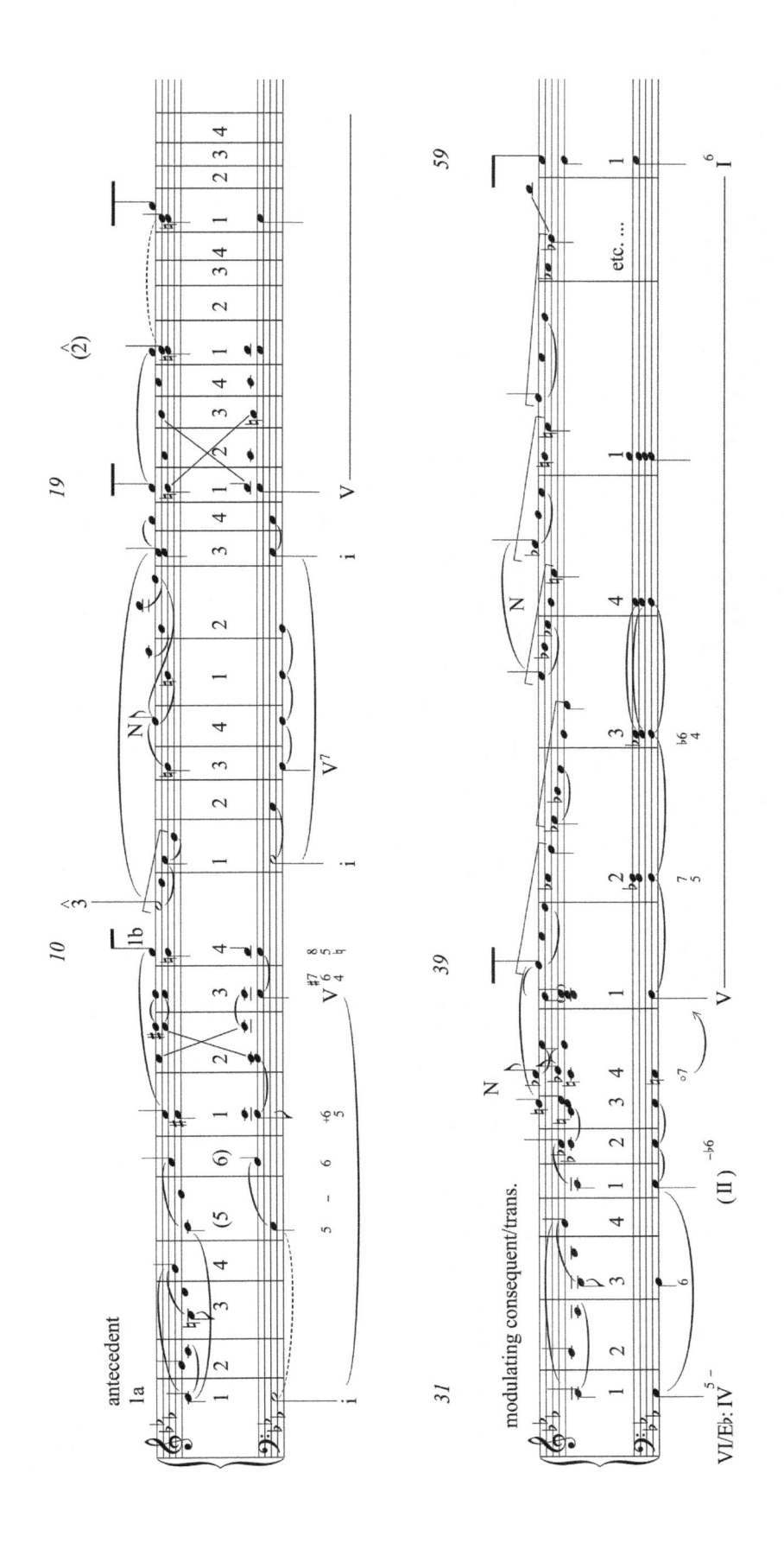

EXAMPLE 8.13 *continued*

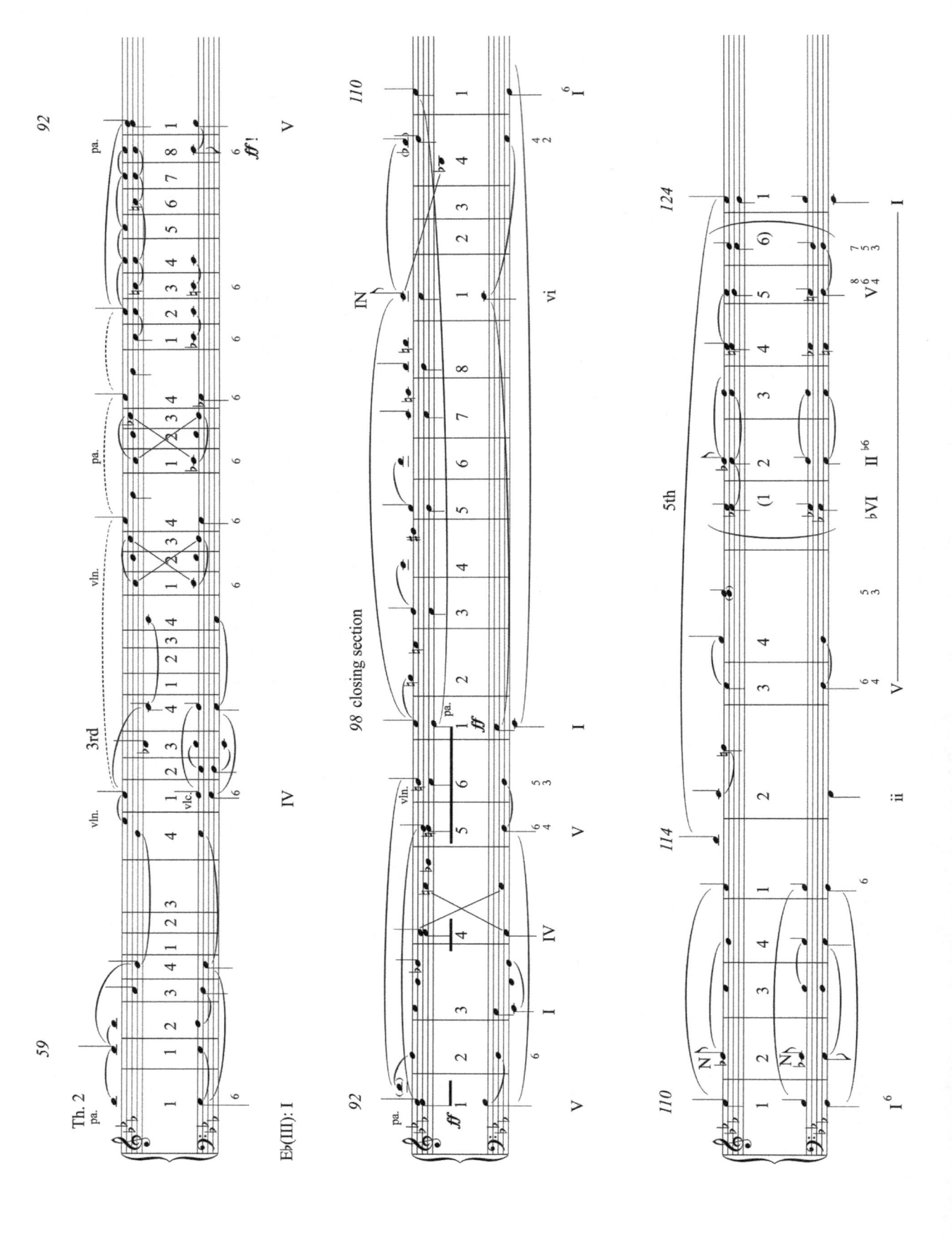

EXAMPLE 8.14 Middleground graph of Beethoven Op. 1, No. 3, exposition-development

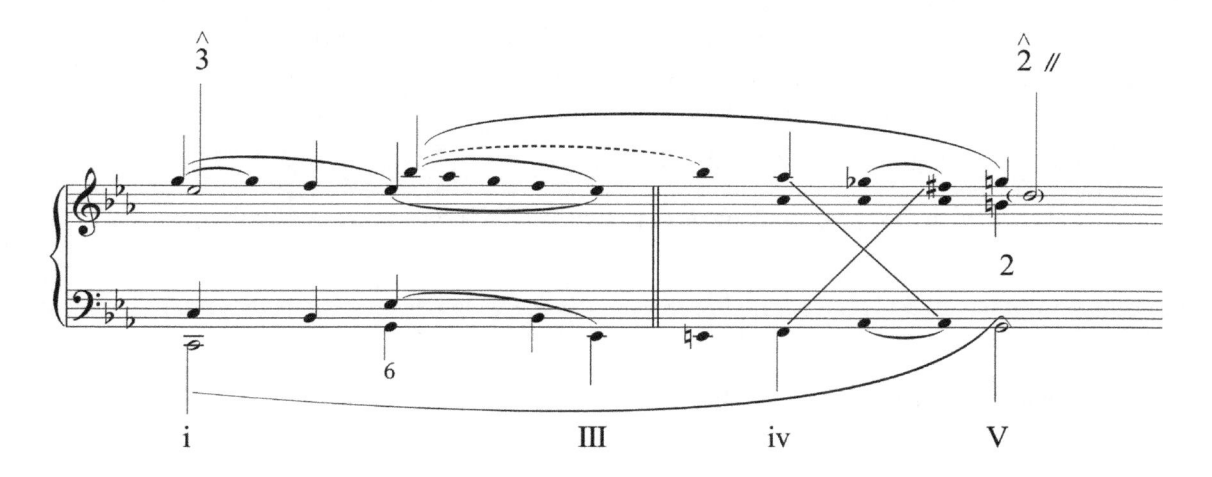

promises the return to B♭5. The next part opens with a prolongation of E♭5 (supported by I⁶) by its chromatic upper neighbor, a reference to the modal mixture associated with the second theme, after which the promised B♭5 is finally introduced. We are now back to where we were at the outset of theme 2, B♭5 supported by tonic harmony in first inversion in the local key. This time there will be a clear descent of a fifth from this covering tone to local closure, delayed however by a parenthetical insertion, once again involving modal mixture. Example 8.13 does not include the final phrase of the exposition, which is based on the motive from 1b.

Example 8.14 provides a middleground graph of the movement up to the recapitulation. The connection between first and second themes involves a descending third from the covering tone G5 back to the primary tone E♭5, now supported by I⁶ in the new key, and the second theme involves the descent of a fifth from the local covering tone B♭5 to local closure on E♭5. The development section opens with the 1a idea, which leads eventually to the subdominant, which is subsequently prolonged by a chromatic voice exchange before leading to the dominant. Here the fundamental line resolves by implication to $\hat{2}$ at the interruption while the top-sounding part descends back to the covering tone G5. The fact that the fundamental line is covered throughout by middleground progressions is most likely a common characteristic of sonata movements of this prototype.

SUGGESTED ASSIGNMENTS

Mozart, Piano Sonata in F, K. 332 (I)

1. I suggest you begin by preparing sketches of the individual parts of the exposition, where appropriate comparing to equivalent places in the recapitulation.

   a. Theme 1. The primary tone is $\hat{5}$. As in the first movement of K 280, keep track of the progress in different melodic registers.

b. Transition to theme 2. Consider the motion C–C♯–D in the bass as an inner voice above an implied F. This will help you discover the underlying pattern, which is controlled by F leading to G as V of the dominant. Compare to the transition in the recapitulation.

c. Theme 2. This theme consists of an antecedent-consequent pair. What is the function of the F5 in the fifth measure?

d. Transition to the closing theme and the closing theme.

2. Do a separate sketch of the development section, paying careful attention to registral connections.

3. Do a middleground sketch from the beginning through the development.

Mozart, Piano Sonata in A Minor, K. 310 (I)

1. Exposition.

a. Theme 1 and transition. This theme consists of an antecedent phrase and a modulating consequent that is extended at the end. How do you explain and notate the dissonant Ds that appear to resolve upward? Compare to the equivalent passage in the recapitulation.

b. Theme 2. Review the discussion in Chapter 3.

2. Development. Do a separate sketch paying careful attention to important registral connections.

3. Develop a middleground sketch through the development section. This movement is an example of our prototype d (minor key).

NOTES

1. An analysis of this movement was published in an earlier article by this author, "The Initial Movements of Mozart's Piano Sonatas K. 280 and K. 332: Some Striking Similarities," *Integral* 8 (1994), 125–146.

2. For a more detailed discussion of this passage, see Examples 4.3 and 4.4 and the accompanying discussion.

3. This variant is described by Ernst Oster in an extended footnote to his English translation of *Free Composition* (Longman, 1979), p. 139.

4. An analysis of this movement is contained in David Beach and Ryan McClelland, *Analysis of 18th- and 19th-Century Musical Works in the Classical Tradition* (Routledge, 2012), 211–231.

9 Sonata Form 2

Motivic Development

Introduction

An interesting exercise for an instructor is to ask the members of a music analysis class to define the term "motive". Traditionally, the term has referred to a short musical figure, often having a recognizable rhythmic pattern that is repeated and developed in the course of a musical composition. Motivic repetition and transformation are fundamental tools of Western art music, and our understanding of the music of a particular composer—let's choose Beethoven as a prime example—depends in part on our recognition of this aspect of a composer's technique and of how this is represented in a particular composition. But it is also important for you to understand that the term "motive" has quite a different meaning within the context of Schenkerian analysis. For Schenker, the concept of motive is linked to his notion of structural levels. Once an idea is repeated at a deeper level of structure, it is no longer associated with a particular rhythmic articulation. What defines it as a motivic repetition is the particular succession of pitches, or, in the case of a transposition of the original idea, a particular succession of scale degrees. In essence, then, "motive" in this context is really a succession of pitches that can appear at different structural levels, not just at the surface. But I want to make it clear that this conception does not deny the importance of our understanding of surface motivic manipulation any more than his ideas on structure and form deny the value of traditional formal analysis. They just deal with different aspects of musical organization.

Schenker's concept of motive and motivic repetition at different structural levels is explained in detail in an excellent article by Charles Burkhart.[1] Of the several examples he cites, the most spectacular is Schenker's analysis of the first movement from Beethoven's Piano Sonata Op. 2, No. 1, in which he shows that the melodic content of the opening phrase, the rising third A♭5-B♭5-C6 followed by the descending sixth C6-E♮5, becomes the framework for the entire development section leading to the dominant. In this text, we have already encountered several examples of motivic parallelism (Schenker's term), beginning with our brief examination of excerpts from Mozart's Piano Sonata in B♭, K. 333 in Chapters 1 and 2, where the motivic associations between the opening ideas of the first and third movements as well as the entire development section of the former were noted. We have also noted clear motivic associations between the first and third movements of Mozart's Piano Sonata in F, K. 280, as well as parallels within each of these movements in Chapter 8. The repetitions of a descending fourth at multiple levels in the third movement provide a particularly clear demonstration of what I have called a pitch motive. See Examples 8.8 and 8.9. The descending fourth also plays a crucial role in the second movement of this same sonata—see Examples 7.2–7.6.

Analyses

Mozart, String Quartet in F, K. 590 (I), Excerpts

Though I have recently published an article dealing in part with motivic enlargement in Mozart's String Quartet in F, K. 590, one of the ideas expressed in that article is worth repeating here.[2] The opening phrase of the first movement of this work with analytic overlay is provided in Example 9.1. The score of the development section of the same movement is provided in Example 9.2 and a graph of its voice-leading structure in Example 9.3.

EXAMPLE 9.1 Mozart, String Quartet K. 590 (I), 1–8

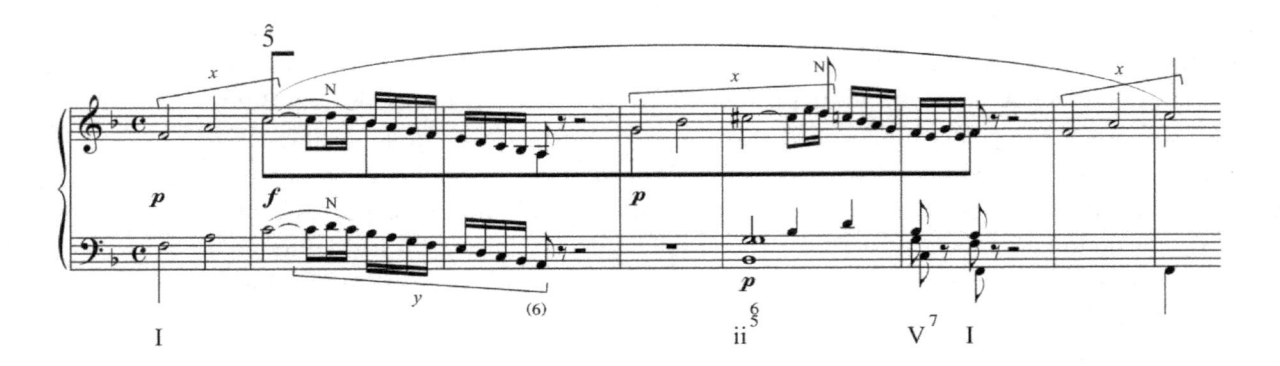

I have identified two motivic ideas in the opening phrase, both of which are developed in the course of the movement: the ascending arpeggiation of the tonic triad stated by all four instruments as the opening gesture (x), and the dramatic descending tenth, stated *forte*, immediately following (y). A subcomponent of this second gesture is the decoration of $\hat{5}$ by its upper neighbor, an idea that is immediately developed by the statement of motive x a step higher in measures 4–5 and then answered at the original pitch level at the beginning of the next phrase (measures 7–8). Note the emphasis given to D5, the neighbor note, in measure 5 by the accented passing tone C♯5. This detail also becomes an important element later in the movement. Finally, note the descending fifth over the course of this initial phrase, which is a motion to an inner voice prolonging $\hat{5}$: C5 (measure 2)-B♭4/B♭3 (measures 2–3)-A3 (measure 3)-G4 (measure 4)-F4 (measure 6).

As shown in Example 9.2, the repeat of the exposition is introduced by the chromatic motion to the upper neighbor of the primary tone (C5-C♯5-D5), which is answered by motive x at the return. As we progress into the development, this same motion leads to an inverted statement of motive x from this same D5. The following passage, in which a sense of tonal direction is temporarily suspended, leads eventually to the A major chord (III♯) in

EXAMPLE 9.2 Mozart, String Quartet K. 590 (I), 73–113

EXAMPLE **9.2** *continued*

measures 90–93. This prepares a descending fifth sequence involving imitative statements of motive y. The goal of this sequence is the subdominant harmony in measure 100, at which point the sequence changes to a series of 5–6 motions above an ascending step progression in the bass leading to G (V of V) and then V, above which successive statements of y inverted arpeggiate to C6 in measure 103. This C6 introduces the seventh of the dominant while the lower octave prepares the return to the beginning in the original register.

Let's return our attention to the opening measures and for a moment think like a composer. How might we utilize the opening phrase to become the framework for the entire development section? Since the development section prolongs the dominant, the first change must be to eliminate the initial tonic and begin with the dramatic gesture from C— that is, motive y. The remaining bass line of these opening measures (without the initial tonic) consists of the descending tenth (compound third) C-B♭-A and then a return through B♭ to C (V⁷) leading to F(I). If we now look at the middleground structure of the development section in relation to its larger context, we see that it follows precisely this same path. The first part of the development section involves an expanded statement of motive y leading to III♯. The passing tone B♭ within this gesture is temporarily abandoned beginning in measure 83, but picked up again in measure 89, now supporting an augmented sixth chord, which resolves to III♯. Though the bass has not descended the entire tenth of motive y, it spans the same interval. As already noted, the next part of the development section is a sequence by descending fifths involving imitative statements of motive y. The goal of this sequence is the subdominant harmony (B♭ bass), at which point there is a change of surface design and a second sequence, an ascending sequence, leading to the dominant. In short, the notes of the bass line from the opening phrase become the middleground bass progression within the larger prolongation of the dominant spanning the entire development section. The first part of this progression, the motion to III♯, is a clear example of motivic enlargement.

I will keep my comments about the melodic structure of the development section brief, since the main purpose of this example is to demonstrate motivic expansion. The second theme of the exposition involves a descending fifth prolonging $\hat{2}$, which is represented in Example 9.3 by the vertical interval of a fifth prior to the development. Scale degree 2 is subsequently prolonged by a motion to the seventh of the dominant, where the passing tone A5 (measure 94) is provided consonant support by III♯. The seventh, B♭5, is not resolved in that register until several measures later, but in the immediate context may be understood to resolve to A4 as part of motive x. Meanwhile, it is the inner voice—which had introduced the development section by the motion C5-C♯5-D5 and the following inverted statement of motive x—that prepares the restatement of $\hat{5}$ by way of the answering statement of that motive.

Beethoven, Piano Sonata Op. 110 (I)[3]

The first movement of Beethoven's Piano Sonata Op. 110 provides a fascinating study of motivic development. The formal design of the movement is sonata form, though different in some respects from the model we find in Haydn's and Mozart's music or for that matter in early Beethoven. For one thing, there is no repeat of the exposition. There are distinct ideas and themes, but once we examine them closely, we will see that they are all derived from a single pitch motive, suggesting that the compositional process is one

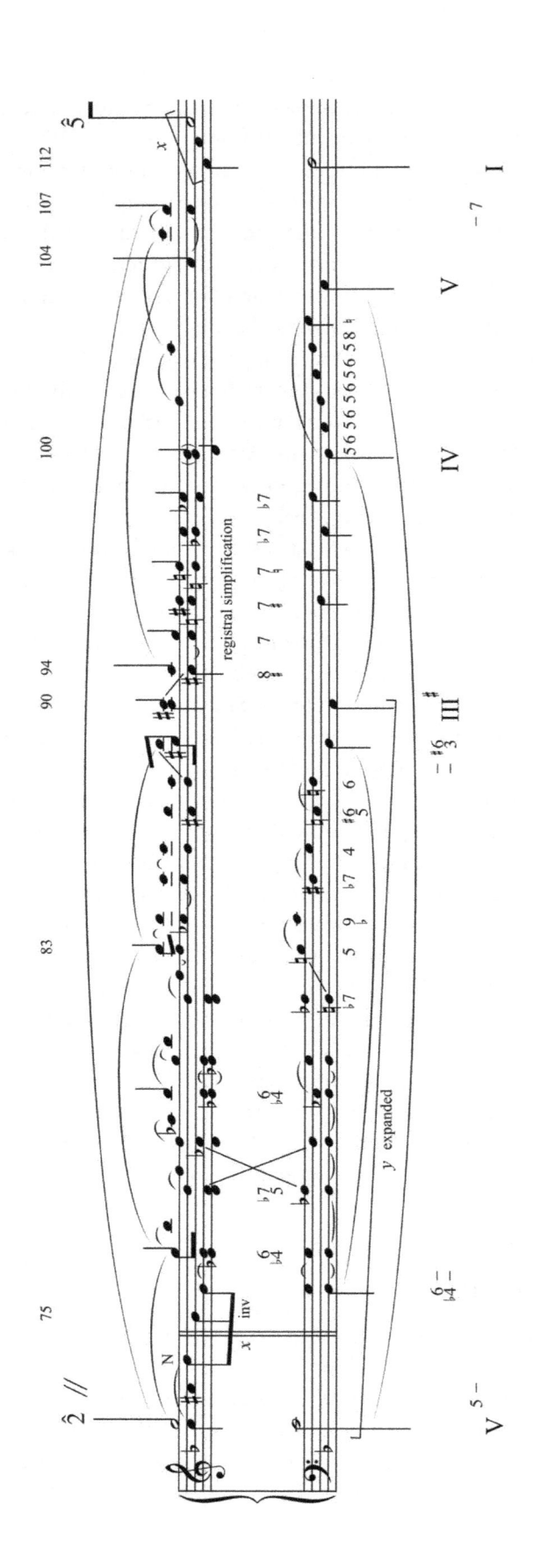

EXAMPLE 9.3 Graph of K. 590 (I), 73–113

of continual variation within the framework of sonata form. A score of the movement with formal designations is provided in Example 9.4, and a separate chart of the form is provided in Figure 9.1. This chart shows that the movement follows a traditional path until the recapitulation, where Beethoven surprises us with an unexpected digression prolonging the subdominant.

A graph of themes 1a and 1b plus the following transition is provided in Example 9.5, which is arranged so one can see the correspondence between 1a and 1b. The initial idea (1a) opens with an ascending melodic motion of the third C5-D♭5-E♭5 progressing in parallel tenths with the bass, where the first two notes are prolonged locally by voice exchanges between the outer voices. This is followed by a third voice exchange between D♭5/F and F5/D♭ moving the top voice to the upper neighbor note of E♭5. From there the line descends back to C5 supported by I via E♭5 and D♭5. The chromatic passing tone D♮5 is also an important aural marker that makes this idea immediately recognizable in its repetitions. Beethoven's written-out embellishment of the trill on D♭5 is also significant in that it summarizes the melodic content of the phrase: an initial ascending third, C5-D♭5-E♭5, answered by a third a step higher, D♭5-E♭5-F5, and the descending third back to C5, E♭5-

EXPOSITION			
1–5	theme 1a		I (A♭)
5–12	theme 1b		I
12–20	transition		
20–28	2 prefix (2p)	E♭: IV – V – I	V
28–38	theme 2		V
DEVELOPMENT			
40–55		vi – IV – ii – V	V
RECAPITULATION			
56–62	theme 1a extended		I
63–70	theme 1b		IV
70–76	transition		(♭VI)
76–78	2 prefix (2p)		(IV of ♭VI)
79–87	2 prefix (2p)		IV – V
87–96	theme 2		I
97–105	closing phrase		I
105–111	transition		I
111–116	final reference to motive		I

FIGURE 9.1 Formal Plan of Beethoven's Op. 110 (I)

EXAMPLE 9.4 Beethoven, Piano Sonata Op. 110 (I)

EXAMPLE 9.4 *continued*

EXAMPLE 9.4 *continued*

EXAMPLE 9.4 *continued*

EXAMPLE **9.4** *continued*

EXAMPLE 9.4 *continued*

EXAMPLE 9.4 *continued*

Db5-C5. I have identified the primary tone as C5 ($\hat{3}$) and, as we shall see, the movement is an example of our prototype b. I have identified the covering line Eb5-F5-Eb5-Db5-C5 as the pitch motive that is developed over the course of the movement.

On the surface, the idea immediately following (theme 1b) offers a contrast to the opening idea in that it consists of a melody plus accompaniment as opposed to the more uniform rhythmic character among the parts in the opening measures. But once we look (and listen!) more carefully, we realize that this idea is derived from the preceding one. The bass opens with the same third as before but an octave higher, above which the top two parts progress much as in measures 1–3, except they are inverted. That is, the original inner voice has been transposed an octave, placing it temporarily above the main voice on C5. This inner line progresses from C5 to Eb5, while the top part decorates Ab5 by a double neighbor-note figure. In the following measure, which consists of a secondary dominant of the following subdominant harmony, the position of the top two parts is inverted once again, placing Eb6 on top. At this point, a slightly varied though clearly recognizable statement of the motive emerges, complete with the voice exchange between the outer voices of the subdominant harmony. This statement of the motive is complete, though the resolution of the dissonant Db6 is transferred to an inner voice on the downbeat of measure 12.

At first the transition appears as if it might be difficult to sketch, but in fact it is based on a common tonal pattern involving exchange of neighboring and passing functions that *look* complex because of the octave changes. However, once we "normalize" octave position, the opening five measures may be represented as shown in Example 9.5. Though I have not marked it as such, the melodic progression in the top part of these measures is the inversion of our motive: Ab5-G5-Ab5-Bb5-C6. From measure 16 to measure 20 this top voice ascends an octave from C6 to C7, internal to which there are two voice exchanges C6/Ab3 to Ab5/C3 to C7/Ab4. The controlling harmony is Ab, but because of the augmented sixth chord

Example 9.5 Graph of Op. 110 (I), 1–20

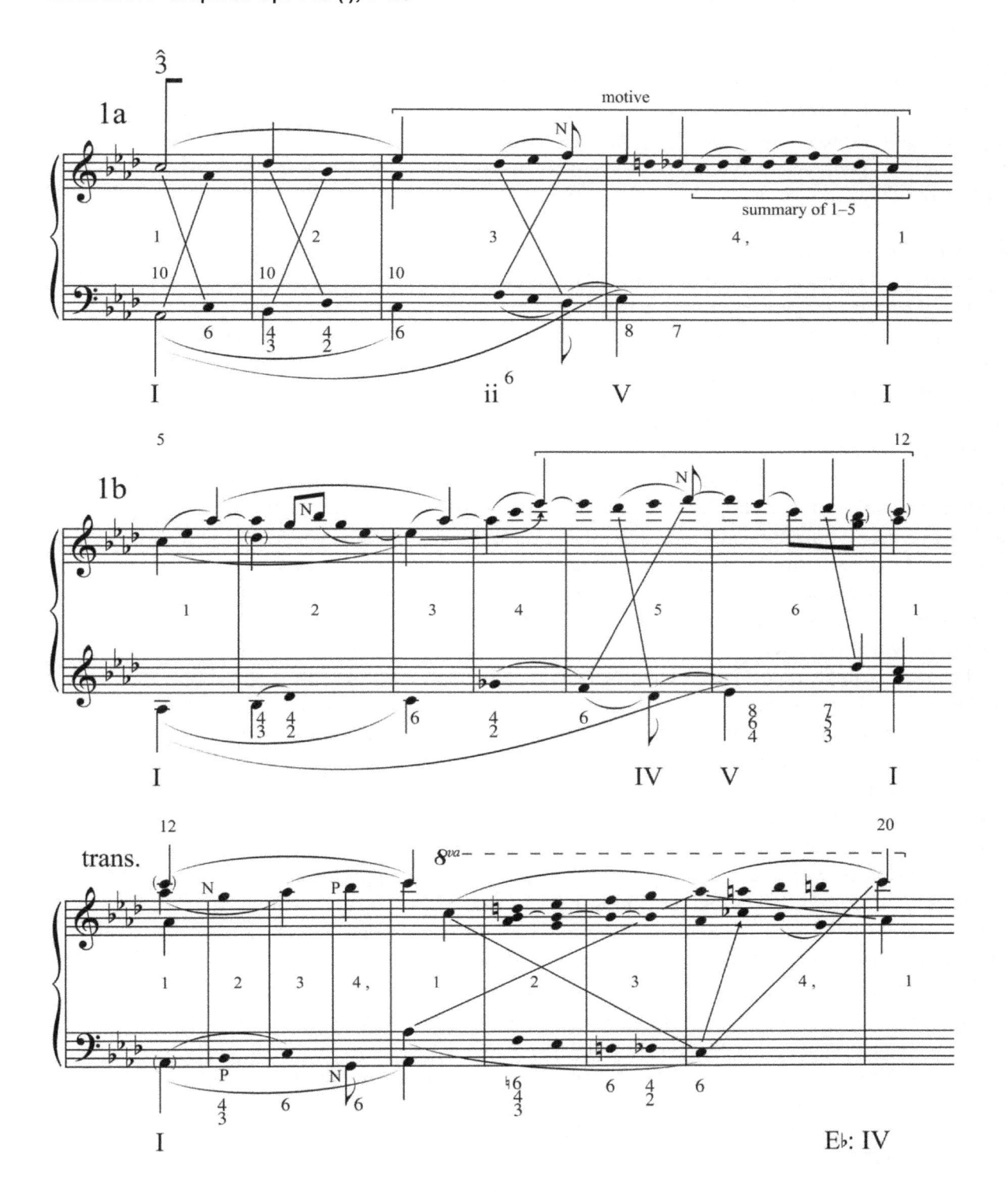

in measure 19, we hear the implied chord in measure 20 as the subdominant in the key of the dominant rather than tonic.

Before progressing further, we should stop for a moment to consider ways in which Beethoven might treat this motive. Here I have the advantage of hindsight. He might state only parts of it—for example, $\hat{6}$ to $\hat{5}$ or $\hat{6}$ $\hat{5}$ $\hat{4}$ $\hat{3}$. Here I am using scale degree designations in a local (non-fundamental) meaning rather than pitches, since we are now headed into the second tonal area where the motive will appear transposed. Second, Beethoven might (and does!) use registral connections—in the extreme upper register—to associate notes that are not in close proximity, while he might make large leaps between events that are close together without disturbing our ability to grasp their meaning. With these thoughts in mind, we are prepared to tackle the next portion of the movement.

The short idea in measures 20–21, which I have labeled 2 prefix (2p), opens with the same harmonic interval as the beginning, C/A♭. In an abstract sense, this idea is related to our motive in that its melodic succession C7-B♭6-A♭6-(B♭6-A♭6)-G6 is $\hat{6}$ $\hat{5}$ $\hat{4}$ $\hat{3}$ in the key of the dominant. I have given considerable thought to finding the most appropriate label for this idea, which plays an important role here, but particularly so in the recapitulation. On the one hand, this is no longer part of the transition, but on the other hand, we have not yet arrived at the new key. It functions really as a prefix to the second theme beginning in measure 28. As shown in Example 9.6, the motion C7-B♭6 of measures 20–21 anticipates the longer-range connection *in the same register* between C7 (measure 20) and B♭6 ($\hat{2}$) eight measures later. Internal to this longer-range connection this prefix idea in measures 20–21 is repeated an octave lower in embellished form followed by a passage connecting the two registers. Harmonically this passage establishes the new tonic. Note the unfolding in the bass D♮-A♭ (V), which is answered by G-E♭ (I). This takes us to the second tonal area and $\hat{2}$.

Theme 2 is, in fact, our motive transposed to the dominant. Following B♭6, the right-hand part skips down to G4 (an inner voice), initiating a series of rising gestures within the local tonic harmony, the first involving a voice exchange with the bass. The third rising scale segment reaches C7, the upper neighbor of B♭6 from measure 28, harmonized by ii$^{6}_{5}$. This is followed immediately by a skip to B♭4 and completion of the motive, including the chromatic passing tone (A♮4) that makes the association to the original statement of the motive even clearer. So, in this statement, the initial part, the $\hat{5}$ $\hat{6}$ $\hat{5}$ neighbor-note motion, is drawn out over four measures, with the first two notes stated in the extreme upper register, and the remainder, $\hat{5}$ $\hat{4}$ $\hat{3}$, in the lower register. This is followed immediately by the reintroduction of the upper neighbor note C6 by E♭6-D♮6-D♭6, a clear reference to measure 4, which is followed by a descending scale leading to B♭4 and completion of this partial statement of the motive on the downbeat of measure 35. The continuation leads to E♭4 on the downbeat of measure 36, completing by implication the descending fifth of the second tonal area. This is followed by an embellished ascending arpeggiation of the local tonic triad terminating at E♭6, the point of departure for the statement in octaves of the descending third E♭-D♭-C leading to the development. Again the reference to the opening idea could not be much clearer.

A graph of the development section is provided in Example 9.7. The opening segment suggests a dual interpretation. On the one hand, if we look just at measures 40–43 over the C pedal as a closed unit, it seems that the third C6 over A♭5 is prolonged by its upper and lower neighbors. But once we consider these measures in relation to their continuation, we hear B♭5 as passing to A♭5 on the downbeat of measure 44. This second interpretation is certainly

EXAMPLE 9.6 Graph of Op. 110 (I), 20–38

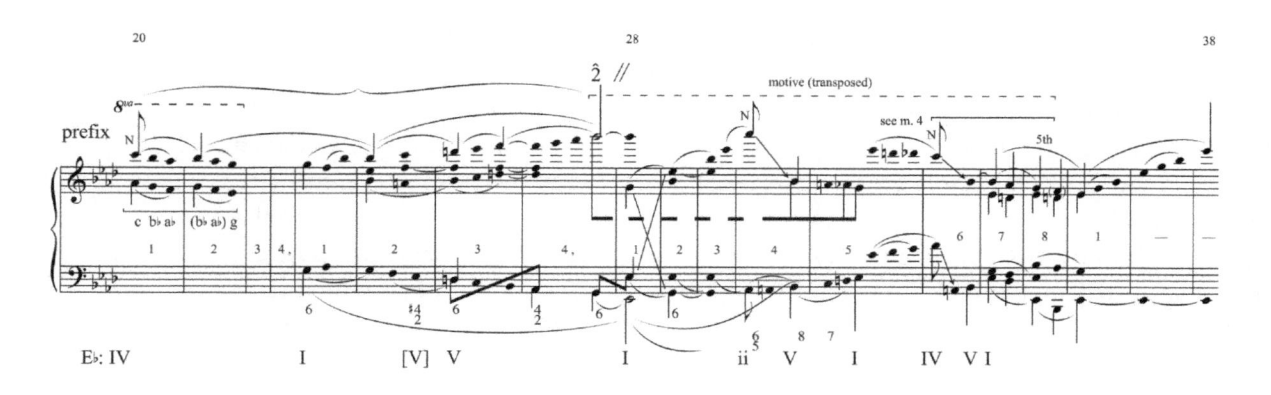

EXAMPLE 9.7 Graph of Op. 110 (I), 38–56

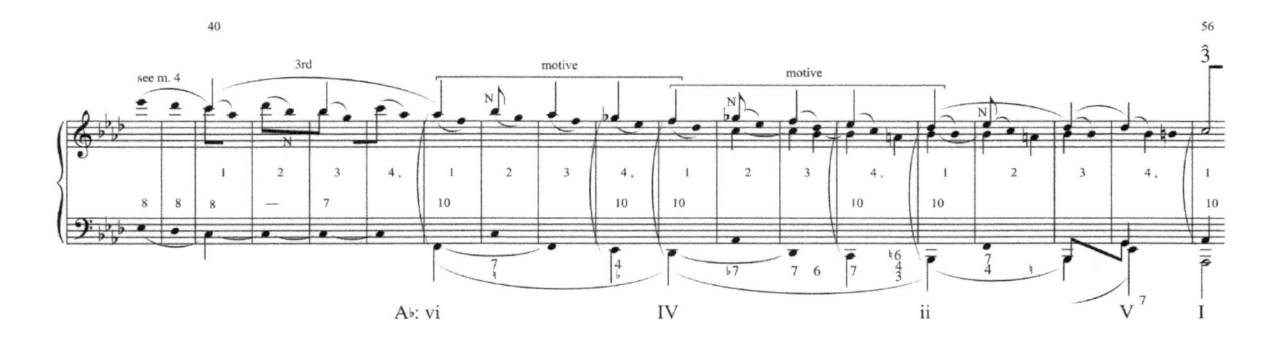

EXAMPLE 9.8 Middleground graph of Op. 110 (I), 1–56

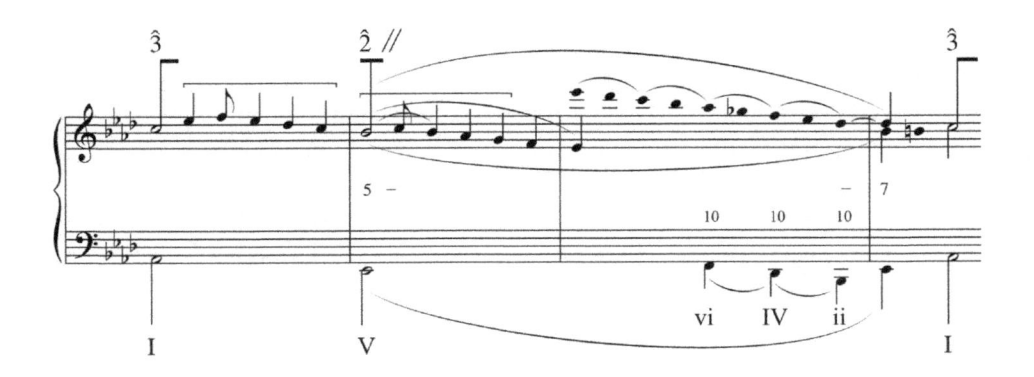

the overriding one. Arrival at A♭5, supported by an F minor harmony (vi), initiates two overlapping statements of the motive: A♭5–B♭5–A♭5–G♭5–F5 (vi) and F5–G♭5–F5–E♭5–D♭5 (IV). What begins as a third statement is altered to maintain D♭5 above B♭4 as the harmony changes from ii to V⁷ to lead to C5 ($\hat{3}$) and tonic harmony.

A brief overview of the movement to m. 56 is provided in Example 9.8. Both the tonic and dominant areas are shown to contain statements of the motive, the second one extended to local closure in V. This is followed by a series of descending thirds leading eventually to D♭5. Overall, then, the prolongation of the dominant involves a motion from the fifth to the seventh (5–7) to reintroduce the primary tone at the beginning of the recapitulation. At the same time, the trill on B♭4 and B♮4 in measure 55 draws our attention back to this important pitch. If we now look back over the movement to this point, we will see that the motive in its various guises has been present almost continuously throughout.

A middleground sketch of the recapitulation is provided in Example 9.9. The statement of 1a begins as it did in the first few measures of the movement, with the obvious change of accompaniment pattern to the thirty-second notes previously employed only with the transition passage. However, as the motive begins its descent back to C5, the resolution of D♭5 is transferred to the bass while the right-hand part leads to A♭5 on the downbeat of the fifth measure, thereby inverting their expected positions. This change leads to an extension of the phrase, in which the dotted rhythmic pattern of the theme is taken by the left-hand while the right-hand part repeats A♭ in two registers, A♭5 and A♭6, descending eventually through G♭5 to F5 as the harmony leads to the subdominant on the downbeat of measure 63. A motion to the subdominant at this point is most significant, since it would allow Beethoven to transpose the remainder of the exposition to end eventually on the tonic.[4] With an octave adjustment, this would have led him to measure 79. But Beethoven does not take the easy path; he has something else in mind.

Theme 1b begins as before, here with F5, the upper neighbor of E♭5, as the main note covered by D♭6, but in the fifth measure Beethoven makes a beautiful enharmonic change (D♭ becomes C♯), from which point the top voice descends a fourth to G♯5 supported by an E major chord in measure 70. We hear E major as ♭VI (F♭), but I have followed Beethoven's notation for ease in reading. I have placed a bracket above the descending fourth C#6 – B#5 – A#5 – G#5 ($\hat{6}\,\hat{5}\,\hat{4}\,\hat{3}$ in E) to indicate its association with the motive, and likewise with the inverted form leading back to C♯6 in measure 76, the goal of the transition passage. The A major chord in measure 76 is the subdominant in E (F♭). The idea stated here is the prefix to the second theme, but not in the correct key, leaving Beethoven the task of finding a way to get back to the subdominant. This leads to the abrupt transition in measures 77–78, a potentially tricky place for the performer to execute convincingly. The voice leading is interesting here. The top voice leads from C♯6 in measure 76 through E♭6 (measure 78) to F6 (measure 79), while the inner voice descends chromatically from G♯5 through G♮5 to F5 over a chromatic change in the bass. This is a tricky spot, and you should examine the voice leading carefully.

So Beethoven has taken a circuitous route to get exactly where he could have gotten much easier. Why? I'm not sure we can answer this question definitively, but a possible explanation has to do with the motive. Beethoven's digression begins from measure 63 and the subdominant harmony supporting F5 and D♭6 above it. Following the enharmonic change and the subsequent transition, we end up at measure 76 on C♯6 (=D♭6) over A♮ for

EXAMPLE 9.9 Graph of Op. 110 (I), 56–116

a statement of the prefix idea, which, following the brief transition, is then repeated at the "correct" pitch level three measures later. What the repetition seems to articulate within the prolonged subdominant harmony is the motion from D♭6 to F6, that portion of the motive originally occurring in voice exchange with the bass. Based on our understanding of the following material from our examination of the exposition, we can predict that this F6 will lead to E♭6 at the outset of theme 2 in the tonic key. Indeed, this is what follows. What I am suggesting is that a possible explanation for Beethoven's interesting digression is expansion of a part of the motive that had so far not been developed. Is it a coincidence that the voice exchange of measure 3 is replaced by parallel motion between the outer voices at the equivalent spot in the recapitulation (measure 58)?

I will not describe in detail the voice leading of the next few measures—the prefix to theme 2 and theme 2 itself—since we have dealt with this material earlier. However, it is important for you to note that statements of the motive will now be at the original pitch level since we are now back in the tonic key. The F6-E♭6 motion of the prefix in measures 79–80 foreshadows the connection between these same two pitches in the same register over a span of eight measures leading to theme 2, which consists of two consecutive statements of the motive, the second one extended through an implied B♭4 to local closure in measure 95. The continuing sixteenth-note motion and displacement of notes of the tonic triad carry us beyond this point to a closing phrase, where Beethoven once again takes advantage of the extreme upper register by restating B♭6 three times, almost insistently, over E♭6, which is first prolonged by its lower neighbor D♮6, and then by its upper neighbor F6, at which point there is a sudden change in surface articulation. This is a fascinating spot. The left-hand part has already begun a statement of the motive, which is marked in the graph, and now the right-hand part follows in quasi-stretto fashion. Note the isolation of the E♭6-F6-E♭6 neighboring portion of the motive in the upper register as had happened before. This is followed by a leap down to E♭5 and continuation of the motive in the original octave. Beethoven's harmonization of C5, the final note of the motive, by an F minor chord (vi) precludes writing B♭4 ($\hat{2}$) over the following dominant chord. However, I hear closure on the downbeat of measure 105, so I have added the B♭4 in parentheses over the preceding dominant. We have heard B♭ stated three times in the upper register in measures 97–99, but it is never stated in this lower octave.

The transition beginning in measure 105 leads to a final partial statement of the motive in measures 111–115. The statement begins on the upper neighbor F5, harmonized by the subdominant. Following a resolution of F5 to E♭5, the upper neighbor is restated again on the downbeat of measure 113. As shown in the graph, the C5 on the downbeat of measure 114 may be considered the resolution of an inner voice D♭5 from the preceding measure. And though the following D♭5 is introduced as a neighbor note to C5, I believe we also hear it as passing down from the E♭5 of the previous measure to C5 and tonic harmony to end the movement. Do not confuse this C5 as a note of the fundamental line, which has already reached its goal. While it might be explained as the product of a final reference to the motive, its practical function is to prepare the first note of the second movement. Also significant here is the employment of the chromatic passing tone F♭, a reference to the earlier digression to ♭VI, but also possibly a foreshadowing of the beautiful *arioso dolente* in A♭ minor (with a Dorian key signature requiring the written flat before each F) that leads to the fugue.

SUGGESTED ASSIGNMENT

Since this chapter has dealt largely with motivic repetition from a Schenkerian perspective, I suggest you analyze the *Arioso* from this same sonata, paying particular attention to how Beethoven weaves statements of this same motive into the fabric. Though the *Arioso* is an introduction to the fugue, you may treat it as a separate unit, in which case you should read the local primary tone as $\hat{5}$. The *Arioso* consists of four phrases. Here are some clues, comments and two questions.

1. Phrase 1: the motive is in the top part.

2. Phrase 2: there is a partial transposed statement covering the main line.

3. Phrase 3: prolongs the upper neighbor.

4. Phrase 4: the main voice is moved to an inner voice to prepare for the statement of the fugue subject.

Two questions:
1. Can the entire *Arioso* be explained as a giant statement of the motive?

2. How is the fugue subject related to the motive?

NOTES

1. Charles Burkhart, "Schenker's 'Motivic Parallelisms'," *Journal of Music Theory* 22/2 (1978), 145–175.

2. David Beach, "Motivic Enlargement and Phrase Expansion: Illustrations From Two Works by Mozart," *Journal of Schenkerian Studies* 3 (2008), 1–17.

3. An analysis of this movement by this author was published in *Integral* 1(1987), 1–29.

4. The composer must always do some rewriting in the recapitulation to end in the tonic. One solution is to rewrite the transition to the second theme, but another is to modulate to the subdominant and from there to progress up a fifth to the tonic, reproducing the tonal relationship from the exposition.

10 Music and Text

In this chapter we will examine vocal works—an aria and three songs—by four different composers: Mozart, Schubert, Schumann and Brahms. While our primary concern here is understanding musical structure from a Schenkerian perspective, we must also deal with the text, since the music is really an interpretation of the text. So, with each work we examine, we will first consider the text, and then the music, and in our analysis of the music we will discuss not only the tonal structure but also how it enhances and musically interprets the text. In some instances, we are talking about details—word painting, for example—but in other instances the representation of more abstract concepts, such as musically representing hesitation or a question. In this regard, we must pay particular attention to the accompaniment and its relationship to the vocal line. The piano introduction not only sets the mood, often portraying features central to the text—for example, the horn call in Schumann's "Waldesgespräch"—but also frequently anticipates elements of the structure, such as the primary tone, as well as establishing the tonality. And the accompaniment occasionally plays a crucial role in the structure by completing a motion left incomplete in the vocal line.[1]

Analyses

Mozart, "Dies Bildnis ist bezaubernd schön", The Magic Flute (Schikaneder)

This aria occurs near the beginning of the opera, which opens with Prince Tamino being pursued by a giant serpent. Tamino faints, but his life is spared by the three ladies, servants of the Queen of the Night, who slay the beast. Tamino eventually awakens to find himself miraculously still alive, whereupon he encounters the bird catcher Papageno, who is more than willing to accept credit for killing the serpent, with his bare hands, no less! Enter the three ladies, who remonstrate Papageno for this and other lies, and they deliver to Tamino a portrait of the Queen's beautiful daughter. Tamino is immediately enchanted.

Dies Bildnis ist bezaubernd schön,	This portrait is enchantingly beautiful
wie noch kein Auge je gesehen!	as no eye has ever seen!
Ich fühl'es, ich fühl'es	I feel it, I feel it
wie Göttesbild mein Herz mit neuer Regung füllt.	how this image fills my heart with new emotion.

Dies Etwas kann ich zwar nicht nennen,	I cannot put a name to this thing,
doch fühl'ichs hier wie Feuer brennen.	Yet I feel it burning here like fire.
Soll die Empfindung Liebe sein?	Could this sensation be love?
Ja, Ja! Die Liebe ist allein!	Yes, yes, it can only be love!
O wenn ich sie nur finden könnte!	Oh, if only I could find her!
O wenn sie doch schon vor mir stünde!	Oh, if she but stood before me now!
Ich würde, würde, warm und rein—	I would, would, warm and chastely—
was würde ich?	what would I do?
Ich würde sie voll Entzükken an diesen	Rapturously I would press her to
heissen Busen drücken,	this ardent breast,
und ewig wäre sie dann mein.	and then she would be mine forever.

A significant feature of Mozart's setting of this text is his repetition of certain words and phrases to create emphasis, and we must consider the possible effects of these repetitions on the phrase structure. In some instances, they signal a phrase expansion, but in other cases, their setting is integral to the phrase. So how can we tell the difference? When a text repetition occurs in conjunction with an exact or a varied repetition of the same music, it is safe to assume it is part of an expansion, whether external or internal, depending on the circumstances. However, the matter is by no means as clear when the text repetition occurs with a new musical setting. In this case, we must check to see if the musical setting is necessary to the tonal progression of the phrase. If it is, then the answer is no, but if it can be omitted without disturbing the progress of the phrase, the answer is most certainly yes.

The aria is divided into three expanded phrases, corresponding to the division of the text given above. These phrases are indicated by Roman numerals on Example 10.1, an annotated copy of the piano-vocal score, and on Example 10.2, a detailed graph of the three phrases. The first, which ends with a perfect authentic cadence in measure 15, is expanded externally by a two-measure introduction and internally by Mozart's setting of the initial statement of the fourth line of the first verse, "mein Herz mit neuer Regung füllt".

The opening orchestral introduction states the arpeggiation B♭4-E♭5-G5 as the voice enters with the initial leap to G5 falling on the downbeat on measure 3. Subsequent events will confirm this pitch, G5, as the primary tone ($\hat{3}$). As shown in Example 10.2, the opening four measures of the vocal part consist of two separate strands—that is, a compound melody. Following the initial leap to G5, the melody descends a sixth back to B♭4, which then progresses by step to A♭4 over a change of harmony. This is followed by a leap up to F5 and then a descent back to A♭4, which then progresses by step to G4 over the return to tonic harmony. The final note in this progression, E♭5, follows on the last eighth note of the same measure. The result is a progression in parallel sixths, G5-F5-E♭5 over B♭4-A♭4-G4. This is followed by a two-measure setting of the repeated text "Ich fühl'es", in which the E♭5 is sustained above the incomplete neighbor-note progression C5-B♭4, harmonized by the progression IV-I⁶. This is followed by a leap of a seventh up to A♭5, the seventh of the dominant. Here we encounter our first internal phrase expansion. The signal to us that there is an expansion comes from the treatment of this dissonance, whose resolution does not follow *in the same register* until measure 13. Measures 10–12 could be omitted without

EXAMPLE 10.1 Mozart, "Dies Bildnis ist bezaubernd schön", *The Magic Flute*

EXAMPLE **10.1** *continued*

Example **10.1** *continued*

EXAMPLE **10.1** *continued*

EXAMPLE 10.2 Graph of the Mozart aria

EXAMPLE 10.2 continued

EXAMPLE 10.2 *continued*

disturbing the meaning of the text or the tonal progress of the phrase to its conclusion. In the immediate context from measure 9 to measure 10, the resolution of the seventh is transferred to the bass, indicated by the arrow. The other important feature of this three-measure expansion is the ascending fourth Bb4-Eb5, marked with a bracket because this idea, the stepwise ascent from scale degree 5 to 8, is important later on as a substitute for the more normal descent to closure.

The graph of this phrase shows the overall melodic motion as a descent from the primary tone to local closure in measure 15, where scale degree 2 is approached from a third above at the cadence. Internal to this overall motion $\hat{3}$ and tonic harmony are first prolonged by the descending third of measures 3–6 and then by the neighbor-note motion G5–Ab5–G5 of measures 3–13. The hypermeter is shown initially to be duple, an outgrowth of the two-measure introduction, changing to quadruple only later in conjunction with the expansion. The metric organization of these seven measures is shown as: 1 (2 3 4) 2 3 4.

The second phrase is written in the key of the dominant, and, as before, the vocal entrance is preceded by a two-measure orchestral introduction, this time featuring the clarinets. The main feature of this introduction is the descending third F5-Eb5-D5, an idea that is subsequently repeated twice by the voice as settings for the rhymed lines "Dies Etwas kann ich zwar nicht nennen" and "doch fühl'ich's hier wie Feuer brennen". The following line of the text, "Soll die Empfindung Liebe sein?", is then repeated, but to different music, so this does not signal a phrase expansion; rather, there is a clear continuation of the established duple hypermeter. The first statement of this repeated question progresses from the inner voice tone Bb4 back to F5 before resolving to Eb5. Note the orchestral flourish here as Tamino mentions the word "love" for the first time. The repetition begins from the upper neighbor of F5, G5, and by implication this G5 would lead back to F5 as the vocal line settles on C5 in measure 25. However, Mozart will save F5 until two measures later for the statement of "Ja". ·

The winds enter for a brief interlude leading from this C5 back to F5. This one measure of interlude is heard as a hypermetric downbeat in the established pattern, and the next measure has been interpreted as a weak measure despite Tamino's sudden triumphant interjection of "Ja, ja".[2] Here there is a clear re-articulation of F5 and tonic harmony (I⁶) in the local key. The large slurs in the graph show the prolongation of F5 ($\hat{2}$) and dominant harmony in the original key from the beginning of the phrase to this point (measure 27). Here we encounter the second instance of phrase expansion involving the repetition of text. As shown in Example 10.2, the main feature of this passage leading to the cadence in measure 34 is the descending fifth F5-Bb4, where D5 and C5—the 6 and 5 of the cadential six-four to five-three—are replaced by the ascent to Bb4 from below, marked on the graph with a bracket. This is the idea first introduced as part of the expansion of the first phrase. As occurred in that initial phrase, the final metric unit of this one is an expanded group of four, but here the insertion itself is four rather than three measures in length. The first two measures of the expansion are shown to be 3 and 4 in the established pattern, the last being reinterpreted as 1 in the continuation.

The final measure of the second phrase (measure 34) is the first measure of the following two-measure orchestral interlude introducing the final phrase. Once again this brief interlude sets the pattern for the continuation with the soaring reach up to Bb5, followed by the staggering Lombardic rhythm of the following descent, representing, it would seem, the conflict between Tamino's soaring emotions and his uncertainty and ensuing hesitation. This is the passage where Tamino speculates about what he would do if this beautiful woman were here before him. The vocal line twice soars up to A♭5, the seventh of the dominant, but as his uncertainty grows the vocal line becomes more fragmented as the accompaniment focuses entirely on the Lombardic rhythmic pattern. Finally, as Tamino asks himself what he would do if she were here, everything stops for a measure of silence, the final hesitation before he musters his courage and hesitantly at first begins to tell us what he would do. These ten measures consist of a single harmony, V⁷; the seventh, A♭5, which is an extension of F5 ($\hat{2}$), predicts the return to G5 ($\hat{3}$). There is certainly a sense of relief when this extended dominant resolves to the tonic in measure 45, though the relief is only partial as the vocal line and accompaniment vie for supremacy in the following measures until Tamino tells us several times that once he has embraced her she would be his forever. The status of this return to tonic harmony in measures 45–48 is not entirely clear. The vocal line is clearly grounded in tonic harmony, but the accompaniment refuses to relinquish the A♭5, in essence denying the expected return to $\hat{3}$. This creates an interesting problem of how best to represent what Mozart is doing here in a musical graph. Because of the tonic harmony, the A♭5 is now locally the upper neighbor of G5, but this G5 is weakly stated. Mozart is saving the definitive return to G5 ($\hat{3}$) until measure 55. My solution to this notational dilemma is to show a return to G5 in measure 45, but only at a lower structural level. This seems a reasonable compromise as a way to represent a return that nevertheless maintains some of the tension, saving the stronger return to $\hat{3}$ until several measures later.

The four-measure tonic return of measures 45–48 leads to measure 49, where voice and accompaniment come together. This measure is heard as a hypermetric downbeat and it leads to the cadential progression ii⁶-V⁷. The text here is "und ewig wäre sie dann mein", which is repeated not once but four times, extending the phrase and avoiding closure until the downbeat of measure 61. Initially, we are faced with the same situation as occurred in the first phrase—namely, that the resolution of A♭5, first supported by ii in measure 50 and then by the dominant in measure 51, does not resolve *in the same register* until measure 55. The intervening three measures are the initial part of the expansion. Measures 55–56 are now the fourth and fifth measures of this expanded six-measure unit. Twice in the following measures closure is avoided by restating G5 in place of the expected E♭5 and tonic harmony, which finally comes on the downbeat of measure 61. This is the second part of the expansion of the underlying six-measure unit to thirteen measures as follows: 1 2 3 (4 5 6) 4 5 (4 5, 4 5) 6. This aria could, in fact, be performed omitting this and all other passages enclosed in parentheses in Example 10.2 without disturbing the flow of the text or the tonal progress of the phrases, but the result would greatly diminish the effect of what Mozart has written. The purpose of our discussion of phrase expansion is to reveal the underlying structures and in doing so to reveal how Mozart has masterfully embellished them, thereby enhancing the meaning of the text.

Schubert, "Der Neugierige", Die schöne Müllerin (Müller)

One should read through all the poems in *Die schöne Müllerin* to understand the context for individual songs, but in a nutshell the collection chronicles the tragic infatuation of the young miller for the beautiful maid of the mill. In this song, he is asking the mill stream, his confidant but also ultimately the vehicle of his death, if the maid loves him. The poem, written in five stanzas, is divided into two parts, a division articulated in Schubert's setting by changes of meter, tempo and accompaniment pattern. In the first two verses, the young miller tells us whom he will not ask (the flowers and the stars) and why, and then he announces that he will ask the brook whether his heart has deceived him. When he addresses the mill stream in the second part, the accompaniment pattern changes appropriately to represent the running water. This second part has the form a–b–a′, where the middle verse is set in the character of a recitative. Though a hint of negativity is present from the very beginning, where the young man starts by telling us whom he will not ask, here in the second part real doubt begins to creep in with the introduction of D♮, first in verse 3 when he observes that the brook is "silent" and later in verse 5 that it is "strange". But in verse 4 the real meaning of D♮ becomes clear. It is the pitch that represents the dreaded word "nein" as the answer to his question, while F♯ represents "ja". Fearful as the young man may be of a negative answer, hope persists until the end.[3]

Ich frage keine Blume,	I ask no flowers,
ich frage keinen Stern	I ask no stars;
sie können mir alle nicht sagen	they cannot all tell me
was ich erfuhr so gern.	what I so dearly want to know.
Ich bin ja auch kein Gärtner,	I am no gardener,
die Sterne stehn zu hoch;	the stars are too far away;
mein Bächlein will ich fragen,	I will ask my little brook
ob mich mein Herz belog.	if my heart has deceived me.
O Bächlein meiner Liebe,	O brook of my love,
wie bist du heut so stumm!	how silent you are today!
will ja nur eines wissen,	I want to know only one thing,
ein Wörtchen um und um.	one little word one way or the other.
Ja, heisst das eine Wörtchen,	Yes is one word,
das andre heisset nein,	the other is no.
die beiden Wörtchen schliessen	These two words encompass
die ganze Welt mir ein.	the entire world for me.
O Bächlein meiner Liebe,	O brook of my love,
was bist du wunderlich!	how strange you are!
will's ja nicht weiter sagen,	I will not repeat it,
sag, Bächlein, lieb sie mich?	tell me, brook, does she love me?

The score of "Der Neugierige" is provided in Example 10.3, and Example 10.4 provides voice-leading graphs of the four-measure piano introduction and of verses 1 and 2. As indicated between the staves, the hypermeter is quadruple, which persists throughout, the only real exception coming in the last verse when the young miller finally asks his question and then immediately repeats it, the second time leading to closure. Prior to this point, phrases 2 and 4 are extended by the linkage passages in the accompaniment and phrase 3 by repetition of the final line of the verse. All three of these result in extensions of their respective phrases, while the expansion in the last verse is internal to the phrase.

The short piano introduction provides a wealth of information. First, note that the left-hand part anticipates the fundamental structure, including a passing reference to D♮, which plays such an important role in this song. Above this, the top part arpeggiates from B4 to G♯5, following which Schubert writes a rest, a gesture that some writers have suggested represents a question because of the way the G♯5 is left hanging. Certainly it is significant that its resolution to F♯5 is missing, since that pitch is the one that will come to represent a positive answer to the young miller's question. The bracket in the inner voice, where G♯4 is resolved, identifies this as an idea that is repeated later.

The vocal line opens with a linear ascent to the primary tone D♯5 (3̂), which is approached not only from below, shown by the beam, but also from above. This linear ascent will be repeated in the opening four measures of the second verse and in a modified form leading to D♮5 (♮3̂) at the beginning of verses 3 and 5. While this opening gesture may be relatively simple to interpret, the continuation is not. The harmony in the second half of measure 9 is a D♯ seventh chord in four-three position, and we might expect the Fx to lead to G♯ as root of a submediant harmony. Though this chord does not function in that capacity here, it will much later in the song at the crucial point where the young man asks his question.[4] Here the chord is passing, leading to the diminished seventh chord B♯-D♯-F♯-A, which does not resolve to a C♯ chord, but to an F♯ chord in first inversion. What appears to have taken place is the delayed entrance of B♯-C♯ in the bass in the next measure to imitate the same motion in the melodic part just before, which is indicated by the brackets and the arrow. A "normative" progression—but one in which the imitation is lost—is provided to the right in parentheses. Here the resolution of the diminished seventh chord, arrived at via a chromatic voice exchange, to the cadential six-four is standard. Returning now to the way Schubert has written these four measures, we can see that the "tenor" voice descends by step from B3 to F♯3, below which the B♯-C♯ is brought in to prepare the cadence in V. Above this the vocal line progresses from D♯5 (3̂) to C♯5 (2̂). This is a motion repeated several times in this song, raising the question of what level of the structure the interruption occurs. My opinion is that the only real interruption of the fundamental line might occur at the end of verse 4, so I have chosen to notate these other interruptions as belonging to more immediate levels in the structural hierarchy.

The first four measures of verse 2 are the same as verse 1, after which the descent from B3 in the "tenor" voice follows the same path as before: B3-F♯3. Here the bass added below is B♮-C♯, supporting ii in six-five position to V in the key of the dominant. Above this the top voice progresses once again from 3̂ to 2̂, this time with an elaborated transposition of the motion of the "alto" line from the introduction. This parallel is indicated in the graph by the brackets. This phrase is extended by the piano interlude preparing the second part of the song. This brief interlude prolongs the dominant, transforming it from stable to active by the addition of the seventh. Above this there is another statement of the idea from the piano introduction, this time in the upper register and resolving the G♯5, the note left unresolved

EXAMPLE **10.3** Schubert, "Der Neugierige", *Die schöne Müllerin*

EXAMPLE **10.3** *continued*

EXAMPLE 10.4 Graph of the Schubert song, verses 1 and 2

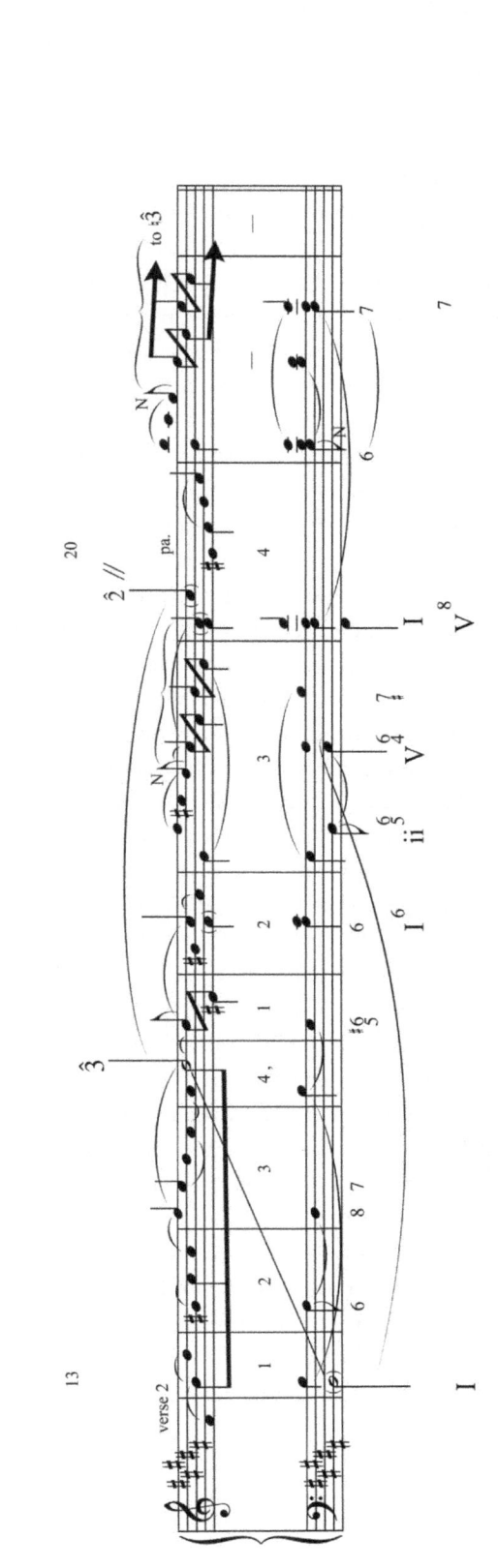

before. Here, however, the statement is cut short, and we have a measure of silence. It seems as if the young miller is hesitating before summoning up the courage to address the brook and ask the crucial question.

Graphs of Schubert's setting of verses 3 and 5 are provided in Example 10.5. Both phrases open the same way, with a linear progression leading to D♮5 (♮3̂), followed immediately by a motion to C♯5 supported by V (local interruption). In verse 3, D♯3 (3̂) is immediately reinstated, and following an immediate descent of a third, the line is led to local closure, where 2̂ is approached from above, supporting the text "ein Wörtchen um und um" (one word one way or the other). This phrase is then repeated. Note that Schubert specifies an accent on the F♯5 where the word "ein" is placed. The miller wants to hear one word, and it is surely no accident that the word "ja" (yes) at the beginning of verse 4 also falls on F♯5. He wants to hear one word and that word is yes. But, as noted earlier, doubt has already crept in.

The continuation in verse 5, a masterful interpretation of the text, is more complex and thus more difficult to graph. From the D♯5 in measure 47, the melodic line descends a third to B4 in measure 50, harmonized by a motion to vi and covered by a descending line from F♯5 (a motion we have heard several times already in this song) that reinstates D♯5. In other words, D♯5 is retained, and the descent initiated in measure 47, where both the D♯5 and the C♯5 are prolonged by their own third progressions, is a motion into an inner voice. By harmonizing the end point as he does—that is, by the secondary dominant of vi in six-five position on the downbeat of measure 50, which then leads to vi⁵—Schubert interjects a subtle twist to the question being posed. This chromatic change falls at the word "mich" (me). So possibly the young miller is not asking simply "does she love me", but "does she love *me*". If you know the rest of the cycle, this emphasis on "me" has considerable significance. As shown by the simplification of this passage, this progression to vi is interpreted as part of a descending third progression initiated from I and leading to ii⁶.⁶ The last line of the verse, the question, is then repeated as the melody descends to closure.

Example 10.6 is a graph of Schubert's setting of the fourth verse, which is shown to prolong the dominant and 2̂. As already noted, "ja" is set as F♯5 and "nein" as D♮5. The introduction of D♮5 gives rise to a descending fifth leading to G♮4, temporarily stabilized by a cadence on G♮, the upper neighbor of F♯ (V). Note that the elaboration of D♮5 in measure 36 involves the temporary cancelation of F♯5 ("ja") by F♮5. In the repetition of this idea, Schubert indulges in a bit of word painting. The verb used by Müller here is "einschliessen", which can mean to "encircle" or to "surround", though translated earlier as "encompass" to fit the context. Note how Schubert in this elaborated repetition circles around F♯5, reinstating it once again to interject a ray of hope. Following the second cadence on G♮, Schubert directs the harmony back toward the tonic by a beautiful enharmonic modulation, where G is spelled as a German augmented sixth chord in B resolving to its dominant. Though buried in an inner part, this progression supports the line shown in the graph, D♮4-D♯4-C♯4, which leads to B3 at the outset of the final verse.

ᴇxᴀᴍᴘʟᴇ 10.5 Graph of the Schubert song, verses 3 and 5

EXAMPLE 10.6 Graph of the Schubert song, verse 4

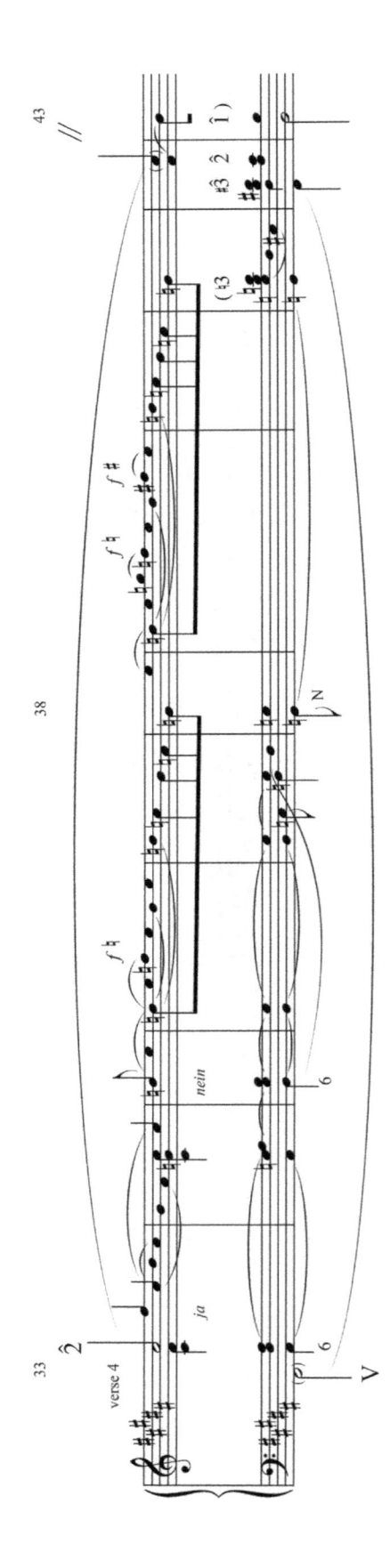

Schumann, "Waldesgespräch", Liederkreis, Op. 39 (Eichendorff)

This poem is one of several based on the legend of Lorelei, the beautiful young woman accused of bewitching men and leading them to their ruin. In the original story by Brentano, the young woman was pardoned of these crimes, and on the way to live out her years in the convent, she climbed a high rock overlooking the Rhine to watch for her unfaithful lover who had abandoned her. She falls to her death, and the high rock overlooking the bend in the river now bears her name. In this version by Eichendorff—a conversation between a young man and the sorceress—Lorelei is alive, living in a castle overlooking the Rhine, and still leading men to their ruin.

Waldesgespräch	Dialogue in the Forest
"Es ist schon spät, es ist schon kalt, was reit'st du einsam durch den Wald? Der Wald ist lang, du bist allein, du schön Braut! Ich führ'dich heim!"	"It is already late, it is already cold, why do you ride alone in the forest? The forest is large, you are alone, you lovely bride! I guide you home!"

"Gross ist der Männer Trug und List
 vor Schmerz mein Herz gebrochen ist,
 wohl irrt das Waldhorn her und hin,
 O flieh'! o flieh'! du weist nicht, wer
     ich bin".
	"Great is man's deceit and cunning,
	 with sorrow my heart was broken,
	 the hunter's horn leads one astray,
	 Oh flee! Oh flee! You know not who
	     I am".

"So reich geschmückt ist Ross und Weib
 so wunderschön, so wunderschön der
     junge Leib;
 jetzt kenn'ich dich, Gott steh'mir bei!
 Du bist die Hexe Loreley!"
	"So richly adorned are steed and woman
	 so wonderfully fair, so wonderfully fair
	     the young form;
	 I know you now, may God help me!
	 You are the sorceress Loreley!"

"Du kennst mich wohl, von hohem Stein schaut still mein Schloss tief in der Rhine. Es ist schon spät, es ist schon kalt, kommst nimmermehr aus diesem Wald".	"You know me well, from the lofty rock my castle looks far over the Rhine. It is already late, it is already cold, nevermore will you leave this forest".

Schumann's setting follows the natural division of the poem into four parts: a b a′ b′. There is a clear differentiation of material of the a and b sections (phrases)—those corresponding to the dialogue by the young man and the sorceress, respectively—by accompaniment patterns, keys and melodic content. The four-measure piano introduction, based on the traditional horn call, establishes the character and fast tempo. It also establishes a quadruple hypermeter that, with exceptions noted ahead, persists throughout the song. The hunting motif is present during the young man's dialogue, and from this we may surmise that he is a stray member of a hunting party. The accompaniment pattern changes when Lorelei speaks. Here Schumann represents two different aspects of Lorelei's personality, the one her calm and reassuring demeanor represented by the soothing character of the ascending arpeggios, and the other the scheming temptress represented by the chromatic descent that follows both in the accompaniment and in the vocal line. The two people are further differentiated by key, the first verse in E major (tonic) and the second in C major

Example 10.7 Schumann, "Waldesgespräch", *Liederkreis,* Op. 39

EXAMPLE **10.7** *continued*

EXAMPLE **10.7** *continued*

EXAMPLE 10.7 *continued*

EXAMPLE 10.7 *continued*

(♮VI). The final two verses remain in the tonic key, however with a brief excursion to E minor/G major when the young man finally realizes that it is the sorceress Lorelei to whom he is speaking. A copy of the score is provided in Example 10.7 and graphs of the first two verses in Example 10.8.

The main features of the piano introduction (with its horn call) are the ascent to G♯4 followed by the descending third leading to F♯4, and then the introduction of the covering B4 by its incomplete upper neighbor. The opening part of this idea then becomes the setting of the first line of the text, "Es ist schon spät, es ist schon kalt". Though G♯4 is clearly the focal melodic pitch of the opening eight measures, I have indicated its statement on the downbeat of measure 9, where it is more stable, as the primary tone. The continuation involves changes in both the accompaniment and the melody. The bass descends by step from E to B, each step supporting a root position triad and each introduced by its applied dominant seventh chord. The graph in Example 10.8 normalizes the octave placement of these notes to show more clearly the continuity of the progression. Above this the melody ascends to D♯5, from which point it descends a third in parallel octaves with the bass, though direct octaves are avoided by approaching each note in the melodic progression from below. Upon reaching B4 and dominant harmony in measure 13, the vocal line arpeggiates to E5, the highest point so far, and then down to G♯4, from which point the line descends to E4, harmonized by ♮VI, thus avoiding harmonic closure. The numbers between the staves in measures 10–13 indicate the intervallic relationship of the upper two parts in relation to the bass. Because of this feature, indication of the hypermetric organization has been temporarily moved above the top part. The numbers indicate that this metric unit has been extended from four to six measures with the end of the phrase falling on a hypermetric downbeat.

The second phrase (b) is preceded by a two-measure introduction establishing the new key and the new accompaniment pattern, the ascending C major arpeggios. The voice then states the ascending fourth G4–C5 twice, a gesture that seems new because of the change of context, but in fact is based on the melodic material beginning in measure 9. The peaceful ambiance projected in these measures is contradictory to the text, which speaks of man's deceit and of her broken heart. This relative calm is shattered suddenly in measure 25 with the sudden shift of dynamic level to *forte* and the descending line generated from E5, which eventually leads all the way to F♯4—a descending seventh, which conceptually replaces an ascending step progression—and interruption of the fundamental line. The first part of the descent is chromatic, involving the progression of a French augmented sixth chord to the dominant, first of E, and then of D. Beginning with the chromatic change of C♯5 to C♮5, the graph shows a local prolongation of an A minor chord by a voice exchange (iv in the key of E major). There are two unusual features of these two measures. First, the E minor chord in first inversion on the third beat of measure 29 strongly suggests an immediate continuation to F♯ and ii$_5^6$, but Schumann avoids arriving at this harmony just yet because there is more text to be set. And second, his slur in the bass in the following measure is contrary to the strong emphasis on A4 above and the indicated voice exchange. Nevertheless, the underlying harmony here is clearly the minor subdominant leading to ii$_5^6$ in preparation for the dominant in the original key.

EXAMPLE 10.8 Graph of Schumann song, verses 1 and 2

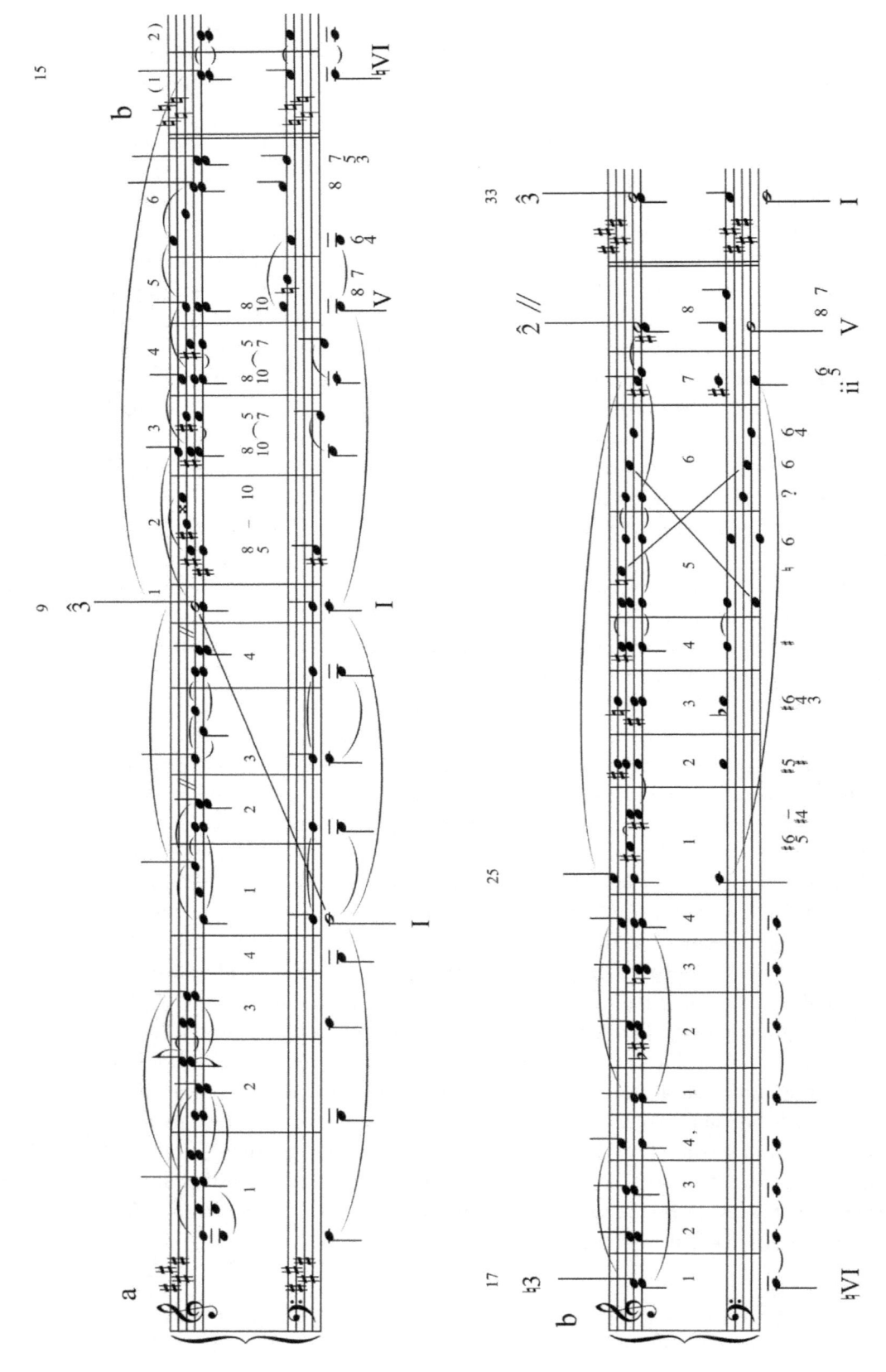

EXAMPLE 10.9 Graph of Schumann song, verses 3 and 4

Graphs of the third and fourth verses are provided in Example 10.9. The third verse opens with a return to the hunting motive and the original vocal material, the only difference being a greater emphasis now on the covering C♯5-B4 motion. This eight-measure section ends with a brief *ritardando* as the realization of the young woman's true identity begins to occur to the young man. This leads to a change to the parallel minor and of the primary tone to ♮3̂, now *forte*. Internal to these four measures, which end on the dominant, there is a brief excursion to G (III) as the young man pleads to God to protect him. Here the covering tone is extended by a continuation of the ascending line to D♮5, the climax of the phrase. The final portion of the text, "du bist die Hexe Loreley", repeats the ascending third G♮4-A4-B4, a motion covering the implied resolution of ♮3̂ to 2̂. The overall motion of this verse, shown by the large slurs in the graph, is 3̂ – ♮3̂ – 2̂ supported by I-i-V.

The final verse is preceded by a two-measure introduction that once again establishes the ascending arpeggio figure associated with Lorelei, now in the tonic. This is followed by the ascending fourth B4-E5, stated twice, the second time increasing in dynamic level. To this point in the song, the upper limit of the vocal line has been E5, but now the voice leaps an additional third to G♯5 (3̂) for the climactic statement of the poem and song. This G♯5 is the initiating point for the chromatic descent, which, as before, is harmonized by the progression of a French augmented sixth chord leading to the dominant, first of iii, then ii. This is followed by [°7] V, which is heard as a downbeat measure, as is the following cadential six-four in measure 60, another example of successive downbeat measures internal to a phrase. The next four measures, which extend the six-four, support the arpeggiation E5-B4-G♯4, which then resolves to five-three leading to closure on the downbeat of measure 64. The voice leading and harmony internal to these four measures, where Lorelei states emphatically several times to the young man that he will never again leave the forest, are interesting. First, the six-four resolves to the four-two chord on the third beat of measure 60, but instead of resolving to I⁶, this leads to a diminished seventh chord of ii in six-five position. Eventually Schumann will get to ii, but in the immediate context the G♯ in the bass, now transferred to the upper octave, leads chromatically through G♮ to F♯ supporting the dominant in four-three position on the downbeat of measure 62. This leads to a return in the bass to the lower octave and the dominant in four-two position for one more statement of "nimmermehr". This dominant passes through a tonic chord in first inversion, leading finally to the promised supertonic chord, which initiates the final drive to closure. The descending third A-G♯-F♯ that finally leads to ii is an answer to the earlier B-A-G♯ that initiates this passage. Not shown in Example 10.9 is the piano postlude, based on the hunting motive, which overlaps with the end of the vocal line and arrival at 1̂.

Brahms, "*Immer leiser wird mein Schlummer*", Op. 105, No. 2 (*Lingg*)

Immer leiser wird mein Schlummer,
nur wie Schleier liegt mein Kummer
zitternd über mir.
Oft im Traume hör ich dich
rufen draus vor meiner Tür,
niemand wacht und öffnet dir,
ich erwach und weine bitterlich.

Ja, ich werde sterben müssen,
eine Andre wirst du küssen,
wenn ich bleich und kalt
eh die Maienlüfte wehn,
eh die Drossel singt im Wald;
willst du mich noch einmal sehn,
komm, o komme bald!

Ever lighter grows my slumber,
like a veil my grief lies
trembling over me.
Often in dreams I hear you
calling outside my door,
no one awakes and opens to you,
I awake and weep bitterly.

Yes, I must die,
you will kiss another
when I am pale and cold
before the May winds blow
before the thrust sings in the forest:
if you want to see me once again,
come, oh come soon!

Hermann Lingg's poem is one of despair but, in the end, one of desperate hope that a loved one will visit one last time. Brahms's setting is divided into parallel sections corresponding to the division of the poem into two verses, and each of these parts consists of two phrases. A copy of the score is provided in Example 10.10.

As a prelude to our analysis of this song, there are two matters to be addressed. The first has to do with Brahms's style in general, some features of which tend to obscure the underlying structure. For example, in this song the bass rarely aligns with the melody, and melodic notes that receive agogic and/or metric stress often serve a lower function structurally than those unstressed. Consider, for example, the first full measure. Are the A4 and F♯4 roots of six-four chords, or are they notes decorating an underlying dominant (cadential six-four) in C♯ minor? The answer may depend on whether you hear moment-to-moment or the underlying gesture, which is at the crux of Schenker's theory. Example 10.11, a graph of the voice-leading structure of the first part, will show the latter. The second matter pertains to Brahms's metric setting of the text. In other songs examined in this chapter, we have observed the presence of hypermetric organization, against which one can judge anomalies, including some very sophisticated phrase expansions. But this song does not exhibit a clear underlying hypermeter. Careful scrutiny suggests that the underlying principle is a very careful adherence to the natural accentuation of the text. Why, for example, does Brahms begin in the middle of the measure? This would seem to result from the natural stress on *lei-ser* and *Schlum-mer*. This also explains the agogic stress on A4 and F♯4 in measure 1 counter to the underlying harmony.

Brahms's setting of the opening line of the text is an embellished descending fifth from G♯4 to C♯4 over a bass arpeggiation connecting G♯2 to G♯1 before resolving to C♯2. As shown in Example 10.11, this bass arpeggiation supports the motion $\frac{8}{6}$ to $\frac{7}{5}$, where the voices exchange positions before resolving. Interpretation of the details of the melodic voices, shown by the slurs, is based on this understanding of the underlying harmonic motion and voice leading. This is followed by the restatement of G♯4 and then a leap to C♯5, from which point the melody descends an entire octave to C♯4 in measure 9. This octave descent occurs at a rather superficial level, however, masking the more structurally significant descending

EXAMPLE 10.10 Brahms, "Immer leiser wird mein Schlummer", Op. 105, No. 2

EXAMPLE **10.10** *continued*

EXAMPLE **10.10** *continued*

EXAMPLE 10.10 *continued*

komm,   o   kom - me bald!

fifth shown in Example 10.11. That is, C♯5 has been interpreted as an important covering tone, from which the melody descends a fifth—a filled-in arpeggiation—to F♯4, which is subsequently prolonged before passing through E4, supported by a passing tonic chord in first inversion, to the perfect authentic cadence in measures 7–9. Following the 5–6 motion above C♯ in measures 3–4, the lower two voices progress in parallel sixths until the ii$^6_5$ chord in measure 7. Thus the support for F♯4 within the descent of a fifth is passing, purely the result of linear motion. As with the opening gesture, the points of stability are at the beginning and at the end (the cadence):

G♯4. . .   D♯4   C♯4

i   ii$^6_5$ V   i

Not shown in Example 10.11 is the displacement of C♯4 by its upper neighbor at the cadence, a gesture that is repeated in the next three measures, creating a direct link between the two phrases. The melodic line begins once again from C♯5, this time descending to G♯4 in measure 14, now harmonized by III. (Harmonically the subdominant in C♯ minor is reinterpreted as the supertonic in this temporary modulation to III.) This is the first time in the song where bass and melody are sounded together on the downbeat. However, this instance of stability is transient as the accompaniment changes to a staggered offbeat pattern and the harmony become temporarily unfocused, together representing the person's agitated dream world where no one wakes to open the door. The vocal line descends a third B4-A4-G♯4 supported by six-four chords, the last of which functions in the immediate context as the cadential six-four in the parallel minor of III. This resolves to the

EXAMPLE 10.11 Graph of Brahms song, part 1

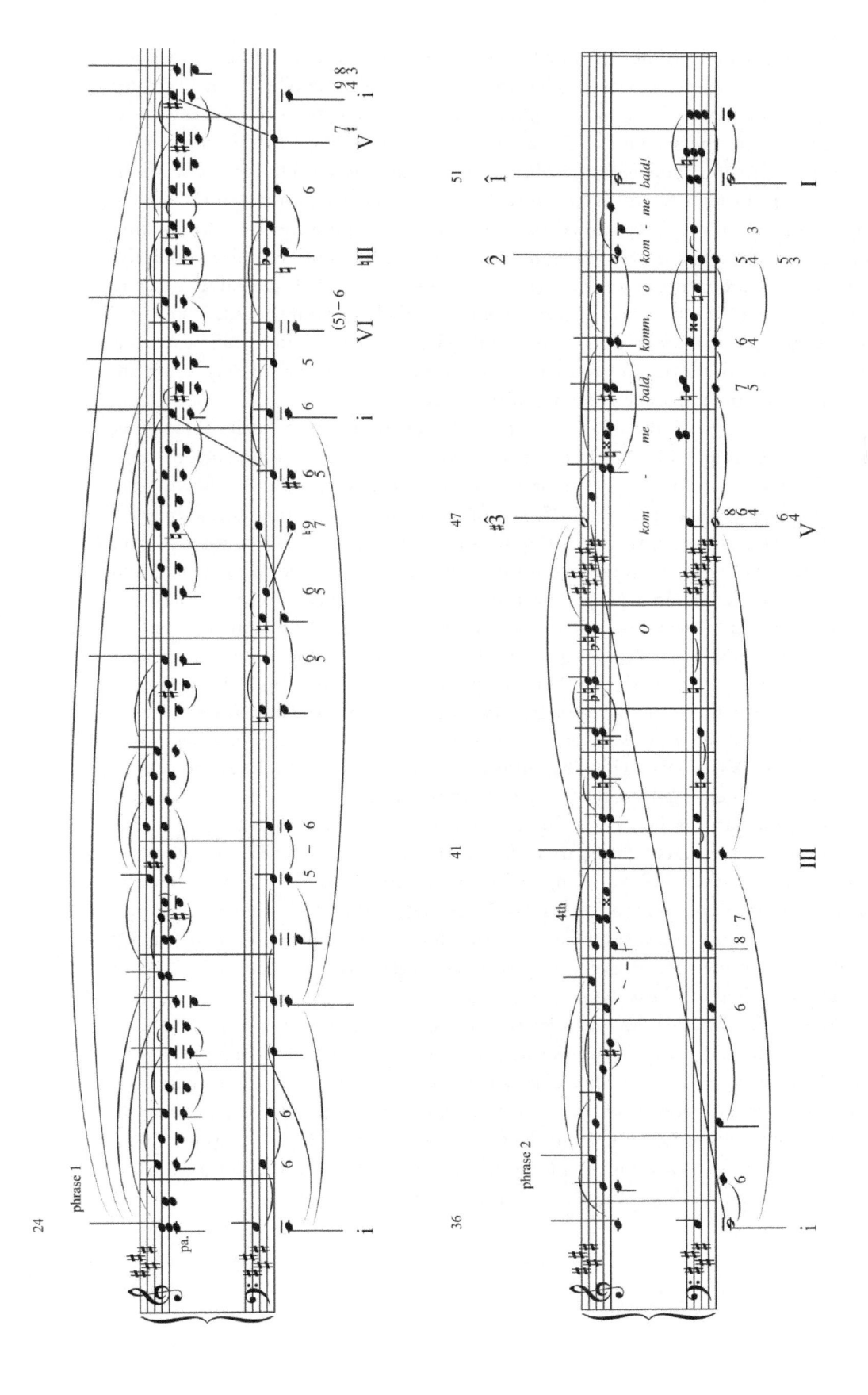

Example 10.12 Graph of Brahms song, part 2

dominant seventh harmony as the dynamic level rises to *forte* for the first time in this song and the text speaks of weeping bitterly. The first statement of "weine" falls on D♯5 (not shown in the graph) at the climax of the phrase before its transfer to the lower octave, where it is covered by the second statement of "weine" on A4-G♯4 as the inner voice resolves D♯4 to E4. Accompanying the resolution of this diminished fifth is the chromatic motion below of B through B♯ to C♯, below which the bass note E2 enters on the downbeat of measure 23. As shown in Example 10.11, the contents of measures 14–23, including the prolongation of G♯4, occur over a 5–6 motion above the bass note E2, after which the phrase continues its progress to closure, missing only E4 to complete the linear descent. Up to the repetition of the final line of text, "weine bitterlich", Brahms's setting has carefully followed the natural accentuation of the words. Here the syncopation, composed-out deceleration, and rests in the accompaniment, which seem to produce a sobbing effect, are most appropriate to emphasize the meaning of the words.

The end of the first part leads directly into the second part, where the piano alone states the opening idea (Example 10.12). Note that the bass arpeggiation is different this time, leading to a different interpretation of the harmony and of the voices above. Following the restatement of G♯4, the voice enters on C♯5. The following material leading to the cadence in measure 36 (measures 27–36) is a variant of measures 3–9. It is divided into three shorter statements corresponding to the three lines of text, ending with repetition of "bleich und kalt". The first is an elaborated arpeggiation from C♯5 to F♯4, and the second, following extension of this F♯4 to A4, leads to a weak cadence in measure 32. Like the previous phrase, the descent to closure is incomplete, missing E4. The harmony supporting this material is initiated by a 5–6 motion above C♯, but here the passing sixth supporting F♯4 is extended by a voice exchange with B leading through B♯ to C♯. This weak cadence is followed by another four measures, this time leading to a stronger cadence. The harmony beginning from measure 32 is i-VI-♮II-V-i, which supports a second "attempt" at a linear descent to closure. This time E4 is emphasized, but not given harmonic support.

The opening measures of the second phrase leading to the internal cadence on III are the same as the equivalent place in the first part, including the repetition of the linking D♯4-C♯4 idea. As before, this is followed by a change of accompaniment pattern, but this time the melody ascends by a series of minor thirds, G♯4-B4, B4-D♮5, D♮5-F♮5, each supported by a six-four chord, the last functioning as the cadential six-four in D♭ major, enharmonically C♯ major. To this point in the song, melodic emphasis has centered on G♯4 and C♯5/C♯4, but here at the climax, where we hear the plea to come one last time, the melodic line reaches up to F♮5 (E♯5) as the dynamic level rises for only the second time to *forte*. This is the long delayed primary tone (♯3̂). Now Brahms's earlier careful avoidance of providing harmonic support for E4 in previous descents to closure makes sense. The song ends in D♭ major, but I have taken the liberty of renotating this passage in C♯ major in Example 10.12. From E♯5 the vocal line arpeggiates to G♯4 and from there progresses by step to E♯4, all as part of an extended six-four, which now leads to closure in the lower octave. This final passage now provides new meaning to the opening gesture of the song.

SUGGESTED ASSIGNMENTS

Mozart

1. Pamina's aria "Ach, ich fühl's" from *The Magic Flute*. Like Tamino's aria examined in this chapter, this one also involves phrase expansions, both external and internal. It is helpful, at least in the beginning, to count written measures as two hyperbeats.

Schubert

1. "Der Müller und der Bach", *Die schöne Müllerin*. Having examined the young miller's earlier encounter with the brook, now look at Schubert's setting of his final meeting. The song is in three parts, with each part also having ternary organization. First sketch the outer two sections, and then the middle one. How does Schubert's setting of the middle one fit into the overall structure of the song?

2. "Du bist die Ruh". Schubert's setting of the third and fourth verses provides a very clear instance of *superposition* (reaching over).

Schumann

1. "Widmung", *Myrthen*, Op. 25. This dramatic song in ternary form may be the easiest one listed here—a good place to start.

2. "Frühlingsfahrt". Though long, this song is repetitive. Schumann's setting of verses 1–5 is structurally continuous. How is his setting of verse 6 a summary and completion of all that came before?

Brahms

1. "Wie Melodien zieht es mir". Op. 105, No. 1. Though this song presents some challenges, it is more accessible than many of his late songs. An analysis of this song by Edward Laufer was published in *The Journal of Music Theory* 15 (1971), 34–57.

NOTES

1. In the following analyses, specification of octave position will follow notated pitch, not sounding pitch with music written for tenor voices.

2. Alternatively one might interpret measures 26 and 27 as successive downbeat measures, in which case the phrase overlap in measure 34 would occur in conjunction with a metric reinterpretation.

3. An analysis of "Der Neugierige," by this author was published as a tribute to Greta Kraus in *Canadian University Music Review* 19/1 (1999), 69–78.

4. One might also speculate that this F× also anticipates the arrival at its enharmonic equivalent G in the fourth verse, where it functions as upper neighbor to F♯.

5. Here the potential of this D♯ seventh chord, first encountered in measure 9, to function as V^7 of vi is finally realized.

6. We encountered this descending third progression earlier in our discussion of the St. Anthony Chorale. See Examples 5.1 and 5.2 and the accompanying discussion.

Schenker's Publications

Writings

Ein Beitrag zur Ornamentik als Einführung zu Ph. E. Bachs Klavierwerke, 1904; rev. 1908 and reprinted 1954. Engl. trans. by Hedi Siegel in *The Music Forum* IV, 1976.

Neue musikalische Theorien und Phantasien

    I. *Harmonielehre*, 1906. Engl. trans. by Elizabeth Mann Borgese, ed. by Oswald Jonas (Chicago) 1954; reprinted 1973.

    II. *Kontrapunkt* I, 1910; II, 1922. Engl. trans. by John Rothgeb and Jurgen Thym (Schirmer), 1987; rev. ed. (Musicalia Press), 2001.

    III. *Der freie Satz*, 1935; rev. ed. by Oswald Jonas, 1956. Engl. trans. by Ernst Oster (Longman), 1979.

Beethovens neunte Sinfonie, 1912; reprinted 1969. Engl. trans. by John Rothgeb (Yale), 1992.

Der Tonwille, 1921–24. Engl. trans. (multiple translators) in two volumes, ed. by Wm. Drabkin (Oxford), 2004–2005.

Beethovens fünfte Sinfonie, 1925; reprinted 1969. Originally published in installments in *Der Tonwille*.

Das Meisterwerk in der Musik

    I. 1925. Engl. trans. (multiple translators), ed. by Wm. Drabkin (Cambridge), 1994.

    II. 1926. Engl. trans. (multiple translators), ed. Wm. Drabkin (Cambridge), 1996.

    III. 1930. Engl. trans. (multiple translators), ed. by Wm. Drabkin (Cambridge), 1997.

Fünf Urlinie-Tafeln, 1932. Revised by Felix Salzer and publ. as *Five Graphic Music Analyses*, 1969.

J. Brahms, *Octaven und Quinten*, 1933. Engl. trans. by Paul Mast, *The Music Forum* V, 1980.

Die Kunst des Vortrags (unpublished manuscript). Engl. trans. as *The Art of Performance* by Irene Schreier Scott (Oxford), 2000.

Editions

C.P.E. Bach, *Klavierwerke*, 1902–03.

G.F. Handel, *Sechs Orgelkonzerte*, 1904.

J.S. Bach, *Chromatische Phantasie und Fuge*, 1910. Engl. trans. and ed. by Hedi Siegel (Longman), 1984.

L. van Beethoven

> *Die letzten [fünf] Sonaten: kritisce Ausgabe mit Einführung und Erläuterungen*, 1913–21; rev. ed. by Oswald Jonas, 1971–72.

> Sonata Op. 27, Nr. 2, 1927.

> *Sämtliche Klaviersonaten, 1934*; reprinted 1975.

Index of Names and Terms

Note: This is a selective index with limited page references for certain entries. Where there are multiple entries, the most important ones are indicated in **bold**.

Index of Musical Works